The Hidden Places of

GLOUCESTERSHIRE, WILTSHIRE AND SOMERSET

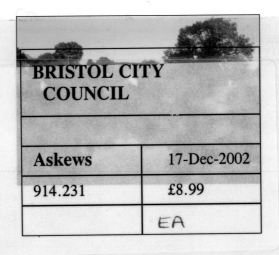

By
Joanna Billing

Published by:
Travel Publishing Ltd
7a Apollo House, Calleva Park
Aldermaston, Berks, RG7 8TN
ISBN 1-902-00777-8
© Travel Publishing Ltd

First Published:	*1990*	*Fourth Edition:*	*1999*
Second Edition:	*1993*	*Fifth Edition:*	*2002*
Third Edition:	*1997*		

HIDDEN PLACES REGIONAL TITLES

Cambs & Lincolnshire
Cornwall
Devon
East Anglia
Heart of England
Highlands & Islands
Lake District & Cumbria
Lincolnshire & Nottinghamshire
Somerset
Thames Valley

Chilterns
Derbyshire
Dorset, Hants & Isle of Wight
Gloucestershire, Wiltshire & Somerset
Hereford, Worcs & Shropshire
Kent
Lancashire & Cheshire
Northumberland & Durham
Sussex
Yorkshire

HIDDEN PLACES NATIONAL TITLES

England
Scotland

Ireland
Wales

Printing by: Scotprint, Haddington

Maps by: © Maps in Minutes ™ (2002) © Crown Copyright, Ordnance Survey 2002

Editor: Joanna Billing

Cover Design: Lines & Words, Aldermaston

Cover Photographs: Cheddar Gorge, Somerset; Castle Combe, Wiltshire; Upper Slaughter, Gloucestershire © www.britainonview.com

Text Photographs: © www.britainonview.com

Foreword

The Hidden Places is a collection of easy to use travel guides taking you in this instance, on a relaxed but informative tour of the counties of Gloucestershire, Wiltshire and Somerset; three adjoining rural counties of outstanding beauty that offer the visitor the imposing chalky heights of the Marlborough downs, the gentler slopes and pretty stone villages of the Cotswolds and the vast heights of the Quantocks Hills and low levels of Somerset. This area is a haven for "hidden places" and the book provides the reader with plenty of interesting historical facts and stories.

This edition of **The Hidden Places of Gloucestershire, Wiltshire and Somerset** is published **in full colour.** All **Hidden Places** titles are now published in colour which ensures that readers can properly appreciate the attractive scenery and impressive places of interest in these counties and, of course, in the rest of the British Isles. We do hope that you like the new format.

Our books contain a wealth of interesting information on the history, the countryside, the towns and villages and the more established places of interest in these counties. But they also promote the more secluded and little known visitor attractions and places to stay, eat and drink many of which are easy to miss unless you know exactly where you are going.

We include hotels, inns, restaurants, public houses, teashops, various types of accommodation, historic houses, museums, gardens, garden centres, craft centres and many other attractions throughout the area, all of which are comprehensively indexed. Most places are accompanied by an attractive photograph and are easily located by using the map at the beginning of each chapter. We do not award merit marks or rankings but concentrate on describing the more interesting, unusual or unique features of each place with the aim of making the reader's stay in the local area an enjoyable and stimulating experience.

Whether you are visiting the area for business or pleasure or in fact are living in the counties we do hope that you enjoy reading and using this book. We are always interested in what readers think of places covered (or not covered) in our guides so please do not hesitate to use the reader reaction forms provided to give us your considered comments. We also welcome any general comments which will help us improve the guides themselves. Finally if you are planning to visit any other corner of the British Isles we would like to refer you to the list of other **Hidden Places** titles to be found at the rear of the book and to the Travel Publishing website at www.travelpublishing.co.uk.

Travel Publishing

Regional Map

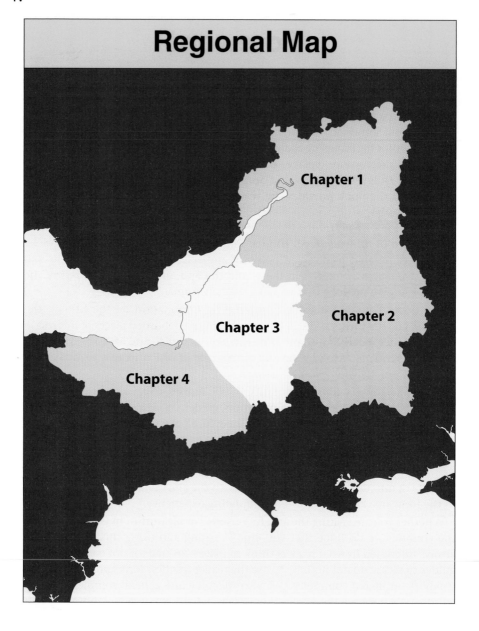

Chapter 1

Chapter 2

Chapter 3

Chapter 4

Contents

FOREWORD   III

REGIONAL MAP   IV

CONTENTS   V

GEOGRAPHICAL AREAS:

Chapter 1:   Gloucestershire   1
Chapter 2:   Wiltshire   57
Chapter 3:   North and East Somerset   102
Chapter 4:   South and West Somerset   147

INDEXES AND LISTS:

List of Tourist Information Centres   193
Index of Towns, Villages and Places of Interest   197
List of Advertisers   205

ADDITIONAL INFORMATION:

Order Forms   211
Reader Comment Forms   215

1 Gloucestershire

For many people the county of Gloucestershire is the Cotswolds, the delightful limestone hills that sweep across the county from Tetbury in the south to Chipping Campden in the north. Along with being home to some of the most glorious scenery and the prettiest villages in England, which are typified by the honey-coloured Cotswold stone, this is also an area that once thrived on the woollen industry. Wool from the sheep grazing on the hillsides and water power provided by the numerous streams, saw the region flourish in medieval times and this was when many of the towns and villages built their grand, and in some cases almost cathedral like, churches. The charming market towns and villages here, such as Tetbury, Stow-on-the-Wold and Bourton-on-the-Water, remain little changed today and here, as elsewhere in the Cotswolds, there are not only picturesque market squares to explore but also glorious surrounding countryside.

Pump Room, Cheltenham

However, the region dates back to long before the Middle Ages and, along with prehistoric remains being found here, the Romans also made their mark. As Corinium Dobonnorum, Cirencester was the second largest Roman town in Britain; to the west of Yanworth is the large and well preserved Chedworth Roman Villa, whilst the Romans established a fort to guard the lowest crossing point of the River Severn in the 1st century AD and so founded Gloucester. However, Gloucestershire's most famous town, Cheltenham, is a relatively late comer and it was just a small and insignificant village until the early 18th century when the discovery of a mineral spring began its rapid development into a spa town. One of Europe's leading Regency spas today, this elegant town is equally famous as being the home of National Hunt Racing and, in March, it is packed with racing enthusiasts from all over the world who come here to watch the very best compete to find that year's greatest steeple-chaser and hurdler.

Lower Slaughter

Gloucestershire, though, is not just the Cotswolds and, bordered by the Severn Estuary to the south and the Wye valley to the west there is the Royal Forest of Dean, one of England's few remaining ancient forests. Today, this rich and varied landscape provides endless interest for walkers, historians and nature lovers and its isolated position gives the area a character all of its own. Over the centuries, the forest has been a wild wood, a royal hunting ground, a naval timber reserve and an important mining and industrial centre and each of these previous uses has helped to shape both the countryside and the towns and villages found here.

Finally, there is the Vale of Berkeley, the fertile strip of land that lies on the southeastern banks of the River Severn. Home to the world famous Wildfowl and Wetlands Trust centre at Slimbridge, this area has been dominated by Berkeley Castle for centuries and it remains the oldest inhabited castle in the country and has been home to some 24 generations of the Berkeley family. First built as an austere Norman castle in the mid 12th century, it has, over the years, become a magnificent, and more comfortable, stately home and also one that has a long and eventful history. Most famously, it was here that the imprisoned Edward II was gruesomely murdered in the 14th century.

PLACES TO STAY, EAT, DRINK AND SHOP

1	Beechworth Lawn Hotel, Cheltenham	Bed and Breakfast	page 4
2	Cheltenham Art Gallery/Museum, Cheltenham	Gallery & Museum	page 5
3	The Courtyard Maisonette, Cheltenham	Self Catering	page 6
4	The Plaisterers Arms, Winchcombe	Pub, Restaurant & Accommodation	page 7
5	Old Station House, Greet, nr Winchcombe	Bed and Breakfast	page 8
6	The Eight Bells, Chipping Campden	Pub, Restaurant & Accommodation	page 10
7	The Crown Inn Hotel, Blockley	Pub, Restaurant & Accommodation	page 12
8	Batsford Park: Arboretum, Batsford Park	Falconry Centre	page 13
9	The Bell Inn, Moreton-in-Marsh	Pub, Restaurant & Accommodation	page 13
10	The Cross Hands Inn, Salford Hill (A44)	Pub, Restaurant & Accommodation	page 14
11	Chancellors Tea Rooms, Painswick	Café and Tea Shop	page 15
12	The National Waterways Museum, Gloucester	Museum	page 17
13	The Rising Sun, Maisemore	Pub and Restaurant	page 18
14	Aubergine Caffe Bar, Tewkesbury	Restaurant	page 19
15	Beckford Inn, Beckford, nr Tewkesbury	Pub, Restaurant & Accommodation	page 20
16	The Crown At Kemerton, Kemerton	Pub and Restaurant	page 20
17	The Berkely Arms, Tewkesbury	Pub and Restaurant	page 21
18	The Nelson Arms Inn, Drybrook	Pub and Restaurant	page 23
19	The King's Head, Birdwood, nr Huntley	Hotel and Restaurant	page 25
20	Harry's Bar & Restaurant, Lydney	Pub and Restaurant	page 26
21	The Miners Arms, Whitecroft, nr Lydney	Pub with Food	page 26
22	The George Inn, Aylburton, nr Lydney	Pub, Restaurant & Accommodation	page 26
23	Garden Café, Lower Lydbrook	Restaurant	page 28
24	Clearwell Caves, Near Coleford	Caves	page 29
25	Speech House Hotel, Coleford	Hotel and Restaurant	page 30
26	Log Cabin At Symonds Yat, Symonds Yat	Café and Tea Shop	page 32
27	The Swan Inn, Stroud	Pub with Food	page 34
28	The Fleece Inn, Lightpill, nr Stroud	Pub with Food	page 36
29	The Old Neighbourhood Inn, Chalford	Pub with Food	page 36
30	Woodcutters Arms, Whiteshill, nr Stroud	Pub with Food	page 36
31	The Bear Inn, Bisley, nr Stroud	Restaurant	page 37
32	Ruskin Mill, Nailsworth	Café, Tea Shop and Craft Shop	page 37
33	Carmella's Restaurant, Nailsworth	Restaurant	page 38
34	The Laurels At Inchbrook, Inchbrook	Bed and Breakfast	page 38
35	The Bell & Castle, Horsley, nr Nailsworth	Pub with Food	page 38

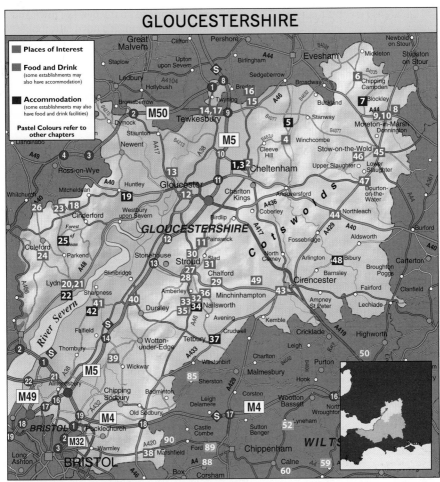

GLOUCESTERSHIRE

■ **Places of Interest**

■ **Food and Drink**
(some establishments may
also have accommodation)

■ **Accommodation**
(some establishments may also
have food and drink facilities)

**Pastel Colours refer to
other chapters**

© MAPS IN MINUTES ™ 2002   © Crown Copyright, Ordnance Survey 2002

36	The Crown Inn, Minchinhampton, nr Stroud	Pub, Restaurant & Accommodation	page 39
37	Stable Cottage, Cutwell, nr Tetbury	Self Catering	page 40
38	The Catherine Wheel, Marshfield	Pub, Restaurant & Accommodation	page 43
39	The Oak Tree Inn, Cromhall	Pub and Restaurant	page 44
40	The Pickwick Inn, Lower Wick, nr Dursley	Pub and Restaurant	page 44
41	The Mariners Arms, Berkeley	Pub and Restaurant	page 46
42	The Jenner Museum, Berkeley	Museum	page 46
43	The Fleece Hotel, Cirencester	Pub, Restaurant & Accommodation	page 47
44	Keith Harding's World Of Mechanical Music	Museum	page 49
45	The White Hart Inn, Stow-on-the-Wold	Pub, Food & Accommodation	page 50
46	The Golden Ball, Lower Swell	Pub, Food & Accommodation	page 51
47	Duke of Wellington, Bourton-on-the-Water	Pub, Food & Accommodation	page 52
48	Hartwell Farm Cottages, Ready Token	Self Catering	page 54
49	The Daneway Inn, Sapperton	Pub with Food	page 55

CHELTENHAM

This smart and fashionable spa town has been welcoming visitors for almost 300 years but, before the accidental discovery of a mineral spring in 1715, by a local man, William Mason, Cheltenham was just a small and insignificant village. Although Mason built a pump room around the spa and began the town's transformation into one of Europe's leading Regency spa towns, it was his son-in-law, the astute Captain Henry Skillicorne who began the development in earnest when he added a meeting room, a ballroom and a network of carriageways and walks. A number of other springs were also discovered, including one in the High Street around which the first Assembly Rooms were built. In 1788, Cheltenham played host to George III, who spent five weeks here taking the medicinal waters with his family, and this royal patronage put the seal of approval on the new spa town and further expansion, at a rapid rate, took place between 1790 and 1840. The resultant Regency town is as charming and elegant today as then but few buildings remain from before that time although one, in particular, is the Church of St Mary that, in parts, dates back to the 12th century.

Still the most complete Regency town in England, much of the centre of Cheltenham lies within a conservation area and this has changed little since the days when such noble and royal visitors as the Duke of Wellington and Princess (later Queen) Victoria stayed here. Today's visitors can still use Skillicorne's walks and rides that are now incorporated into the **Promenade**, which is not only one of the most beautiful boulevards in the country but it is also one of the finest shopping streets. The elm and horse chestnut trees that line the promenade were planted in

BEECHWORTH LAWN HOTEL

133 Hales Road, Cheltenham,
Gloucestershire GL52 6ST
Tel: 01242 522583 Fax: 01242 574800
e-mail: beechworth.lawn@dial.pipex.com
website: www.beechworthlawnhotel.co.uk

Close to the centre of town, **Beechworth Lawn Hotel** is a handsome late-Victorian detached house open all year round for superior Bed & Breakfast accommodation. The hotel is owned and run by Claire and Peter Christensen and their daughter Vicky. The Christensens have run hotels in

Canada, France, London and Bath, and 2002 sees their third season in Cheltenham.

The spacious, centrally heated guest bedrooms are seven in number, all with en suite facilities, tv, radio alarm, hairdryer and hospitality tray; laundry and ironing facilities are available. Two of the rooms are on the ground floor. Guests have the use of an elegant lounge, and a full English breakfast is served in the equally appealing dining room. Ample parking; children welcome; pets by arrangement.

Pump Room, Cheltenham

1818 and its crowning glory is the wonderful **Neptune's Fountain** that was modelled on the Fontana di Trevi in Rome and was built in 1893. Elsewhere in the town formal and less formal gardens were created including **Montpellier Gardens**, which date from 1809 and are framed by lime trees, **Imperial Gardens**, which were planted in 1818 and were exclusively for subscribers of the Sherborne Spa, and **Pittville Park**, the largest ornamental park in Cheltenham that dates from 1825. Housed in Pittville Park is the magnificent Pump Room that overlooks the lake and this elegant Regency building is now one of the few drinking spas still remaining in Britain. Along with taking the waters here, as visitors have done for decades, the Pump Room is also home to the **Pittville Pump Room Museum**, which uses original period costumes to bring to life the story of Cheltenham from its Regency heyday to the 1960s.

Whilst the Regency period dominates the architecture of the centre of Cheltenham, the town is also associated with the Arts and Crafts Movement of the early 20th century and this style is well represented at the **Cheltenham Art Gallery and Museum**, which holds an outstanding collection of William Morris inspired furniture, textiles and silver. On display here, too, are collections of Oriental porcelain, English ceramics and paintings and numerous items that reflect the history of Cheltenham. The Museum and Art Gallery is open all year round except for Bank Holiday Mondays. The composer Gustav Holst was born in Cheltenham in 1874 in a terraced Regency house in Clarence Road that is now the **Holst Birthplace Museum** and, along with housing the original piano of the composer of *The Planets*, the house

---

CHELTENHAM ART GALLERY & MUSEUM

Clarence Street, Cheltenham, Gloucestershire GL50 3JT
Tel: 01242 237431 Fax: 01242 262334
e-mail: artgallery@cheltenham.gov.uk
website: www.cheltenhammuseum.org.uk

Cheltenham Art Gallery & Museum is one of only 52 museums in the country officially designated as a museum with an outstanding collection. In this case it comprises furniture, silver,

jewellery, ceramics, carvings and textiles, produced by the Arts & Crafts Movement, whose members were inspired by the ideology of William Morris. The Museum also has a fine collection of paintings from the 17th century onwards, and 20th century gems. Among other highlights are displays on the history and archae-ology of the area and special events, talks and exhibitions take place throughout the year. There is also a café and gift shop.

contains many mementoes of his life and works. The building also illustrates the way of life in an upper middle class Victorian and Edwardian family house and there is a working Victorian kitchen, a Regency drawing room and a nursery. Another interesting, and famous, establishment in the town is **Cheltenham Ladies College**, which was founded in 1854 and where the pioneering Miss Beale was principal.

Cheltenham Lake

However, the town certainly does not dwell in the past and there are two remarkable pieces of modern public art on display in the centre of Cheltenham. The **Wishing Fish Clock** in the Regent Arcade is a work in metal by the famous artist and craftsman Kit Williams. Below the clock, from which a mouse pops out when disturbed by the arrival of an egg laid by a duck, is suspended a 12 foot long fish that celebrates the hours by swishing its tail and blowing bubbles. The mechanical parts of this extraordinary clock were made by the renowned local clockmaker Michael Harding. Meanwhile, off the High Street, are the **Elephant Murals** that portray an event that occurred here in 1934 when three elephants from a travelling circus escaped and raided a provision shop stocked with corn – an incident that older locals, with long memories, still recall.

Just two miles to the north of the town lies the home of National Hunt Racing, **Cheltenham Racecourse**, which holds numerous top quality race meetings throughout the Autumn, Winter and Spring including the highlight of the National Hunt racing season in March when the Gold Cup and the Champion Hurdle are run to determine the year's best steeplechaser and best hurdler. Several other festivals have found their home in Cheltenham including the International Jazz Festival, the International Festival of Music and the International Festival of Literature.

The Courtyard & Regency Maisonette

22 Montpellier Spa Road, Cheltenham, Gloucestershire GL50 1UL
Tel: 01242 517412
e-mail: jane@22montpellier.co.uk website: 22montpellier.co.uk

Two luxurious self-catering premises in central Cheltenham, managed by owners Jane and Bruce Reynolds. **The Courtyard**, at 22, is a two-bedroom apartment in a listed Regency building, with a large sitting room, kitchen-diner, bathroom with bath and shower, and a small courtyard garden with cast-iron furniture. Along the road at 16 is the **Regency Maisonette**, also with two bedrooms, sitting room and kitchen. Both properties are kept in superb order and are close to the best shops, bars and restaurants of Cheltenham's Montpellier district; the renowned Promenade is a short walk away.

AROUND CHELTENHAM

WINCHCOMBE
6 miles NE of Cheltenham on the B4632

Once the capital of the Saxon kingdom of Mercia, in the late 8th century King Kenulf founded an abbey here and, although the date of the death of the king is unknown, it is believed that his 7-year-old son, Kenelm, succeeded him. However, Kenelm's elder sister, Quendrida, was an ambitious and scheming woman and she sought to rule Mercia herself so she bribed Askbert, her younger brother's tutor, to murder Kenelm. Askbert took the boy out into the forest and, whilst he was resting, dug a grave but, just as the tutor was about to commit the terrible deed, Kenelm woke and, having declared that this was not the place that had been ordained for his death, he then drove an ash twig into the ground that, at once, grew and flowered. Undeterred by this miracle, Askbert took the young king elsewhere, beheaded him and buried his body in another grave. A short while later the Pope came to hear about the tragedy and he alerted the kings of England to the murder. A search was made of the area around Winchcombe, the boy's grave was found and Kenelm's body was taken back to Winchcombe Abbey where he was buried next to his father.

Meanwhile, Quendrida suffered an agonizing death, where her eyes were said to burst from her head, during the funeral procession for her murdered brother. During medieval times, St Kenelm's shrine was a popular destination for pilgrims and, in Britain, it was second in importance to the shrine of Thomas à Becket.

The Middle Ages saw Winchcombe grow in importance and it became a walled town with an abbot who presided over the government of the town. The abbey, along with many others, was destroyed in 1539 after Henry VIII's Dissolution of the Monasteries and all that remains today is a section of a gallery that is now part of the George Inn. Along with pilgrims coming here to pay their respects at St Kenelm's shrine, the abbey also gave rise to a flourishing trade in wool and sheep.

One of the most famous townsmen of this prosperous time was Jack Smallwood, also known as Jack o' Newbury, a leading producer of woollen goods, who sponsored some 300 men to fight at Flodden Field in 1513. Silk and paper were produced here too and, for a few decades, tobacco was grown locally – a fact remembered in place names such as Tobacco Close and Tobacco Field. This activity ceased in 1670 when a law was passed banning home-produced tobacco in favour of imports from the then struggling

THE PLAISTERERS ARMS
Abbey Terrace, Winchcombe, Gloucestershire GL54 5LL
Tel: 01242 602358 Fax: 01242 602360
e-mail: plaisterers.arms@btinternet.com

The **Plaisterers Arms** is an atmospheric inn with a history going back to the 15th century. The interior is full of period charm, with black beams, stone walls, wood panelling and an eclectic assortment of decorative features. At least three real ales are always available, and home-cooked food ranges from bar snacks to full meals, with a traditional roast lunch on Sunday. The inn also has five letting bedrooms with modern facilities in old-world surroundings. Behind the inn, the ground slopes down to a delightful beer garden with a children's play area and pleasant views of the countryside. In spring and summer the garden and the front of the inn are a mass of flowers.

Sudeley Castle

museum contains one of the largest collections of railway equipment in the country and visitors can work the signals, clip tickets and enjoy the nostalgia of the age of steam whilst the surrounding typical Cotswold garden is full of old and rare plants.

To the southeast of the town and standing out against a backdrop of Cotswold hills is **Sudeley Castle**, a place steeped in history that is open to the public during April. However, surrounding the castle are 10 enchanting and award winning gardens (open from March to October) that include a

colony of Virginia, in North America. The decline that followed the enacting of this law, in effect, stopped the town's development and, happily for visitors today, this has resulted in many of the old buildings surviving unaltered. Those that do remain include St Peter's Church, built in the 1460s and known particularly for its 40 grotesques and gargoyles and the so-called Winchcombe Worthies.

The Tudor-style Town Hall is home to the **Winchcombe Folk and Police Museum**, which tells the history of the town from Neolithic times to the present day as well as also housing a collection of British and international police uniforms and equipment. Meanwhile, down a narrow passageway, beside an ordinary looking house is the **Winchcombe Railway Museum and Garden**: the

Sudeley Castle Grounds

OLD STATION HOUSE

Greet, Nr Winchcombe, Gloucestershire GL54 5LD
Tel/Fax: 01242 602283   e-mail: old_station_house@hotmail.com

Step back in time to the elegant age of steam. Jenny and Norman Collier offer guests a truly delightful, relaxing Cotswold Country Break at **Old Station House**. Set in an attractive garden, the Edwardian Cotswold stone former station master's house has two tastefully furnished guest rooms with every modern comfort. The accommodation consists of a double room with separate bathroom and a family room en suite. Both have hospitality trays. There is a lovely lounge with an open fire, tv and lots of information on local places of interest. Breakfast is served in a heated conservatory overlooking a preserved steam railway. The tariff includes a Cotswold country tea on arrival and a full English breakfast. Special three day breaks include a basket of fruit and chocolates.

Wildflower Walk, a Non Soil Terrace Garden, a Mulberry Lawn and the Heritage Seed Library with its rare vegetables.

STANWAY
9 miles NE of Cheltenham on the B4077

This picturesque village, which lies at the foot of a wooded hill, has a particularly unusual cricket pavilion – this one was designed by the playwright JM Barrie, who is perhaps more famous as the creator of *Peter Pan*. Here, too, is the charming Cotswold manor, **Stanway House**, which is best known for its splendid **Baroque Water Garden**, one of the finest in the country. The garden and the house have limited opening in August and September only.

A couple of miles to the south of Stanway are the ruins of **Hailes Abbey** (National Trust), which was founded by Richard, Earl of Cornwall in 1246, and the abbey was created in such a grand style that the Cistercian monks who lived here were hard pressed to keep up the maintenance. However, after a wealthy patron donated a phial said to contain the blood of Christ, the abbey soon became a place of pilgrimage and the monks' money worries were over. The authenticity of the phial was questioned at the time of the

Dissolution, it was destroyed and with the phial went the abbey's main source of income. The buildings fell into disrepair and, today, the only significant parts to survive are the cloister arches. Some of the many artefacts that have been found at the site, including medieval sculptures and decorated floor tiles, are on display in the abbey's museum. The abbey is open throughout the year although times and days vary.

STANTON
10 miles NE of Cheltenham off the B4632

This attractive village of steeply gabled limestone cottages, dating mainly from the 16th and 17th centuries, is widely acknowledged as one of the prettiest of the Cotswolds. Its appearance today though is due to the restoration work carried out by the architect Sir Philip Scott who restored the whole village in the early 20th century and his home, between 1906 and 1937, was **Stanton Court**, an elegant residence that was built by Elizabeth I's Chamberlain. The village Church of St Michael has many interesting features, including some stained glass from nearby Hailes Abbey and a number of medieval pews with scarred ends that were caused, perhaps, by the leashes of the shepherds' dogs.

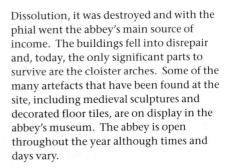

To the east of the village lies **Snowshill Manor** (National Trust), an elegant manor house dating from Tudor times that was once the home of Catherine Parr. Today, the house is home to the fascinating collections of Charles Paget Wade, the last private owner, and visitors can see examples of craftsmanship from around the world, including Samurai armour, musical instruments,

Hailes Abbey

navigational equipment and bicycles. One of the doors in the interior of the house bears the inscription 'Amor et tussis non celantur' (you cannot conceal love or a cough) and, in the room behind the door, in 1604, Anthony Palmer secretly married the heiress Ann Parsons. However, their secret was soon discovered and Palmer was tried before the Court of the Star Chamber for marrying Ann without her relative's permission. The house, which is open on selected days between April and November, is surrounded by a charming cottage garden.

Chipping Campden

CHIPPING CAMPDEN
16 miles NE of Cheltenham on the B4081

Often described as the 'Jewel of the Cotswolds', Chipping Campden is one of the region's best preserved and most historically important towns and, as a regional capital of the wool trade between the 13th and 16th centuries, many of its fine buildings date from that period of prosperity. It was originally planned in the late 12th century and its layout can still be traced today, particularly in the High Street, which follows the line of an important trade route and where long narrow burgage plots can be found on both sides. The oldest properties in the

THE EIGHT BELLS

Church Street, Chipping Campden,
Gloucestershire GL55 6JG
Tel: 01386 840371 Fax: 01386 841669
e-mail: neilhargreaves@bellinn.fsnet.co.uk
website: www.eightbells.co.uk

A distinguished presence just off the High Street for 700 years, the **Eight Bells** was built to accommodate stonemasons working on the town's imposing church and to store the bells for the church tower. Behind the delightful Cotswold stone frontage hung with flower baskets many original features survive, including oak beams, stone fireplaces and a priest hole, and the tradition of hospitality still thrives under licensees Neil and Julie Hargreaves. A wide range of cask-conditioned and local ales, notably the excellent Hook Norton brews, is served in the bar, together with a varied list of wines from around the world to accompany the food for which the inn is justly renowned.

In the separate dining areas - one of them non-smoking - a daily changing menu features top-quality local seasonal produce in superb, imaginative dishes prepared by accomplished head chef Greg Sweet and his talented team. There are usually at least four special fish dishes each day, and game appears in many guises in season. A children's menu is available. The dining room leads to a beautiful terraced garden that's a perfect setting for a private party. A visit here is always a pleasure, and that pleasure can be extended to take in the full Eight Bells experience with an overnight stay or a short break. The four guest rooms, all en suite, comprise a twin room, two doubles and a family room.

Cotswold Cottage, Chipping Campden

town, both dating from the 14th century, are **Grevel's House** and **Woolstaplers Hall**, whilst, in the town centre, is the **Market Hall** that was built in 1627 and that was one of many buildings financed by the noted wool merchant, Sir Baptist Hicks. Hicks also endowed a group of almshouses and built **Old Campden House**, at the time the largest residence in the village, although, later it was burnt down by Royalists during the Civil War to prevent it falling into enemy hands. All that survives today are two gatehouses and the old stable block. The village's 15th century Church of St James was built on a grand scale, reflecting the wealth generated by the wool trade, and inside are several impressive

monumental brasses including one of William Grevel measuring a mighty eight feet by four feet.

Nearby lies **Dover's Hill**, a natural amphitheatre above the town, and this is the scene of the **Cotswold Olympics** that were founded in the 17th century by Captain Robert Dover of Stanway House. The games followed in the traditions of the ancient Greeks although some more down-to-earth activities, such as shin-kicking and bare-knuckle boxing, were added by the Captain. The lawlessness and hooliganism that accompanied the games led to their being closed down in 1852 but they were revived, in a modern form, in 1951 and remain a popular spring attraction today.

HIDCOTE BARTRIM
18½ miles NE of Cheltenham off the B4081

This little hamlet in the north of the county is a must for gardening enthusiasts as it is home to two glorious gardens. One of the country's great gardens, **Hidcote Manor Garden** (National Trust) is a masterpiece of the Arts and Crafts Movement style that was created by Major Lawrence Johnston in the early 20th century. Famous for its rare shrubs and trees gathered from all over the world, the garden is laid out as a delightful series of

Hidcote Manor

Kiftsgate Court Garden

atmosphere. Kiftsgate is open from April to September.

BLOCKLEY
15 miles NE of Cheltenham on the B4479

Silk spinning was the main industry here and, until the 1880s, six mills created the main source of employment. As far back as the *Domesday Book*, water mills were recorded here and the village also once boasted an iron foundry and factories making soap, collars and pianos. Today, the mills are now silent but visitors here will find, set around a mill in a steep-sided valley, **Mill Dene Garden**, a traditional garden that has been designed and planted in the English country style. A series of terraces rising up from the mill pond and with glorious views from the top levels over the Cotswold hills, the gardens include a rose walk, a fantasy fruit garden and a potager. The garden is open from April to October.

smaller gardens or 'rooms'. Hidcote Manor is open most days from April to October.

Also here is **Kiftsgate Court Garden** that reflects gardening throughout the 20th century and, whilst it is perched on the edge of the Cotswolds with wonderful views to the west, the sheltered lower gardens have a real Mediterranean

Just to the southeast and overlooking the Evenlode Valley is **Batsford Arboretum** (see panel opposite), some 55 acres of parkland that contain over 1,500 different species of trees and that is, in autumn, a wonderful riot of rich reds, purples, yellows and golds. Meanwhile, further south again is **Burton House Garden**, which surrounds a delightful 18th century manor house (not open to the public). Open from May to October, this

---

THE CROWN INN HOTEL

High Street, Blockley, Nr Moreton-in-Marsh, Gloucestershire GL56 9EX
Tel: 01386 700245 e-mail: info@crown-inn-blockley.co.uk
Fax: 01386 700247 website: www.crown-inn-blockley.co.uk

The Crown Hotel is a true Cotswold gem, a handsome old building in mellow local stone. Business partners Mandy Eden and Andrew Kertai offer top-quality accommodation in 24 beautifully furnished en suite bedrooms. Each room has its own individual style, but all have tv, telephone, hairdryer and tea/coffee making facilities. The bar has a true country inn atmosphere and in the intimate beamed restaurant the talented chefs prepare a wide variety of superb dishes such as slow braised lamb shank set on a goat's cheese potato cake and stir-fried capsicum coated with a redcurrant and rosemary glaze. A super selection of wines complements the fine food. Lighter meals, including pizza and tapas, are served in the brasserie.

BATSFORD PARK: ARBORETUM

Batsford Park, Moreton-in-Marsh, Gloucestershire GL56 9QB
Tel: 01386 701441 Fax: 01386 701829
e-mail: batsarb@batsford.freeserve.co.uk
website: www.batsford-arboretum.co.uk

Batsford Park is a place of several unique attractions, comprising an arboretum and wild garden, a garden centre and a falconry centre. The Arboretum contains a rare and beautiful collection of over 1,500 species and varieties of trees, shrubs, bamboos and wild flowers set in 55 acres of typical Cotswold countryside. Visitors can wander along magical meandering paths and by the side of streams, discover delights and surprises at every turn, including a Japanese Rest House, a hermit's cave and a number of magnificent bronze statues from the Far East, originally collected by Lord Redesdale. Each season brings its own special magic to this jewel in the Cotswold crown: in spring the snowdrops and daffodils; in early summer the magnolias and the Japanese cherry blossom; in autumn the reds and yellows and golds of the deciduous trees; and in winter the fairyland of frost and the waterfall of icicles suspended above the frozen lake. The Arboretum and gift shop are open daily from the beginning of February to mid-November, otherwise at weekends only.

exciting garden features imaginative topiary, magnificent herbaceous borders and a unique shade house.

MORETON-IN-MARSH

16½ miles NE of Cheltenham on the A429

A still thriving market town that retains much of its original plan from when it was laid out in the 13th century, Moreton-in-Marsh is also well placed at the crossing point of the Roman Fosse Way and the London to Worcester road and so it was an important staging post during the days of coach travel. Of the fine buildings to be found here is the rare Curfew Tower, still with its original clock and bell, which dates from 1633 whilst 18th and 19th century houses and shops line the long and wide High Street.

To the east of the town is the **Four Shires Stone** that marks the old meeting point of the county boundaries of Gloucestershire, Worcestershire, Warwickshire and Oxfordshire. The town's important links with agriculture are maintained with annual **Moreton Show**, a major celebration of farming in this area of the north Cotswolds.

Just to the west of the town is the

THE BELL INN

High Street, Moreton-in-Marsh, Gloucestershire GL56 0AF
Tel: 01608 651688 Fax: 01608 652195
website: bellinncotswold.com

The **Bell Inn** is a Georgian building in honey-coloured local stone, originally a coaching inn, and its tradition of hospitality is being maintained in splendid style by leaseholders Pam and Keith Pendry. Six well-kept real ales are on tap to quench thirsts, and in the restaurant a wide selection of home-cooked snacks and meals, sandwiches and vegetarian options is served. Behind the inn a charming courtyard and a lovely flower-filled walled garden are summer bonuses. The Bell also offers exceptional accommodation in five en suite bedrooms with period features; two of the rooms are wheelchair accessible. An alternative to the in-house rooms is an adjacent self-catering cottage sleeping up to six guests.

THE CROSS HANDS INN

Salford Hill (A44), Moreton-in-Marsh,
Gloucestershire GL56 0SP
Tel: 01608 643106
website: www.crosshandsinn.co.uk

The Cross Hands Inn is a lovely old coaching inn
situated at the junction of the A44 and A436 close to
the county boundaries of Gloucestershire, Warwickshire
and Oxfordshire (the inn is actually just in Oxfordshire).
A popular place with travellers since the 16th century,
it retains many features from those far-off days,
including beams and exposed rough stone for walls and pillars. In this atmospheric ambience
leaseholders Graham and Denise Povey dispense hospitality, real ales and a good selection of draught
keg bitters, lagers, stout and cider.

Home-cooked food is served lunchtime and evening (all day in summer) from a wide-ranging
menu that is made even wider by daily blackboard
specials. The choice runs from lunchtime sandwiches
to lasagne, scampi, steak & ale pie and Cross Hands
Chicken - a chicken breast cooked in a barbecue sauce
topped with caramelised onions. The Sunday choice is
more limited, since the traditional roast is so popular.
Thought to be the highest public house in Oxfordshire,
the Cross Hands enjoys fine views of the surrounding
countryside, and to the rear is a caravan and camping
site with room for up to 18 touring vans; all the stands
have electric hook-ups and there are shower and toilet
facilities on the site.

Cotswold Falconry Centre, which gives
visitors an insight into the ancient art of
falconry as well as offering the opportunity
to see falcons, hawks, eagles and owls fly
freely in the regular spectacular
demonstrations. The centre, where visitors
can also view the breeding aviaries, is open
from March to November.

CRANHAM
7 miles SW of Cheltenham off the A46

Just to the west of the village lies
Prinknash Abbey Park (pronounced
Prinnage), an active monastery with a
chapel, working pottery, gift shop and tea
room. Home to Benedictine monks, they
moved here from Caldey Island in 1928
when the old house was given to them by
the 20th Earl of Rothes in accordance with
the wishes of his grandfather. Although
the monks no longer live in the old house
– they moved into the impressive new
monastery in 1972 – the abbey chapel is

open daily and visitors can tour the
pottery and buy a hand-made Prinknash
pot in the gift shop. Meanwhile, part of
the abbey gardens are now the **Prinknash
Bird and Deer Park**, where visitors can
feed and stroke the fallow deer and view
the waterfowl, peacocks and African
pygmy goats.

PAINSWICK
10 miles SW of Cheltenham on the A46

Known as the 'Queen of the Cotswolds',
Painswick, which is surrounded by some of
Gloucestershire's most glorious
countryside, is a delightful place where
many of the buildings are constructed of
the mellow Cotswold stone that was
quarried from nearby Painswick Beacon.
Flourishing on the back of a prosperous
wool trade, New Street was constructed in
the early 15th century and it contains the
oldest building in England to house a Post
Office – this is also a rarity for the town as

CHANCELLORS TEA ROOMS

Kingsley House, Victoria Street, Painswick,
Gloucestershire GL6 6QA
Tel: 01452 812451 Fax: 01452 810990
e-mail: jan&judy@chancevicst.freeserve.co.uk

Sisters Janet and Judy Parkinson opened here in 2001 serving
morning coffee, light lunches and afternoon teas. **Chancellors
Tea Rooms** occupy distinctive corner premises in local stone,
parts of which were formerly a granary (now available as a
function room), a dairy and a toy shop. Home-made scones and
cakes are major temptations, the latter including some speciality Viennese pastries, but there's also a
good savoury choice, with omelettes always popular. Chancellors Tea Rooms, a non-smoking zone, are
open from 9.30 to 5.30; closed Mondays except Bank Holidays.

it is a timber-framed building. Another example of a building constructed at the height of the town's prosperity is 14th century St Mary's Church, which contains some rare corbels that are thought to represent Richard II and his queen. Meanwhile, the church tower rises to some 172 feet and it acts as a local landmark. Later, during the Civil War, the church was the scene of one of the many local skirmishes when a party of Parliamentary soldiers came under cannon fire that also caused considerable damage to the building. In 1643, Charles I is believed to have spent the night at the Court House (adjacent to the church) before the siege of Gloucester and, at **Spoonbed**, between Painswick and Gloucester, is **King Charles' Stone**, where the king is said to have rested after the siege.

Each year, in September, the children of the town perform the ancient custom of 'Clipping the Church', when, in the afternoon, a procession is led around the boundaries of St Mary's churchyard. After circling around the church and dancing, the traditional Clipping Hymn is sung and the ceremony ends with the vicar reading a Clipping Sermon. This custom is thought to have

originated from an old pagan rite in which the local community shows its faith by embracing its place of worship. The churchyard contains 99 yew trees and legend has it that, whenever a 100th tree is planted, it fails to grow.

Just north of the town lies **Painswick House** and in its grounds, hidden away in this lovely Cotswold valley, is the **Painswick Rococo Garden**, a unique 18th century garden that is home to plants from around the world. Combining formality and informality, this charming garden,

View of Painswick

which is open from January to November, includes a maze, a striking kitchen garden, a breathtaking display of snowdrops in early spring, a specialist nursery, gift shop and restaurant.

The countryside surrounding Painswick is exceptionally beautiful and it also holds a wealth of interest for both birdwatchers and wildlife enthusiasts alike. As well as being on the famous **Cotswold Way** footpath, there are magnificent views from **Painswick Beacon** out across the Severn Valley to the Welsh mountains and, close by, is **Slad Valley** that was made famous by Laurie Lee is his book *Cider with Rosie*.

GLOUCESTER
8 miles SW of Cheltenham on the A417

The capital city of the county, Gloucester first gained prominence under the Romans, who, in the 1st century AD, established a fort here to guard what was then the lowest crossing point on the River Severn. A much larger fortress followed and their settlement of Glevum became one of the most important Roman military bases in their attempts to confine the rowdy Celts to Wales. It was at Gloucester, too, that William the Conqueror held a Christmas parliament, commissioned the Domesday Survey and ordered the rebuilding of the abbey – an undertaking that included the building of a magnificent church that was to become the forerunner of the superb Norman Cathedral. The elaborately carved tomb of Edward II, murdered at nearby Berkeley Castle, is just one of the many historic monuments within **Gloucester Cathedral** whilst another, the work of the Wedgwood designer John Flaxman, remembers Sarah Moreley, who died at sea in 1784. The cathedral is also noted for its superb Norman nave with its

massive cylindrical pillars, the exquisite fan tracery in the cloisters and the magnificent East Window that, at 72 feet by 38 feet, is the largest surviving stained glass window in the country and it was built to celebrate victory at the Battle of Crécy in 1346. Still very much a place of worship today, the cathedral also has an exhibition telling its story, from the founding of the abbey some 1300 years ago to the present day, and there are guided tours of the crypt. More recently, the cathedral was used as one of the locations for the film *Harry Potter and the Philosopher's Stone*.

The old area of the city, centred on Gloucester Cross, boasts some very fine early buildings, including St John's Church and St Mary's Church, whilst, close by, and near to the house Robert Raikes of Sunday School fame lived, is an odd looking tower. Built in the 1860s to honour Hannah, the wife of Thomas Fenn Addison, a successful solicitor, the tower also acts as a memorial to Raikes. During the 14th and 15th centuries several inns were built to accommodate the pilgrims who came to the city to visit Edward II's tomb. One, the galleried New Inn, was founded by a monk in the mid 15th century and it doubled as a theatre and still retains its cobbled courtyard. It was from here that Lady Jane

Gloucester Cathedral

Grey was proclaimed Queen. Another equally ancient inn is The Fleece Hotel that has a 12th century stone-vaulted undercroft. Close by is **Maverdine House**, a four-storey mansion that was the residence and headquarters of Colonel Massey, Cromwell's commander during the Civil War siege of Gloucester in 1643. Although most of the surrounding region was in Royalist hands, Massey and his troops survived a month long assault on Gloucester by a force led by the king himself and so turned the tide of the bitter conflict.

Elsewhere there is **Gloucester City Museum and Art Gallery** that houses exhibits detailing the early history of the city including dinosaur bones, Roman remains and the amazing **Birdlip Mirror** – it was made in bronze for a Celtic chief just before the Roman invasion. The decorative and fine art displays are exhibited in rotation and include English landscape paintings by Turner and Gainsborough. Meanwhile, a timber-framed Tudor building houses the **Gloucester Folk Museum**, one of the earliest folk museums in the country, which concentrates on local history, crafts, trades and industries associated with both the city and county. The city's former fire station is now home to the **Gloucester Transport Museum** with its small collection of well preserved vehicles and baby carriages whilst, in College Court, is the **House of the Tailor of Gloucester**, which was sketched by Beatrix Potter in 1897 and featured in her tale *The Tailor of Gloucester* and it now brings to life the famous children's story.

England's most inland port, **Gloucester Docks** were once the gateway for waterborne traffic heading into the Midlands and the handsome Victorian warehouses are always in demand as

THE NATIONAL WATERWAYS MUSEUM

Llanthony Warehouse, Gloucester Docks, Gloucester, Gloucestershire GL1 2EH
Tel: 01452 318056 Fax: 01452 318066
e-mail: marketing@nwm.demon.co.uk
website: www.nwm.org.uk

There's so much to see and do for all ages at the award-winning **National Waterways Museum** located in a splendid Victorian warehouse in historic Gloucester Docks. The Museum charts the fascinating 300-year story of Britain's inland waterways through interactive displays, touch-screen computers, working models and historic boats. Visitors can find out what made the waterways possible, from the business brains and design genius to the hard work and sweat of the navvies, and try their hand at designing and painting a narrow boat, building a canal and navigating a boat through a lock.

The Museum has a working blacksmith's forge, a floor of displays dedicated to waterway trade and cargoes, a marvellous interactive gallery and family room where weights and pulleys, water playareas, period costume, large jigsaw puzzles and brass rubbings bring history to life in a way that is both instructive and entertaining. The museum shop sells unusual gifts and souvenirs and refreshment is provided in the café. There are computerised information points throughout the Museum and visitors can even take to the water themselves on a 45-minute boat trip running along the adjacent Gloucester & Sharpness Canal between Easter and October. The National Waterways Museum is owned by the Waterways Trust, which preserves, protects and promotes our waterway heritage while giving new life to their future.

location sites for period films. Today, the restored warehouses are now home to several award-winning museums: the **National Waterways Museum** (see panel above), which tells the fascinating story of Britain's canals with films, displays and historic boats; the **Soldiers of Gloucestershire Museum**, where displays describe the life of those who served in The Glosters and the Royal Gloucestershire

THE RISING SUN

Hiams Lane, Maisemore, Gloucestershire GL19 3DQ
Tel: 01452 700392

Tucked away off the A417 north of Gloucester, the **Rising Sun** is a cheerful white-painted pub that once saw service as a Methodist church. With Tom and Jan Madden at the helm, it attracts regulars from Gloucester, the surrounding countryside and further afield with its top-quality food and the extensive selection of draught and bottled ales. Jan is a super cook, and among her many excellent dishes are fish specials and the Sunday roasts. Children are very welcome, and there's a play area and a family beer garden. A big attraction of the Rising Sun is the skittle alley, which is available with notice when not in use by the many local teams who play here.

Hussars for the past 300 years; and the **Museum of Advertising and Packaging: The Robert Opie Collection** – a comprehensive collection of British packaging and advertising that dates back to 1963 and where, also, visitors can see exhibits that portray a social history of Britain from the 1870s to the present day.

Close to the centre of Gloucester are the ruins of **Llanthony Abbey**, which was the only monastic community in England that, curiously, bore a Welsh name. The priory of Llanthony was originally founded in the Black Mountains of Wales at the beginning of the 12th century but the monks were so frightened of the local Welsh that they begged the Bishop of Hereford to find them a safer place for their community. The bishop passed their plea to Milo, Earl of Hereford, who granted the monks this plot of land for a second priory bearing the same name as the first and Llanthony Secunda was consecrated in 1136. On a nearby hill, the monks built **St Ann's Well** whose waters were, and still are, believed to cure eye complaints.

WALLSWORTH
6½ miles W of Cheltenham off the A38

Housed in **Wallsworth Hall**, a fine Georgian mansion, is **Nature in Art**, the world's first museum that is dedicated entirely to art inspired by nature. Open all year round, the works of art on display range from Flemish masters to contemporary abstracts whilst both Picasso and David Shepherd are also represented along with ethnic art. The gallery has a programme of exhibitions throughout the year whilst visitors also have a chance to watch artists at work.

PAUNTLEY
10 miles NW of Cheltenham off the A417

This hamlet is home to **Pauntley Court** where, in around 1350, Richard Whittington, one of three sons of landowner Sir William de Whittington was born. Contrary to the pantomime, Dick was neither poor nor an orphan although he did become apprenticed to a merchant in London, went on to become a famous financier who lent large sums of money to Richard II, Henry IV and Henry V and was three times Mayor (although not Lord Mayor as that title had not been invented) of London. He married Alice Fitzwarren, the daughter of a wealthy landowner from Dorset and died in 1423. The origin of the cat connection is unclear but an event that could have contributed to the myth was the discovery, in 1862, of the carved figure of a boy holding a cat in the foundations of a house in Gloucester. This carving can now be seen in Gloucester Museum.

DEERHURST
6½ miles NW of Cheltenham off the B4213

Found on the eastern bank of the River Severn, the village church here has a distinct Celtic feel and it is also one of the oldest in England with parts dating back to the 7th century. The treasures inside include a unique double east window, a 9th century carved font and a Saxon carving of the Virgin and Child. Some 200 yards from the church is another Saxon treasure, **Odda's Chapel**, which was dedicated in 1056 and was lost for many centuries before being rediscovered in the late 19th century.

TEWKESBURY
7 miles NW of Cheltenham on the A38

A town of historic and strategic importance at the confluence of the Rivers Severn and Avon, Tewkesbury is an ancient settlement whose expansion has been restricted by the rivers and, therefore, it remains one of the best medieval townscapes in the country. Its early prosperity was based on the wool and mustard trades along with the movement of corn by river and many fine

half-timbered buildings still remain from those days.

At the heart of the town lies **Tewkesbury Abbey**, one of the largest parish churches in the country, which was founded in the 8th century although it was completely rebuilt in the 11th century. One of the last religious houses to be dissolved by Henry VIII, in 1540, it was saved from destruction by the townspeople, who raised £453 to buy it from the Crown. Many of the building's features are on a grand scale: the colossal double row of Norman pillars, the six-fold arch in the west front and the vast tower – at 132 feet it is the tallest surviving Norman tower in the world.

Housed in a 17th century building, the **Town Museum** is home to a fascinating collection that illustrates the history of the town and where there is also a model of the Battle of Tewkesbury on display. Close by and in part of a row of late 15th century

AUBERGINE CAFFE BAR

73 Church Street, Tewkesbury,
Gloucestershire GL20 5RX
Tel/Fax: 01684 292703

Aubergine Caffe Bar is a Grade II listed building dating from the late 15th century. Behind its black-and-white timbered frontage squeezed between taller buildings on one of the town's main streets, Aubergine has immense charm, with masses of wood everywhere - pillars, beams, panelling, slatted floor - and the occasional modern picture making a splash of colour on the snow white walls. Owned and run by business partners Graham Thornton and Nathan

Beauchamp, Aubergine is a place to eat, a place to drink, a place to meet friends, a place to escape.

The printed menu and blackboard specials provide plenty of choice lunchtime and evening, typified by home-made broccoli soup, moules marinière, supreme of chicken with wild mushrooms, white wine and cream, and venison sausages with mash, braised red cabbage and onion gravy. There's a good wine list, including some by the glass, and a wide variety of bottle beers. Aubergine's opening times are 11.30-2 (Sunday till 2.30, Saturday from 10.30) and 7-9. Closed Monday except for Bank Holidays and pre-booked parties of 10+; also closed Sunday evening.

BECKFORD INN

Cheltenham Road (A46), Beckford, Nr Tewkesbury,
Gloucestershire GL20 7AN
Tel: 01386 881532/881254 Fax: 01386 882021

Looking more like a country mansion than a typical inn, **Beckford Inn** is a superb Cotswold stone building with its origins in the 18th century. It's run by the Fenn family - Kevin and Margaret and sons Jamie and Matt - and offers all the facilities of a public house and restaurant, as well as comfortable Bed & Breakfast accommodation; it also makes a splendid venue for parties and conferences. Three or four real ales, including a local brew, are on tap in the bar, along with a full range of other beers, lagers, stout and cider. These can be enjoyed on their own or to accompany a meal in the well-appointed 70- cover restaurant (non-smoking).

The printed menu and the specials board offer a fine choice; among the latter could be red snapper with a chive and vermouth sauce, pan-fried medallions of beef with a peppercorn and armagnac sauce and the impressive Beckford 'Big' Grill. Food is served every lunchtime and evening except Sunday evening in winter. Picnic tables are set out on the spacious lawned garden at the front of the inn. Children are welcome, and for guests staying overnight the eight first-floor twin or double bedrooms all have en suite shower, tv, radio-alarm and tea & coffee making facilities. The inn is open all day, every day except between 3.30 and 5 on Monday, Tuesday and Wednesday out of season.

THE CROWN AT KEMERTON

High Street, Kemerton, Nr Tewkesbury,
Gloucestershire GL20 7HP
Tel: 01386 725293
e-mail: crown.kemerton@dial.pipex.com

With a history going back to the 16th century, the **Crown** is a welcoming sight on the main street of Kemerton. Behind the long white-painted facade with a slate-roofed porch, the inn has abundant atmosphere and a wealth of character provided by old flagstones, stripped oak and a Cotswold-stone fireplace. The Crown has been run since 1994 by Tim Barber and Marion New, who bring experience and a real feel for what keeps the customers happy to their work.

A minimum of three real ales is always available, and a long blackboard menu in the 30-seat

restaurant changes daily to reflect what's best and freshest in the markets. Typical choices run from smoked seafood paté and home-made minestrone for starters to plaice fillets in a cheesy prawn and dill sauce, casseroled rabbit and roast rack of lamb with a mint gravy. Room should certainly be left for a scrumptious home-made pudding such as gooseberry and ginger crunchy crumble, and the excellent food is complemented by a wide selection of wines. Food is not served on Sunday evening out of season. Darts and cribbage are the favourite games, and the pub holds regular quiz nights. At the back of the Crown is s delightful south-facing walled garden.

cottages are two other museums. The **John Moore Countryside Museum** is concerned with both issues of conservation and matters relating to the countryside and it is named after the well-known writer, broadcaster and naturalist, who was born in Tewkesbury in 1907. The adjoining **Little Museum** is a restored merchant's house that retains many of its medieval features. Meanwhile, down by the River Avon is the **Abbey Mill**, whose foundations are believed to date back to the 12th century although the present building was constructed in the 18th century. No longer a mill today, it did features as Abel Fletcher's mill in *John Halifax, Gentleman*. Another building here with literary connections is **The Royal Hop Pole Hotel**, one of the town's coaching inns, where Mr Pickwick, of Charles Dickens' creation, had a thoroughly enjoyable meal.

Tewkesbury Abbey

The **Battle of Tewkesbury** was one of the fiercest in the Wars of the Roses and it took place in 1471 in a field to the south of the town that has, ever since, been known as Bloody Meadow. Following the Lancastrian defeat here, those who had not been slaughtered on the field fled to the abbey, where the killing began again.

Abbot Strensham intervened to stop the massacre but the survivors, who included the Duke of Somerset, were handed over to the King and executed at the Market Cross. The 17-year-old son of Henry VI, Edward Prince of Wales, was killed in the conflict and a plaque marking his final resting place can be seen in the abbey. Tewkesbury was again the scene of military action almost two centuries later during the Civil War. The town changed hands several times during this period and, on one occasion, Charles I began his siege of Gloucester by requisitioning every pick, mattock, spade and shovel in Tewkesbury.

THE BERKELEY ARMS

8 Church Street, Tewkesbury, Gloucestershire GL20 5PA
Tel: 01684 293034

The **Berkeley Arms** is a historic black-and-white timbered building with a history going back to the 15th century. The interior has an old-world charm in keeping with the inn's age, and at the rear of the premises is a wonderful old beamed barn that has been refurbished and now serves as an overspill for the restaurant. Five real ales head the long list of beers, and blackboards display the day's dishes. The tenants at this most atmospheric of inns are Ian and Jo Phillips, and Jo is queen of the kitchen. Everything she cooks on an across-the-board selection is worth trying, but her beef and Guinness pie really is extra special. There's live music on Saturday evening and a quiz every Tuesday.

CINDERFORD

First recorded as 'Sinderford', in 1258, the name is thought to have been derived from the term 'sinders' or slag left behind by an early Roman iron works in the area whilst 'ford' refers to a crossing over the Cinderford Brook. In 1674, following improvements made after the Civil War, the ford at Cinderford was replaced by the Cinderford Bridge. At that time, the settlement was little more than a collection of dwellings but, in 1795, the establishment of the first coke furnace here, by Thomas Teague, began the expansion that was finally realised in the 1820s when financial problems were overcome and the ironworks finally began to thrive. The output of the Cinderford Iron Company reached its peak in 1858, when four blast furnaces were working simultaneously, but, by 1890, the ironworks had closed as they could not compete with the larger works in South Wales and the Midlands. Many of the buildings in the town date from those prosperous days of the ironworks and, along with the parish Church of St John that dates from 1884, there is Belle Vue House (1840) that is now the Belle Vue Centre and the market house that was set up in 1869.

Today, the town, which lies at some 800 feet above sea level, provides some spectacular views across the River Severn to Gloucester and the Cotswold hills. Meanwhile, much of the town's industrial heritage can be traced at **Linear Park** that incorporates part of the former network of old railway lines and a former open cast mining site. Now a place of woodlands and wetlands, the park is home to a wide variety of both flora and fauna and it is a tranquil place for a quiet walk and seems far removed from the heavy industrial past of the 19th century.

Forest of Dean

Away from its industrial past, Cinderford can also claim fame as holding the last witchcraft trial in Britain, in 1906, when Ellen Hayward, a local herbalist was charged with unlawful deception by pretended witchcraft when she is said to have put a spell on a Mr Davis who had brought his sick pig to see her. However, the bizarre case was, after the magistrates had received many letters telling of Ellen's good deeds, dismissed but not before Ellen herself had suffered great financial hardship.

Cinderford lies in the heart of the **Forest of Dean**, an area of unspoilt wilderness between the Rivers Wye and Severn, which was once called the 'Queen of Forests all', that is one of the country's few remaining ancient forests. A peaceful and tranquil place, today the forest is not only rich in natural history but also, from prehistoric times onwards, it has been inhabited. Plundered for its timber and other natural resources such as iron, stone and coal, the Forest of Dean has been a place of industry right from the times of the Romans who established some of the first iron works here.

To the southwest of Cinderford lies **Cyril Hart Arboretum**, which is named after the local historian and forestry expert. This small but excellent collection of rare conifer and broadleaf species was started in 1910 and there are various trails amongst the woodland plantings.

AROUND CINDERFORD

MITCHELDEAN
3 miles NE of Cinderford of the A4136

Just a mile to the south of this quiet community that is situated on the northern fringe of the forest, is **St Anthony's Well**, whose water is invariably icy cold and bathing in it is said to cure skin diseases. St Anthony's Fire was the medieval name for a rampant itching disease. Meanwhile, in Mitcheldean lies **Wintle's Brewery** that once supplied the public houses within the forest. During World War II, the brewery became a dispersal factory for British Acoustic Films and, now, as Rank Precision Industries, it is, with the closure of the area's collieries one of Forest of Dean's largest employers.

KEMPLEY
10 miles NE of Cinderford off the A449

Famous for its cider, this village is home to two churches, of very different ages – the sandstone Church of St Edward dates from 1903 and was built by the 7th Earl Beauchamp in the style of the Arts and Crafts Movement. Meanwhile, the **Church of St Mary**, one of the most popular in the area, dates from the 11th century and is a delight. However, what makes this small Norman church so special are the superb frescoes that it contains. The oldest, found in the chancel, date from 1130 and were restored to their original condition in the 1950s; they depict various scenes including Christ sitting on a rainbow blessing the world.

DYMOCK
11 miles NE of Cinderford on the B4216

At the centre of this village is the early Norman **Church of St Mary** that, along with a 13th century stone coffin lid and a 17th century turned oak font, also contains an unusual collection of artefacts and memorabilia including the last ticket issued at Dymock station in 1959. The village boasts some other interesting old brick buildings, including the White House and the Old Rectory whilst, just outside, the Old Grange incorporates the remains of the Cistercian Flaxley Abbey.

THE NELSON ARMS INN

Morse Road, Drybrook, Gloucestershire GL17 9AH
Tel: 01594 544860
e-mail: bookings@thenelsonarms.co.uk
website: www.thenelsonarms.co.uk

North of the A4136 in the heart of the Forest of Dean, the **Nelson Arms Inn** is finding a new lease of life in the capable hands of owners Ian and Diane. Arriving here in December 2001, they have totally refurbished the 18th century inn, and the growing reputation for hospitality and good food and ale is proving a magnet for both local residents and visitors to the Forest. Three real ales are always available, and Diane's excellent food is served in the bar areas and in the 28-cover restaurant, where booking is recommended for Friday and Saturday evenings and Sunday lunch. The Nelson Arms is closed on Mondays except Bank Holidays.

In the years before World War I, Dymock became the base for a group of writers who became known as the **Dymock Poets**. Amongst the group were Rupert Brooke, Wilfred Gibson, Edward Thomas, Lascelles Abercrombie and Robert Frost and they sent out their *New Numbers* poetry magazine from Dymock's tiny post office. It was whilst here that Brooke published his *War Sonnets* that include *The Soldier*. Both Brooke and Thomas were killed during the Great War, which led to the dissolution of the group, and, today, there are two circular walks from the village that take in places associated with the poets.

In 1892, a lead tablet was found here on which was written the name Sarah Ellis – backwards. Known as the Dymock Curse, it is believed that the unfortunate girl had, for an unknown reason, a curse placed upon her and this knowledge, according to legend, sent the young woman insane and she finally committed suicide. As was the custom at the time, suicides were buried at a crossroads and she was buried at such a point on the boundary of Dymock and Oxenhall parishes at what was to become known as Ellis's Cross. Though both her identity and the reason for the curse remain a mystery, the tablet can be viewed at Gloucester Folk Museum.

NEWENT
8½ miles NE of Cinderford on the B4216

Appearing in the *Domesday Book* as 'Noent', Newent lies in an area that is dominated by farming and, therefore, is different in character from the other towns of the Forest of Dean region. A conservation area today, Newent has not only managed to retain much of its medieval street pattern but also some of its original black and white timbered buildings. However, excavations in the area have revealed that Newent dates back to long before the Norman Conquest and a large Roman industrial site has been found

just outside the town. Later, in medieval times, Newent was the property of the Abbey of Cormeilles in Normandy and the legacy of those days remains the fine churches that the monks built on their land, including **St Mary's Church** whose spire rises to some 153 feet in height. Other interesting features here are the shaft of a 9th century Saxon cross found in the churchyard and the 17th century nave (that was needed to replace the one damaged severely during the Civil War), which was started after Charles II agreed to donate 60 tons of timber from the Forest of Dean. Another legacy of the Normans is its market – the 17th century Market House still dominates the medieval market square – and the annual **Onion Fayre**, which is believed to be the only such fayre in the country.

The Market House is now home to the **Newent Heritage Centre**, which is open every summer's day afternoon, whilst, close by, is **The Shambles of Newent, a Museum of Victorian Life** that is almost a complete reconstruction of a small Victorian town, with cobbled streets and alleyways, cottages, shops and even a mission chapel and a Victorian conservatory. Meanwhile, at the old magistrates' court, in Nicholson House, is the unique **Crime Through Times, the Black Museum** that houses an outstanding private collection of world-wide interest.

Newent is the capital of the area of northwest Gloucestershire that is known as Ryelands and it is also the most important town in the **Vale of Leadon**, an area of market gardens, rolling farmland and vineyards that is a perfect example of a traditional English countryside landscape. In this surrounding area, just north of the town, lies the **Three Choirs Vineyard**, the largest vineyard in the country and where visitors can take a guided tour before enjoying a wine tasting. To the south lies

May Hill, on National Trust land, whose 1,000 foot summit has been, at various times, planted with trees to celebrate Queen Victoria's Golden Jubilee in 1887, Queen Elizabeth II's Silver Jubilee in 1977 and, three years later, the Queen Mother's 80th Birthday. The reward for climbing to the top is a quite magnificent view that stretches over Gloucestershire, and, on a clear day, as far as Bristol. Close by is the **National Bird of Prey Centre**, which houses one of the world's largest and most extensive collections of birds of prey – over 110 aviaries are home to eagles, falcons, owls, vultures, kites, hawks and buzzards. Open from February to November, between 20 and 40 birds are flown daily in thrilling free flying demonstrations.

UPLEADON
10 miles NE of Cinderford off the B4215

This straggling village is home to **St Mary's Church** that, as well as having some fine Norman and Tudor features, is probably well over 1,000 years old and stands on a huge mound of clay that may have been an ancient place of worship. However, the church is best known for its unique half-timbered tower that was added in the 16th century whilst, inside, is its greatest treasure – an early example of the Authorised Version of the Bible printed by the Royal printer, Robert Barker. It was Barker who later issued an edition with a small but rather important word missing:

the so-called Wicked Bible of 1631 in which Exodus 20.14 reads "Thou shalt commit adultery."

WESTBURY-ON-SEVERN
4 miles E of Cinderford on the A48

This village is best known as the home of **Westbury Court Garden** (National Trust), a fully restored, formal Dutch water garden that was originally laid out between 1696 and 1705. Historic varieties of apple, pear and plum, along with many other species introduced into England before 1700 and a 400-year-old evergreen oak, make this an extremely interesting place for gardening enthusiasts. The house has long since been demolished and the only surviving building is an elegant two-storey brick pavilion with a tower and weather vane. The gardens are open from March to October.

Several centuries ago, in this area particularly, it was believed that witches could turn themselves into hares or rabbits and folk tales of women appearing as such animals are commonplace. However, there is another local legend that is unusual in that it concerns a man rather than a woman. An old widower lived with his beautiful daughter in the nearby village of Elton and, protective of his only child, he discouraged the attentions from the local young men. One such young man, deeply in love with the daughter, was desperate to see the object of his love and, one

THE KING'S HEAD

Birdwood, Nr Huntley, Gloucestershire GL19 3EF
Tel/Fax: 01452 750348

Hospitality is the name of the game at the **King's Head**, an excellent place to pause on a journey and a perfect base for exploring the attractions of the region. Marg and Mike Jefferies, here for 21 years, really know how to look after their guests, offering convivial bars with beams, brasses and military memorabilia, a comfortable dining area serving hot and cold bar meals and a speciality Sunday roast, pleasant gardens and a children's play area. The bedrooms are either doubles or family rooms; all have en suite facilities, tv, central heating and tea/coffee makers. The skittle alley doubles as a function room that's a popular venue for private parties and receptions. On the main A40, 6 miles from Gloucester and 7 miles from Ross on Wye

HARRY'S BAR & RESTAURANT

Regents Walk, Lydney, Gloucestershire GL15 5RF
Tel: 01594 845916

Warmly traditional, with polished wood and a pleasantly old-fashioned air, **Harry's Bar & Restaurant** has a first-floor location in a shopping arcade. A place for all ages, tastes and appetites, it was created in 1994 by Robin Johnson and has been managed since then by Wendy Williams. The restaurant offers plenty of variety on its menus, from lunchtime sandwiches and 'loaded jackets' to Thai chicken wings, sausage & mash, fish pie and stilton & pasta bake. A full range of drinks is served in the bar, where happy hour is from 7 to 9 every evening; disco and live entertainment from 9.30 Friday and Saturday.

THE MINERS ARMS

Whitecroft, Lydney, Gloucestershire GL15 4PE
Tel: 01594 562483 e-mail: birkinshaw@hotmail.com
website: www.minersarms.org

The Miners Arms is an outstanding free house in the village of Whitecroft, a couple of miles north of Lydney and within the beautiful Forest of Dean. In the early days this was an alehouse, and under owners Stuart and Elaine it still maintains a fine reputation for real ales, with three or four usually available along with a wide selection of beers from local, national and international breweries. Sandwiches and ploughman's platters provide solid sustenance, and for entertainment there are skittles, boules and other traditional pub games. A really appealing pub with lots of character, real fires in winter and a pleasant beer garden for warmer times.

THE GEORGE INN

High Street, Aylburton, Nr Lydney,
Gloucestershire GL15 6DE
Tel: 01594 842163

In the heart of the village of Aylburton on the busy A48, the **George Inn** is a fine place to pause on a journey or to enjoy a longer stay in an area that's full of interesting things to see and do. The Victorian building, constructed of local dressed stone, is very attractive, and in the comfortable, cosy bar regulars and occasional visitors can enjoy a choice of real ales that changes constantly, adding up to over 100 in any year.

In the bar and in the non-smoking 40-cover restaurant, the printed menu and daily specials list provide a good, varied choice of well-prepared dishes; food is served from 12 to 2 and from 7 to 9 daily, and booking is recommended for Saturday evening and Sunday lunch. Children are welcome at the George if eating. Leaseholders Gillian and Derek have added another string to their bow by creating 14 excellent guest bedrooms in the adjacent property, which was originally a brewery. These rooms are stylish and comfortable, and all have en suite facilities, tv and hospitality tray.

summer's afternoon, he passed by their cottage in the hope of catching a glimpse of the girl. The old man was outside tending his garden and, seeing that the youth had passed by, he fell asleep in his chair whilst his daughter prepared dinner. Later, the old man awoke and saw, in a nearby field, a hare staring at the house. Thinking of what a fine meal the animal would make the old man collected his gun and took a shot at the hare. Rather than killing the animal the gun shot wounded it in the leg and the hare ran off into hiding across the field. Later, the same young man who had passed by the cottage earlier came out of the field into which the hare had fled and he appeared to be limping as one of his legs was injured! The explanation of the story, which has been told to generations of children down the years, is simply that the youth had turned himself into a hare in order to see his beloved.

LITTLEDEAN
1 mile SE of Cinderford on the A4151

Along with a 13th century church and an 18th century prison, this village is also home to **Littledean Hall**, reputedly the oldest inhabited house in the country, which lies just to the south. The claim seems genuine as there are both Saxon and Celtic remains in the cellars and it is thought to have its foundations in the 6th century. Meanwhile, other highlights here include a Roman temple site, a Victorian garden and a number of ancient chestnut trees.

UPPER SOUDLEY
2 miles S of Cinderford off the B4226

Close to the village is the **Dean Heritage Centre**, the museum of the Forest of Dean, which has numerous displays on the history of the forest and the people who have lived and worked here. Near to the centre is a corn mill that dates from 1876

whilst **Soudley Ponds,** also in the vicinity, were created by the industrialist William Crawshay as fishponds. There is a pleasant walk beside the ponds and those following the path will also be able to see the old charcoal hearths that supplied the early generation of ironworks.

PARKEND
4½ miles SW of Cinderford on the B4234

This community, like so many in the area, was once based on the extraction of minerals and New Fancy Colliery is now a delightful picnic area with breathtaking views out over the forest. Meanwhile, the village was also the site of the Parkland Ironworks, which closed in 1877 and were demolished in the 1890s, although the engine house still survives and can be seen beside the station. To the northwest of Parkend is the RSPB's **Nagshead Nature Reserve** that has several footpaths and waymarked trails to help visitors make the most of this interesting site.

LYDNEY
7½ miles SW of Cinderford on the B4231

Situated on the western bank of the River Severn, the name Lydney is believed to have been derived from 'Lydeney' meaning 'travellers' island' and there is evidence that this area has been inhabited since the Bronze Age. Meanwhile, Camp Hill, the site of an Iron Age hill fort, was also the site of a great Roman mansion with an elaborate bath systems. The proximity to the River Severn, along with the waterways high tides, made it possible for quite large vessels to navigate as far as Lydney and the harbour here became an important trading centre from which timber, coal and iron were shipped from the region. However, in the 17th century, the area around Lydney Pill (the early harbour) began to silt up and Admiralty ship building was moved from here to Portsmouth. This did not prevent, with the help of a new harbour built in

1810, Lydney remaining an important port until the 1920s. Meanwhile, throughout the 19th and early 20th centuries, Lydney was also an important railway centre, with goods being transported to the harbour for export, and, although the local railway network declined with the end of the Forest of Dean's mining industries, the nostalgic days of steam can be recaptured at the **Dean Forest Railway**, which runs steam trains between Lydney Junction and **Norchard Railway Centre**, the headquarters of the line, where there is also a railway museum and a souvenir shop.

One of the chief attractions here is the **Lydney Park Spring Gardens and Museum**, to the south of the town, and, particularly in May and June, the gardens are a riot of colour. The grounds also incorporate the Iron Age hill fort and the remains of a late Roman temple (mentioned earlier) that was excavated by Sir Mortimer Wheeler in the 1920s. The builders of this unusual temple are thought to have been wealthy Romanised Celts and the mosaic floor (now lost) depicted fish and sea monsters and was dedicated to Nodens, the Romano-Celtic god of healing. The nearby museum houses a number of Roman artefacts discovered on the site, including the famous Lydney Dog, and a number of interesting items brought back from New Zealand in the 1930s by the 1st Viscount Bledisloe. Also in the park traces of Roman iron mine workings and earth workings can be found. The gardens are open from March to June on selected days.

Housed in the restored coach house and farm buildings of the Lydney Park estate, **Taurus Crafts** offers all the family the chance to view a vibrant range of crafts and visitors can also try their hand at throwing a pot.

ST BRIAVELS
8½ miles SW of Cinderford on the B4228

Named after a 5th century Welsh bishop, whose name appears in various forms throughout Celtic Wales, Cornwall and Brittany but nowhere else in England, this historic village was, in the Middle Ages, an important administrative centre and a leading manufacturer of armaments. In 1223 it is believed that Henry III ordered 6,000 crossbow bolts (quarrels) from St Briavels.

The substantial Norman **St Mary's Church**, which provides panoramic views over the Wye Valley, is thought to be sited on a place of worship that dates back to the 5th century. However, the church, which was remodelled by the Victorians, is best known for the curious and very English annual **Bread and Cheese Ceremony**. After evensong on Whit Sunday, a local forester stands on the Pound Walls and throws small pieces of

GARDEN CAFÉ
Lower Lydbrook, Gloucestershire GL17 9NN
Tel/Fax: 01594 860075
e-mail: gardencafe@supanet.co.uk
website: www.gardencafe.co.uk

The Garden Café is a superb restaurant in a glorious setting in the Forest of Dean, a short drive from Symonds Yat. It is set in a substantial period country house amid all kinds of greenery - lawns at the front, trees and shrubs on the patio, creeper on the facade, tall trees rising behind. In this lovely atmospheric ambience owner Paul Hayes offers visitors a fine selection of dishes from a menu that changes constantly to reflect what is best and freshest in the local markets. Preparation and presentation both take high priority in this outstanding restaurant.

bread and cheese to the villagers and the ceremony is believed to have originated more than 700 years ago when the villagers successfully defended their rights of estover (collecting wood from commonland) in nearby Hudnalls Wood. As they were collecting the wood, the villagers would take bread and cheese in their pockets to sustain them and, in celebration of the rights being continued, each villager paid a penny to the churchwarden to help feed the poor and this act led to the founding of the ceremony.

Situated on a high promontory, and in an almost impregnable position, is **St Briavels Castle**, which was founded by Henry I and enlarged by King John who used it has a hunting lodge. Two sturdy gatehouses are among the parts that survive today and they, like some of the actual castle buildings, are still in use though now as a youth hostel.

CLEARWELL
6½ miles SW of Cinderford off the B4231

On the outskirts of this historic village and set in an area of special landscape value, are the **Clearwell Caves** (see panel below), the only remaining working iron mine in the Forest of Dean and this particular mine produces ochres for use as paint pigments by artists or those wishing to decorate their homes with natural paints. Before the 19th century only Freeminers were allowed to enter the mines of the Forest of Dean and any Freeminer allowing access to a non-member of the fellowship would have been brought before the mine law court, their fellowship withdrawn, their tools broken or confiscated and the miner would never again be allowed to mine within the Forest of Dean. Today things are different and at Clearwell Caves there are nine impressive caverns open to visitors who are allowed to descend over 100 feet underground although the mine itself goes down to a depth of 600 feet.

Back in the village is **St**

CLEARWELL CAVES

Near Coleford, Royal Forest of Dean, Gloucestershire GL16 8JR
Tel: 01594 832535
Fax: 01594 833362
e-mail: rw@clearwellcaves.com
website: www.clearwellcaves.com

Clearwell Caves are set in an area of special landscape value, on the outskirts of the historic village of Clearwell, which boasts good walks, a castle, a handsome church, as well as several good pubs and hotels. The Caves are part of the last remaining working iron mine in the Forest of Dean and the last ochre mine in the UK. The Caves are part of a natural cave system that became filled with iron ore around 180 million years ago. Working for ochre began by at least the Bronze Age, over 4000 years ago and as a result the Caves complex now consists of many miles of passageways and hundreds of caverns.

Visitors are offered a wide range of activities, from a leisurely and fascinating self guided under-ground walk, descending over 100 feet, to a more strenuous

adventure caving trip or even a Natural Paint workshop. The Cave shop is a treat in itself with unusual gift ideas, books, souvenirs and a wide range of spectacular minerals and crystals from around the world. And of course you can buy ochre mined here.

Don't miss the Tearoom, which provides a good range of freshly prepared lunches and refreshments, and some very interesting mining artefacts displayed around the ceiling and walls. An unusual day out for all ages and a great underground experience.

SPEECH HOUSE HOTEL

Nr Coleford, Forest of Dean,
Gloucestershire GL167EL
Tel: 01594 822607 Fax: 01594 823658
e-mail: relax@thespeechhouse.co.uk
website: www.thespeechhouse.co.uk

On the B4226 Cinderford road three miles northeast of Coleford, **Speech House** is a top-notch hotel offering an impressive range of facilities in extensive grounds in the Forest of Dean. Built in 1676 as a hunting lodge for Charles II, it is now a hotel of universal, year-round appeal, with 33 en suite bedrooms, cottage apartments, two restaurants, an informal bar and superb meeting and conference facilities. The bedrooms range from singles through doubles and twins to four-posters, family rooms and a luxury spa suite. In the grounds, three cottage apartments provide self-contained accommodation for up to 14 guests in total. Rooms can be hired on a Bed & Breakfast or Dinner, Bed & Breakfast basis.

The main restaurant contains a unique feature in the Verderers Court, the court of the Foresters of

Dean. The Verderers still meet here four times a year, making this Britain's oldest functioning court room and providing the hotel with a fascinating judicial history. The second, more intimate Freeminers Restaurant remembers another historical aspect of the Forest. The menu offers a regularly changing choice of classic dishes with some contemporary influences, typified by salmon with asparagus and hollandaise sauce, Welsh lamb cutlets served on a bed of aubergine and caper tapenade, or chicken breast marinated in lemon juice, mint and yoghurt, fried and served with the pan juices. A separate menu is available in the bar, which is open round the clock for residents. The Speech House is licensed to conduct civil wedding ceremonies, which take place in the picturesque and historic setting of the Verderers Court.

The hotel has conference facilities both within and outside the main building, and the six meeting rooms can be configured for banquets, theatre-style or as boardrooms or classrooms. One of the most impressive of the hotel's amenities is the health and beauty studio, comprising sauna, solarium, spa bath, showers and a mini-gym; in the treatment room, beauty therapy, massage, nail care, aromatherapy and hydrotherapy are among the services offered. With the Forest of Dean on the doorstep, the hotel is an ideal base for individual outdoor activities, management training and survival/ team building courses. Typical activities include climbing, canoeing, orienteering and falconry; Speech House has its own cricket pitch, and golf is available at the nearby Forest Hills golf course. The hotel's General Manager is Lewis Scott, the restaurant manager Jackie Holder.

Peter's Church, a fine example of a mid 19th century building in the French Gothic style that was designed by John Middleton at the request of the Dowager Countess of Dunraven of Clearwell Castle.

NEWLAND
7½ miles SW of Cinderford off the A466

This beautiful village is home to All Saints Church that is often known as the **Cathedral of the Forest** because of its impressive size. Built during the 13th and 14th centuries, and remodelled by the Victorians, this spacious building has many beautiful furnishings but it is most famous for its miner's brass that depicts a medieval Forest miner with a pick, hod and a candle in his mouth.

COLEFORD
5½ miles SW of Cinderford on the B4136

First recorded as 'Colevorde' in 1275, this settlement grew up around three streams and it may well have first been inhabited by the Romans as remains have been discovered close by. As the mining industry in the local area expanded so the population of Coleford grew and, in 1661, Charles II granted the town a Market Charter allowing a weekly market to be held every Friday along with two annual fairs. A Market House was built in the 1670s although an earlier house is thought to have existed and been burnt to the ground during the Battle of Coleford in 1643. Close to where the Market House once stood is the **Clock Tower**, all that remains of an old church that was constructed in 1821 and then demolished in the 1880s after the parish church had been built elsewhere in Coleford. Today, the centre of the town remains much as it did during the 18th and 19th centuries and it is now a conservation area with several listed buildings including some classical Georgian properties.

Before the granting of the market charter, Coleford had already become an important iron processing centre, partly due to the availability of local ore deposits and partly due to the ready supply of timber for converting into charcoal that was used in the smelting process. It was here, in the 19th century, that the Mushet family helped to revolutionise the iron and steel industry when Robert Forest Mushet, a Freeminer, discovered how spiegelsisen, an alloy of iron, manganese, silicon and carbon, could be used in the reprocessing of 'burnt iron' and then went on to develop a system for turning molten pig iron directly into steel – a process that predated the more familiar Bessemer process.

Still regarded as the capital of the Royal Forest of Dean, this busy commercial centre is also home to the **Great Western Railway Museum**, housed in an original GWR goods station, and where the exhibits include several large-scale steam locomotives, railway relics and memorabilia, and a miniature locomotive for children. Another treat for railway fans is the **Perrygrove Railway**, a narrow gauge steam railway that also has a children's indoor village with secret passages.

STAUNTON
7 miles W of Cinderford on the A4136

This village is home to one of the Forest's oldest churches, **All Saints' Church**, which dates from the early 12th century. The most striking feature here is the unusual corkscrew staircase leading past the early 16th century stone pulpit to the belfry door. Meanwhile, in the churchyard is a memorial to David Mushet, a metallurgist whose experiments, along with work undertaken by other family members, revolutionised the steel industry.

Close to the village are two enormous mystical stones, the **Buckstone** and the

Log Cabin At Symonds Yat

Symonds Yat, Gloucestershire GL16 7NZ
Tel: 01594 834479

Walking, rock climbing, canoeing, bird watching.....all these and more attract visitors to the famous Symonds Yat, and the **Log Cabin** is an excellent spot to start or finish a day spent in the open air and to revel in the glorious views. It's very much a family affair, with Anne Ireneus and daughters Karen and Ingrid providing the warmest of welcomes, along with their close friend Dawn. Home-made cakes and preserves with a refreshing cup of tea are popular orders, and the menu of the day always includes the speciality meat or vegetarian pasties. Souvenirs and local information are also on sale at the Log Cabin, which is open daily from March to October and at the weekend in winter (closed January).

Suck Stone: the former, looking like a great monster, used to buck or rock on its base but is now firmly fixed in place whilst the other is a real giant, weighing many thousands of tons.

RUARDEAN
3 miles NW of Cinderford off the A4136

Like many old villages on the fringe of the forest, Ruardean also has a church with some interesting features and here, in particular, is a rare tympanum depicting St George and the Dragon whilst, on a stone plaque in the nave of **St John's Church**, is a curious carving of two fishes. Believed to be the work of craftsmen from the Herefordshire School of Norman Architecture and completed in around 1150, the carving is part of a frieze that was removed with rubble when the south porch was being built in the 13th century. Thought to have been lost, the carving of the two fishes was found in the lining of a bread oven in a cottage at nearby Turner's Tump in 1985. Meanwhile, the church's tower provides panoramic views across the Wye Valley and to the Welsh Mountains.

This village is also famous as being the birthplace of James and William Horlick who were born here in the 1840s. The two brothers moved to the United States separately sometime later and, in 1885, in Wisconsin, they founded the Horlicks Food Company that manufactured the 'malted milk' that they had patented in 1883. Soon their drink (made from the malted milk powder mixed with hot milk or water) was to become world famous and it was supplied to the famous Arctic and Antarctic explorers of the early 20th century – Amundsen, Evens, Scott and Shackleton.

WOTTON-UNDER-EDGE

There has been a settlement here since 940 and throughout much of its history the wealth of this pleasant market town has been based upon wool – indeed until 1830 over half the residents of the town, including children, were involved in making woollen cloth. This industry is not really surprising as the raw materials are all close to hand: wool from the Cotswold sheep, dyes from local plants, water from the area's streams and fuller's earth for finishing the cloth. Such was the town's dependence on cloth manufacture that inside the parish **Church of St Mary** is a chapel dedicated to St Katherine, the patron saint of weavers who is depicted in the stained glass window from the Catherine Wheel upon which she was martyred. However, in the 19th century the town became well known as the home of Isaac Pitman, inventor of the shorthand system in 1837, and his terraced house can still be seen along with numerous houses and cottages that were once occupied by mill owners and their workers. Today, Wotton remains a thriving shopping centre, with many traditional shops, and it also boasts its own independent cinema where the latest block busters are shown in a charming atmosphere of a bygone age.

To the east of Wotton lies **Newark Park** (National Trust), a compact hunting lodge that was built by the Poyntz family in the mid 16th century. Extended in the late 17th century and remodelled in a Gothic style by James Wyatt in around 1810 for Lewis Clutterbuck, the result is a country house with a delightful mix of styles set in a marvellous position overlooking the western escarpment of the Cotswolds. Viewing is by guided tour only and the house is open two afternoons a week between April and September. The countryside surrounding Newark Park is excellent walking country and one particularly fine walk takes in the **Midger Wood Nature Reserve** on the way up to **Nan Tow's Tump**, a huge round barrow whose tomb is said to contain the remains of a local witch, Nan Tow.

AROUND WOTTON-UNDER-EDGE

SLIMBRIDGE
6½ miles N of Wotton-under-Edge off the A38

This village is synonymous with the **Wildfowl and Wetlands Trust** centre that lies to the northwest on the banks of the River Severn. Here tame birds can be hand fed whilst there are also some 14 hides from which visitors can watch the centre's vast wildfowl populations. By contrast, in the Tropical House, there are humming birds and, at the visitor centre, the 'Wonder of Wetlands' exhibition explains the importance of the work undertaken here.

FRAMPTON-ON-SEVERN
8½ miles N of Wotton-under-Edge off the B4071

This village is home to one of the largest village greens in England and its 22 acres were formed when marshy ground was drained in the 18th century. Known as Rosamund's Green, this expanse of grass is believed to have been named after Rosamund Clifford, the mistress of Henry II, who was born at nearby Clifford Castle. According to legend, Henry hid Rosamund in a house at the centre of a maze in Woodstock Park but the King's jealous wife, Eleanor, found her way to the house by following a silken thread and, confronting her husband's mistress, offered her a choice of death by dagger or poison. Rosamund is said to have chosen poison but, contrary to this fanciful tale, she is believed to have died a natural death in 1176.

The gates of **Frampton Court**, an outstanding example of a Georgian country house, stand on the edge of the green and it has been the home of the Clifford family ever since it was built in the Palladian style by Vanbrugh in the 1730s. The house is filled with fine porcelain, furniture and paintings, whilst peacocks strut around the grounds where there is a superb Dutch Orangery and a 17th century octagonal tower that is a dovecote. The court is open by appointment only. Meanwhile, on the opposite side of the green is the Clifford family's former home, **Frampton Manor**, which was built between the 12th and the 16th centuries. A handsome timber-framed house with a lovely old walled garden containing some rare plants, the manor is believed to have been the birthplace of Rosamund. The manor is open by appointment only.

At the southern edge of the village is the **Sharpness Canal** that was built to allow ships to travel up the Severn Valley as far as Gloucester without being at the mercy

THE SWAN INN

Swan Lane, Stroud,
Gloucestershire GL5 2HF
Tel: 01453 763917
website: www.swaninn.net

On the banks of the Frome, where five valleys meet, Stroud is a town of many attractions, and a stroll around town reveals some interesting old buildings, notably the Subscription Rooms in neo-classical style and the Old Town Hall (1594) in the Shambles.

Opposite the Shambles, in the main pedestrianised shopping area, is another fine old building, the **Swan Inn**, with a smart white and green facade and a large sign that straddles the street. The Swan dates from 1822, and in the convivial bars

handsome old wooden panelling and beams are distinctive features.

Since their arrival at the end of 2001, joint leaseholders David and Kelly have enhanced the inn's reputation for friendship and hospitality to regulars and visitors alike, and it is one of the most popular places in town for enjoying a chat and a glass or two of something refreshing - at least three real ales are usually on tap, Tetleys and two guests, along with Boddington's Keg and a good choice of lagers and ciders.

David is a talented cook, and his dishes, served from 11 to 3, are a treat that should not be missed; his pies and roasts are the

specialities, but there's something for all tastes, with a daily specials board augmenting the printed menu.

On Sundays, it's roasts only, and that's an occasion that many of the regulars particularly look forward to each week. The citizens of Stroud will be pleased to know that within the lifetime of this edition David intends to make food available in the evenings, too.

The Swan is open all day, every day. Local talent clears its throat on the first Thursday of each month, when the karaoke session starts at about 8.30.

of the estuary tides. The canal has several swing bridges and at some of these, as at Splatt Bridge and Saul Bridge here, there are splendid little bridgekeepers' cottages.

To the west of Frampton, on a great bend in the River Severn, is the **Arlingham Peninsula**, which lies on part of the **Severn Way** Shepperdine-Tewkesbury long-distance walk. The trail passes close to Wick Court, a 13th century moated manor house whilst the land on which the village of **Arlingham** stands once belonged to the monks of St Augustine's Abbey in Bristol who believed it to be the point where St Augustine crossed the river on his way to converting the heathen Welsh tribes. The Severn naturally dominated life hereabouts and at **Saul**, a small village on the peninsula, the inhabitants decorated their houses with carvings of sailors, some of which, in bright, cheerful colours, can still be seen today. Further round the bend in the river, **Epney** is the point from which thousands of baby eels are exported each year to the Netherlands and elsewhere to replenish their own stocks.

ULEY
3½ miles NE of Wotton-under-Edge on the B4066

Once a busy centre of commerce based on the textile industry, Uley is now a quiet peaceful village that is home of one of the most distinguished houses in the area, **Owlpen Manor**. Set in a wooded valley, this handsome Tudor country house was built between 1450 and 1616 and, along with the Great Hall, it has a Jacobean solar wing, a fine William Morris inspired Arts and Crafts collection and unique painted cloth wallhangings that can be found in a room said to be haunted by Queen Margaret of Anjou who visited Owlpen in 1471. Outside there is a formal 16th century terraced garden whilst the outbuildings include a Grist Mill of 1728, a 17th century Court House and a 15th

century barn that is now a licensed restaurant.

Overshadowing the village to the northwest is **Uley Bury**, a massive Iron Age hill fort where evidence has been found of a prosperous community of warrior farmers dating from the 1st century BC. Another prehistoric site, a mile along the ridge, is Uley Long Barrow, which is known locally as **Hetty Pegler's Tump**. This chambered long barrow, 180 feet in length, takes its name from Hester Pegler, who came from a family of local land-owners and adventurous visitors can crawl into this Neolithic tomb to reach the burial chambers, whose walls and ceilings are made of huge stone slabs infilled with drystone material. A little further north, at the popular picnic site of **Coaley Peak** with its adjoining National Trust nature reserve, is another spectacular chambered tomb, **Nympsfield Long Barrow**.

STROUD
9 miles NE of Wotton-under-Edge on the A46

Situated at the point where five valleys converge, Stroud (whose name is derived from the Old English word Strod meaning 'marshy ground overgrown with brushwood') was the capital of the Cotswold woollen industry and the surrounding hill farms provided a constant supply of wool whilst the Cotswold streams supplied the water power. By the 1820s there were over 150 textile mills in the area but, today, only six survive – one specialising in the green baize for snooker tables and the felt for the tennis balls used at Wimbledon. The town's dependence on the textile trade also led to one Stroudie, Edwin Budding, inventing the lawnmower, in 1830, after watching the way that the cloth was shaved in the local mills.

In 1779, Stroud was connected to the River Severn by the **Stroudwater Navigation** and, just ten years later, to the River Thames by the **Thames and Severn**

Canal. Passing through some of the most glorious Cotswold countryside on route to Lechlade, the canal's main feature is the impressive **Sapperton Tunnel** that, at over two miles in length, was for many years the longest canal tunnel in the country.

The centre of the town has several interesting buildings including the **Old Town Hall**, which dates from 1594, and the **Subscription Rooms**, which were built, in 1833, as a venue for political and social events. The building's unusual name comes from the manner in which it was financed: entirely by public subscription with over 60 people buying shares worth £50 each. Today the rooms remain a focus for the town's social and artistic life and, now refurbished, they host top class arts events.

Just a short walk from the town centre is **Stratford Park** that started life as an arboretum in the 19th century and still has a number of large and exotic trees. Along with the lake and miniature railway laid out by the Victorians, the park has a

THE FLEECE INN

106 Bath Road, Lightpill, Nr Stroud, Gloucestershire GL5 3TJ
Tel: 01453 764432

The Fleece Inn is a charming cream-painted presence right on the A46, a mile south of Stroud. Open every session and all day at the weekend, the Fleece is family run by Paul and Jill, who number many families among their regular customers. One, sometimes two real ales head a good choice for the thirsty, and good food is served throughout opening hours. Paul and Jill both cook, and the Fleece's repertoire runs from sandwiches and light snacks to big juicy steaks; a takeaway service is also available. The inn has a pool table and a skittle alley that doubles as a function room; at the back is a secure beer garden with a bouncy castle. Every other Saturday is either disco or karaoke night at this most sociable of inns.

THE OLD NEIGHBOURHOOD INN

Chalford Hill, Chalford, Nr Stroud, Gloucestershire GL6 8EN
Tel: 01453 883385

In a secluded location on Chalford Hill (well signposted from Chalford), the **Old Neighbourhood Inn** is a spick and span Cotswold stone building with very comfortable and roomy public and lounge bars. Owned and run since the summer of 2001 by keen rugby player Roland Gabriel, the inn attracts a local and passing trade with its pleasant ambience - it really is neighbourly - and its good food served all day, from simple starters and light snacks to steaks. Wednesday is curry night, and senior citizens enjoy a special deal for Thursday lunch. The inn, which has a beer garden, is open every day (Monday to Thursday flexible out of season) and all day Friday, Saturday and Sunday.

WOODCUTTERS ARMS

Whiteshill, Nr Stroud, Gloucestershire GL6 6JS
Tel: 01453 764870
e-mail: granvillej@btinternet.com

The Woodcutters Arms stands a mile north of Stroud in the village of Whiteshill, overlooking the picturesque Stroud Valley. Built of Cotswold stone in the early 1900s, the pub is run by local couple Granville and Brigitte Jones, who like to see regulars and visitors chatting together in the spotless bar/ lounge. A great selection of real ales is guaranteed to break the ice, and a good selection of pub grub ensures something for everyone, including vegetarians. The Woodcutters holds a children's licence and has a beer garden with play fort. There is also a car park. The pub is open every lunchtime and evening and a warm welcome is guaranteed.

THE BEAR INN

Bisley, Nr Stroud, Gloucestershire GL6 7BD
Tel: 01452 770265

In the picture postcard village of Bisley, **The Bear Inn** is a former courthouse with a history going back to Tudor times. The classic Cotswold stone facade has a pillared portico on one side and inside there are exposed black beams on low ceilings, flagstones, big open fireplaces and dark oak furniture. Simon and Susan are very proud of the Bear, which attracts a wide cross-section of regulars as well as tourists who come to see the impressive All Saints Church and the renowned Seven Wells. Freshness and value for money are paramount in the cooking, which provides an excellent choice for lunch and dinner seven days a week, with daily specials adding to the options. Opening hours are 11.30-3 & 6-11; 12-10.30 on Sunday.

modern leisure complex with a range of indoor and outdoor facilities as well as being home to the **Stratford Park Museum**, which was once a private residence but is now a state of the art museum charting the history of the town.

BISLEY

11½ miles NE of Wotton-under-Edge off the A419

This delightful village, which stands 780 feet above sea level, is known locally as 'Bisley-God-Help-Us' because of the biting winter winds that sweep across the hillside. The village's impressive All Saints Church dates from the 13th century and it was restored in the early 19th century by Thomas Keble, whose brother, the poet and theologian John Keble, gave his name to Keble College, Oxford. The churchyard is the Poor Soul's Light, a stone wellhead beneath a spire dating from the 13th century that was used to hold candles that were lit for those whose souls were in

purgatory. Below the church are the **Seven Wells of Bisley** (also restored by Thomas Keble) that are blessed and decorated with flowers each year on Ascension Day.

However, the village's main claim to fame is the story of the Bisley Boy that dates from the time when it was a rich wool town and had a royal manor, Over Court, where the young Princess Elizabeth (later Elizabeth I) often stayed. During one of her visits the young princess fell ill and died and, fearing the wrath of her father, Henry VIII, her hosts looked for a substitute and found a local child with red hair and remarkably similar physical characteristics. Unfortunately the child was a boy named John Neville! Although the story is unlikely, it does explain why the Virgin Queen was reluctant to marry.

NAILSWORTH

6½ miles NE of Wotton-under-Edge on A46

This small residential and commercial town was once, like so many of its

RUSKIN MILL

Old Bristol Road, Nailsworth, Gloucestershire GL6 0LA
Tel: 01453 837537 Fax: 01453 837512
e-mail: maria.fischer@ruskin-mill.org.uk

Ruskin Mill, originally built as a woollen mill in the 1820's, is a vibrant centre for the arts, crafts and cultural development. Visitors can enjoy the stunning walks along the trout ponds, through the gardens or into the woodlands. Delicious organic cakes and lunches are available at the coffee shop. The gallery and craft shop are open daily. Day and evening classes and weekend workshops range from rug making, plant dyes, spinning, felting, drawing and watercolours to soap making, wood sculpting, leather work and paper maché, to name but a few. The Ruskin Mill Further Education Centre, ½ mile up the road, offers individual learning programs to students with special learning needs.

neighbours, a centre of the wool trade and several of the old mills have survived and been modernised: some playing new roles whilst others plying their original trades – **Ruskin Mill** is a thriving arts and crafts centre. Found on Cossack Square is an unusual 17th century building, **Stokescroft**, where, during restoration work in 1972, scribblings were found on an attic wall suggesting that soldiers had been billeted here between 1812 and 1815. It is also thought to have housed Russian prisoners during the Crimean War, which accounts for the name of the square.

AVENING
8 miles NE of Wotton-under-Edge on the B4014

Before the Norman Conquest, the manor of this ancient village belonged to Brittric of Avening, Lord of Gloucester who, in 1050, was sent by Edward the Confessor as

CARMELLA'S RESTAURANT

Albino's Cottage, 28 George Street, Nailsworth, Gloucestershire GL6 0AG Tel/Fax: 01453 834802

Chris and Hilary Freeman, daughter-in-law Clare and righthand lady Sarah make a winning team at **Carmella's**, a lovely little restaurant in a 17th century house. Breakfast starts the day, and home-made cakes are a popular day-long order, but the main offering is the light lunch menu with dishes such as chicken liver or mushroom & herb pâté, rainbow trout fillets with prosciutto and sage, herb-marinated chicken breast with spinach and leeks, or loin of pork served with grilled mango and creamed celeriac - all fresh, wholesome dishes full of natural flavours. There are seats for 50 inside, and a pretty garden area for fine days. Carmella's, a non-smoking restaurant, is open from 8.30 to 5.30, closed Sunday. Booking is recommended on Saturday.

THE LAURELS AT INCHBROOK

Inchbrook, Nailsworth, Gloucestershire GL5 5HA
Tel/Fax: 01453 834021 e-mail: laurels@inchbrook.fsnet.co.uk

The Laurels at Inchbrook offers comfortable Bed & Breakfast accommodation in a relaxed atmosphere. Run by Lesley, Richard and Emily Williams-Allen, the Laurels and an adjacent cottage have a total of six en suite bedrooms, all with central heating, tv, radio alarms and beverage facilities; one room on the ground floor is accessible to disabled guests. Children are welcome, and high chairs are available. The panelled study has a piano, a fire on chilly evenings and a selection of books, and in the games room there's tv, snooker and board games. Breakfast, with a choice of English, Continental, Vegetarian or Healthy Option, is served in the dining room. Outside attractions at the Laurels include a peaceful garden and a swimming pool. This is a non-smoking establishment.

THE BELL & CASTLE

The Cross, Horsley, Nailsworth, Gloucestershire GL6 0PR
Tel: 01453 832155

Close to the church in a picturesque village on the B4058, **The Bell & Castle** is Horsley's only public house. It's a pub of immense character, both outside, with Bath stone walls topped by ancient tiles, and within, where thick stone walls, beams and heavy old wooden furnishings paint a traditional picture in the bar. Georgie and David Vening are the leaseholders, and Georgie prepares an excellent variety of dishes on a menu that ranges from bar snacks to fish specials and Sunday roast lunches. Booking is advised at the weekend. The Bell & Castle is home to many sporting teams and has its own skittle alley. Happy hour is 5.30 to 6.30 on Saturday.

an ambassador to Baldwin, Count of Flanders. Whilst away, Brittric met Matilda (who was later to become the wife of William the Conqueror) and she fell in love with him although, to her great disappointment, her approaches were rejected. After the Norman invasion and now married to William, Matilda asked her king to take the manor from Brittric who was then thrown into prison in Worcester where he died. In remorse for her persecution of Brittric, Matilda and William stayed at Avening Court whilst she, as penance, commissioned the rebuilding of the village church so that masses could be said for Brittric's soul. Consecrated in 1080, Avening Church is one of the best preserved of the ancient churches in the Cotswolds.

The village's long history does not end there as, each September, it celebrates Pig Face Sunday, a festival that goes back to the days when wild boar roamed the region causing damage to crops, livestock and even humans. One rogue animal caused such havoc that, when it was caught, it was hung from an oak tree before being roasted and eaten.

Meanwhile, to the northeast of the village is the extraordinary **Avening Long Stone**, which stands 8 feet high and is pierced with holes. Local legend tells that, on Midsummer's Eve, this prehistoric standing stone moves.

RODMARTON
12 miles NE of Wotton-under-Edge off the A433

Mentioned in the *Domesday Book*, on the edge of this small village is an important Roman and prehistoric site, the **Long Barrow** on **Windmill Tump** (English Heritage). Meanwhile, **Rodmarton Manor** features furniture that was specifically commissioned for the house by Arts and Crafts Movement cabinetmakers. The

THE CROWN INN

High Street, Minchinhampton, Nr Stroud, Gloucestershire GL6 9BN
Tel: 01453 852357
e-mail: crown@minchinhampton.fsbusiness.co.uk

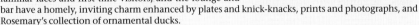

Overlooking the market place in historic Minchinhampton, the 17th century **Crown Inn** is one of the most popular and pleasant places to meet for a drink and a chat, to enjoy a quiet game of darts or bar billiards, to linger longer over a meal or to pass a comfortable night or two. Tenants Rosemary and Richard have an equally warm welcome for familiar faces and first-time visitors, and the lounge and bar have a homely, inviting charm enhanced by plates and knick-knacks, prints and photographs, and Rosemary's collection of ornamental ducks.

There is always a variety of real ales to enjoy, and Richard keeps a well-stocked cellar. Both he and Rosemary cook, and their menus provide a good selection, from light bites to classic pub dishes, including a rightly acclaimed steak & kidney pie. The main dining area seats 34, with a non-smoking section, and booking is advisable for Sunday lunch (no food Sunday night). A senior citizens menu, available Monday to Friday lunchtimes, offers two or three courses at a bargain price. At the back of the inn is a secluded lawn and beer garden. Five comfortable, well-appointed guest bedrooms with en suite or private bathroom, tv, radio/alarm, tea/coffee tray and hairdryer make the Crown an excellent base for an extended stay or for exploring the many attractions the region has to offer.

house and gardens are open to the public in the summer.

TETBURY
8 miles E of Wotton-under-Edge on the A433

A charming Elizabethan market town and another that prospered from the wool trade, Tetbury's origins go back to the 7th century and there is also evidence that it might have been a prehistoric defended hilltop site. Today the focus of the town remains its market place and the most famous building here is the **Market House** that was built in 1655 and is supported on three rows of bulging stone pillars. The ancient **Chipping Steps** connecting the market house to the old trading centre are also worth a visit as is **Tetbury Police Museum**, which is housed in the original cells of the old police station. The fascinating collection here includes artefacts, memorabilia and uniforms from the Gloucestershire Constabulary.

To the northwest of the town stands **Chavenage House**, a beautiful Elizabethan mansion built of grey Cotswold stone, which stands on the foundations of a monastery, and that has the characteristic E shape of the period. The elegant front aspect has remained virtually unchanged down the centuries and the present owners, the Lowsley-Williams family, can

Market House, Tetbury

trace their lineage back to the original inhabitants. Of the treasures found within, there are two rooms covered with rare 17th century tapestries and the house also contains many relics from the Cromwellian era. Cromwell is known to have stayed here and, during the Civil War, he persuaded the then owner, Gloucestershire MP Nathaniel Stephens, to vote to put Charles I on trial. After the trail that led to the execution of the king, Stephens is said to have been so troubled by his conscience that he died and his soul is said to have been taken away in the black coach driven by a headless horseman. However, Stephens did not die until 1660. Believed to be Gloucestershire's second most haunted house – Berkeley Castle is the most haunted – in 1970 an astonishing find was

---

STABLE COTTAGE

Cutwell Farm, Cutwell, Tetbury, Gloucestershire GL8 8EB
Tel: 01666 502026

Just outside Tetbury off the A433 Bath road, **Stable Cottage** is a lovely conversion in Cotswold stone on a small working farm. The cottage has been tastefully decorated throughout by owner Jill Price and equipped with everything needed for a pleasant self-catering holiday. On the ground floor are the lounge, dining area and fully fitted kitchen, while upstairs is a large family bedroom sleeping up to 5, and a large bathroom with bath and shower. The farm enjoys a quiet, secluded location, yet the town of Tetbury, with its shops, pubs, restaurants and historic buildings, is only a short walk away. The cottage is available from Easter to November.

made in the attic when a portfolio of watercolours by George IV were found that turned out to be his plans for the restoration of Windsor Castle.

WESTONBIRT
6½ miles SE of Wotton-under-Edge on the A433

To the north of the village lies **Westonbirt Arboretum**, which contains one of the finest collections of trees and shrubs in Europe and the 18,000 specimens, planted between 1892 and the present day, are spread over 600 acres of glorious Cotswold countryside. The arboretum was founded by wealthy landowner Robert Stayner Holford for his own interest and pleasure and his work was continued with equal enthusiasm by his son, Sir George Holford, until his own death in the 1920s. Opened to the public in 1956, there are over 17 miles of waymarked trails and, throughout the year, there is always something to marvel at: from the glorious display of rhododendrons, azaleas and magnolias in spring to the glorious reds, oranges and golds of autumn. Open daily, all year round, the arboretum also has a plant centre, shop and courtyard café.

Westonbirt Arboretum

BADMINTON
7½ miles SE of Wotton-under-Edge off the B4040

The **Badminton Park** estate was founded by Edward Somerset, the son of the Marquis of Worcester, whose 25 foot monument stands in the little church next to the main house. The central section of the house dates from the 1680s and contains some marvellous carvings in limewood by Grinling Gibbons whilst the rest of the house, along with the grounds and the many follies and gateways, is the work of the mid 18th century architect William Kent. The game of badminton is said to have started here during a weekend party in the 1860s when the Duke of Beaufort and his guests wanted to play tennis in the entrance hall but were worried about damaging the paintings and a member of the party came up with the bright idea of using a cork studded with feathers instead of a ball. In such a moment of inspiration was the game born and it was one of these guests who later took the game to Pakistan, where the first rules were formalised.

Many of the buildings on the estate, including the parish church and the estate villages of Great and Little Badminton, were designed in an ornate castellated style by Thomas Wright. The park is perhaps best known as the venue of the Badminton Horse Trials, which annually attracts the best of the international riders as well as spectators in their thousands.

HORTON
5 miles S of Wotton-under-Edge off the A46

Norton Court (National Trust) is a 12th century Norman hall that was once the home of Ulf, an illegitimate son of King Harold and his mistress, Edith of the Swan

Neck. The hall and its 14th ambulatory, situated in a peaceful valley, are open to the public from March to October.

CHIPPING SODBURY
7 miles S of Wotton-under-Edge on the A432

This pleasant market town was one of the earliest examples of post Roman town planning and the settlement was arranged in strips on either side of the main street in the 12th century. Ever since the market charter was granted, in 1227, this has been a thriving trading centre and the monthly market continues to this day. However, the townsfolk were, in the Middle Ages, so concerned with buying and selling goods that little regard was given to making room in the main streets for a church and, as a result, St John's Church, built in 1284, lies down a side alley between two allotments. However, the size of the church does reflect the prosperity of the town at that time.

Just to the east of the town lies **Old Sodbury**, whose part Norman church contains some exceptional tombs and monuments including a carved stone effigy of a 13th century knight and the tomb of David Harley. Harley was the Georgian diplomat who negotiated the treaty that ended the American War of Independence. A tower just to the east of the church marks a vertical shaft that is one of a series that were sunk to ventilate the long tunnel that carried the London to South Wales railway through the Cotswold escarpment. Opened in 1903, the two mile long tunnel required its own brickworks and took some five years to complete.

There are two fine country houses to be found close by. Medieval **Little Sodbury Manor** has an excellent great hall along with Elizabethan, Jacobean and Queen Anne additions and is open, by appointment only, between April and September whilst, down a lane leading south from Old Sodbury, lies **Dodington**

House. Built between 1796 and 1816 on the foundations of an Elizabethan house, it was designed in lavish neo-Roman style by the classical architect James Wyatt who was killed in a carriage accident before seeing his work completed. The house, whose interior is even more ornate than the façade, is open daily in the summer. Connected to the house by an elegant conservatory is the private Church of St Mary, also by Wyatt, which takes the shape of a Greek cross.

DYRHAM
11 miles S of Wotton-under-Edge off the A46

Situated on the slope of the Cotswold ridge, a little to the south of the site of a famous 6th century battle between the Britons and the Saxons is **Dyrham Park** (National Trust). A striking baroque mansion, which was used as the setting for the film the *Remains of the Day*, it houses a wonderful collection of artefacts that were accumulated by the original owner, William Blathwayt, during diplomatic tours of duty in Holland and North America (he later became Secretary of State to William III) and, in particular, there are several Dutch paintings and some magnificent Delft porcelain. The west front of the house looks out across a terrace to lawns laid out in formal Dutch style and much of the estate is a deer park and, interestingly, the word Dyrham means 'deer enclosure' in Saxon. A charming little church in the grounds has a Norman font, a fine 15th century memorial brass and several memorials to the Winter and Blathwayt families.

During World War II, orphaned children from London came here with their nurses and, whilst the children were given the freedom of the terrace during the day, Lady Islington, who was living here at that time, had a barrier placed beside the front door so that only she, and not her young visitors, could use it. The park is open daily all year round whilst the house and gardens, along with the café and shop, are open from March to October.

MARSHFIELD
12 miles S of Wotton-under-Edge off the A420

This old market town was once the fourth wealthiest town in Gloucestershire and its prosperity was based on the malt and wool industries. As a result its long main street has many handsome buildings dating from the good old days of the 17th and 18th centuries but not many of the coaching inns remain that were here in abundance when the town was an important stop on the London to Bristol run. Among the many notable buildings are the **Tolzey Market Hall** and the imposing Church of St Mary, which boasts a fine Jacobean pulpit and several impressive monuments from the 17th and 18th centuries. Each Boxing Day the **Marshfield Mummers**

take to the streets to perform a number of time-honoured set pieces wearing costumes made from newspapers and accompanied by a town crier.

A lane leads south through a pretty valley to the delightful hamlet of **St Catherine's**, whose church contains a splendid 15th century stained glass window with four lights depicting the Virgin Mary, the Crucifixion, St John and St Peter. The great manor house, St Catherine's Court, now privately owned, once belonged to the Benedictine priory at Bath.

THORNBURY
7½ miles SW of Wotton-under-Edge on the B4461

This attractive and ancient town has been inhabited by both Bronze Age and Neolithic people and Roman coins and pottery have also been found in the vicinity. However, by the time of the Normans both the village and its Norman

THE CATHERINE WHEEL

High Street, Marshfield, Nr Bath SN14 8LR
Tel: 01225 892200
e-mail: info@thecatherinewheel.co.uk website: www.thecatherinewheel.co.uk

Despite its elegant Georgian façade **The Catherine Wheel** is a much older building and it was, originally, a 15th century house. With a highly regarded reputation locally for being one of the best inn's in the area, The Catherine Wheel offers customers friendly and relaxed hospitality in a charming and distinctive setting.

The stylish interior décor complements the exposed stone walls and large open fireplaces of the bar and eating areas. A small patio is also available for eating during the day. Along with a fine range of real ales, including Bellringer from Abbey Ales in Bath, The Catherine Wheel also has an excellent wine list. However, it is for its delicious food that this is inn is best known and, with two chefs on the premises, there is always a wonderful selection of freshly prepared dishes for both lunch and dinner. It is always advisable to book a table at the weekends and for Sunday lunch.

The Catherine Wheel also has four comfortable en suite guest rooms that have each been decorated and furnished in the same elegance as the rest of the inn. All have TV, tea and coffee making facilities. Please contact Jackie or Dave for details.

THE OAK TREE INN

Bibstone, Cromhall, Nr Wotton-under-Edge,
Gloucestershire GL12 8AD
Tel: 01454 260365

The Oak Tree Inn, formerly the Royal Oak, is a very attractive hostelry, part stone, part half-timbered, in the hamlet of Bibstone. The setting is rural and secluded, but only a mile from Junction 14 of the M5, so it's an excellent place to break a journey. The premises date back to the 17th century, and period features inside include a fine stone inglenook surmounted by a beam dated 1674, and a leaded stained-glass window in the snug. New leaseholders Bridie and Jon Paul Collins provide a full range of beer, always including three guest ales, and in the recently created restaurant area food is served daily up to about 9.30. The Sunday carvery is very popular, and Bridie and Jon Paul plan occasional themed food evenings.

church passed into Royal hands and, by the 13th century, the town was important enough to become a borough in its own right – a status it retained until 1883. Today, Thornbury has all the character and charm of a typical English market town and, in the centre, there are several historic buildings to be found that include the parish church whose 130 foot high medieval tower acts as a prominent local landmark. The town also boasts the country's only Tudor **Castle** and it was reputedly used by Henry VIII, Anne Boleyn and Mary Tudor.

TORTWORTH

3½ miles W of Wotton-under-Edge off the B4509

Overlooking the village green is the Church of St Leonard that contains some fine 15th century stained glass as well as a pair of canopied tombs of the Throckmorton family, former owners of the Tortworth Park estate. In a field over the church wall can be found several interesting trees including an American hickory, a huge silver-leafed linden and two Locust tress whilst, nearby, is the famous **Tortworth Chestnut**, a massive Spanish chestnut tree that the diarist John Evelyn called "the great chestnut of King Stephen's time." The tree was certainly well established by the time of King Stephen in the 1130s and a fence was put around it to provide protection in 1800.

Trees seem to dominate this village as it is also home to the **Tortworth Arboretum** that was founded in the mid 19th century as a sister venture to nearby Westonbirt Arboretum.

OLDBURY-ON-SEVERN

9½ miles W of Wotton-under-Edge off the B4461

On the banks of the River Severn lies **Oldbury Power Station** whose visitor

THE PICKWICK INN

Lower Wick, Nr Dursley, Gloucestershire GL11 6DD
Tel/Fax: 01453 810259

The Pickwick Inn is a charming family-run public house in the village of Lower Wick, reached by minor roads southwest of Dursley. Originally a cider house, it was for a long time called the Greyhound Inn, before becoming the Pickwick in the 1980s. In summer the front is a positive riot of colour, and all year round the bars and dining area have an inviting, old-fashioned appeal. A good selection of Young's real ales is always available, and super home-cooked food is served every lunchtime and evening. The non-smoking restaurant has seats for 90, but such is the popularity of the pub that booking is always advisable. Behind the pub is a large lawned space with picnic benches and a children's adventure area.

Oldbury-on-Severn

centre illustrates the story of nuclear energy and the making of electricity through a series of videos, films and hands-on displays. Open throughout the year, with pre booked visitors only between November and February, there is also a nature trail for visitors to follow.

BERKELEY
6 miles NW of Wotton-under-Edge off the B4066

The **Vale of Berkeley**, a fertile strip of land along the southeastern banks of the River Severn, takes its name from this small town whose largely Georgian centre is dominated by the Norman **Berkeley Castle**. Said to be the oldest inhabited castle in Britain and home to 24 generations of the Berkeley family, this wonderful sandstone building was completed in 1153 by Lord Maurice Berkeley at the command of Henry II. Over the intervening centuries, this ancient castle has not only

been preserved but also gradually transformed from a savage Norman fortress into a truly stately home that contains a wealth of treasures including paintings by English and Dutch masters, tapestries, furniture, silver and porcelain. Berkeley Castle, too, has many historic associations and it was in the Great Hall that the Barons of the West Country met before going to Runnymede to force King John to put his seal to the Magna Carta. Meanwhile, in the dungeon of the massive Norman keep is the cell where Edward II was imprisoned and then brutally murdered by his captors with a red hot iron spit in 1327.

The castle is surrounded by sweeping lawns and terraced Elizabethan Gardens that contain many rare plants along with a lilypond and Elizabeth I's bowling green. Another interesting feature here is the deer park and, from the outer bailey, there are panoramic views across the gardens and

Berkeley Castle

THE MARINERS ARMS

49 Salter Street, Berkeley, Gloucestershire GL13 9BX
Tel: 01453 811822

The Mariners Arms is a substantial corner building on the B4066 in the centre of Berkeley. The oldest part dates back to the 14th century, and the interior presents a rich assortment of old-world charm, with polished parquet floor, wooden panelling, beams and a marvellous stone inglenook. Good-value home cooking is served at lunchtime, with baguettes a popular choice for a quicker bite. Hospitality is dispensed in generous measure by tenant Sandra Cooke and her righthand man Steve Mauld. The pub has a skittle alley and games room; live music is performed from 9 every Saturday evening, and there's a quiz on the last Sunday of the month.

meadows to the New Kennels, built in 1730, which are the home of the Berkeley Hunt. Also in the grounds is the delightful **Butterfly Farm** that is housed in a walled garden. Here both British and exotic species of butterflies are farmed and visitors can see over 40 different species, from all over the world, flying freely among the unusual plants and flowers. The castle is open from April to October.

Close to the castle, and also the parish church of St Mary that contains several memorials to the Berkeley family, is the **Jenner Museum** (see panel on opposite), a beautiful Georgian building that was once the home of Edward Jenner, the doctor and immunologist who is best known as the man who discovered a vaccine against smallpox. The son of a local parson, Jenner was apprenticed to a surgeon in Chipping Sodbury in 1763 at

the young age of 14 and this museum, through state of the art displays, shows the importance of the science of immunology as well as telling the story that led up to Jenner's famous and life saving discovery. In the grounds of the house is the rustic thatched hut where Jenner used to

THE JENNER MUSEUM

Berkeley, Gloucestershire BL13 9BH
Tel: 01453 810631 e-mail: manager@jennermuseum.com
Fax: 01453 811690 website: www.jennermuseum.com

Born in Berkeley in 1749, Edward Jenner returned here after completing his medical training and his house, The Chantry, is now home to the **Jenner Museum** where this pioneering doctor and immunologist's life and work is explored. Intrigued by the country lore that said that milkmaids who caught the mild cowpox could not catch smallpox, one of the most feared diseases of all time, Jenner set about developing a means of vaccinating against smallpox, which he successfully did in 1798. In 1967, the World Health Organisation master-minded a final global plan to eradicate the disease and, in 1980, smallpox was declared dead. Not only did Jenner develop the first vaccination but his discovery has now been developed into one of the most important parts of modern medicine – immunology. Along with his work on smallpox, Jenner also made several other important contributions to medicine: he was probably the first to link angina with hardening of the arteries, he described rheumatic heart disease and he purified important medicines. Both Jenner's medical work and also his work as a naturalist and geologist are described here through numerous displays and exhibits.

vaccinate the poor free of charge and which he called the Temple of Vaccinia. The museum is open most afternoons from April to September.

CIRENCESTER

The Capital of the Cotswolds, this lively market town has a long and fascinating history that dates back to the time of the Romans. As Corinium Dobonnorum, it was the second largest Roman town in Britain (Londinium was the largest) and, although few signs of the Roman occupation remain today, the award winning **Corinium Museum** features one of the finest collections of Roman antiquities along with a reconstruction of a Roman kitchen, dining room and garden that give an insight into life in Cirencester almost 2,000 years ago.

Church of St John the Baptist

The main legacy of the town's medieval wealth is the magnificent **Church of St John the Baptist**, one of the grandest of all the Cotswold 'wool churches' and one that is often referred to as the 'Cathedral of the Cotswolds'. Its 120 foot high tower dominates the town whilst, inside, its greatest treasure is the Anne Boleyn Cup, a silver and gilt cup made for Henry VIII's second wife in 1535 – the year before she was executed for adultery. Her personal insignia, a rose tree and a falcon holding a sceptre, is on the cup's lid and it was given to the church by Richard Master, physician to Elizabeth I. The church also has a unique three-storied porch that was used as the Town Hall until 1897. The town also boasts one of the country's oldest open air swimming pools that was built in 1869 and both the main pool and the paddling pool use water from a private well.

In the 9th century it is believed that Gurmund, a Dane, captured Cirencester from the Saxons by trapping a flock of

THE FLEECE HOTEL

Market Place, Cirencester, Gloucestershire GL7 2NZ
Tel: 01285 658507 Fax: 01285 651017 e-mail: relax@fleecehotel.co.uk

The Fleece Hotel is owned by the Barlow family, experienced hoteliers from Cornwall, and personally run by Hazel Hill. They have treated the Grade II listed building to a top-to-toe refurbishment and have created the splendid Bar & Brasserie 1651, whose name commemorates the anniversary of Charles II coming to Cirencester in the Civil War. Food is served here every session except Sunday evening, and booking is recommended for Friday and Saturday evenings; lighter lunches are served in the hotel bar. Accommodation at the Fleece comprises 26 en suite rooms with tv, radio, direct-dial telephone, hairdryer, trouser press and beverage tray. Some rooms are on the ground floor for easier access, some are big enough for families and two boast four-poster beds.

sparrow, tying flaming twigs to the birds and then releasing them over the town and so burning down the town's walls.

AROUND CIRENCESTER

NORTH CERNEY
3½ miles N of Cirencester on the A435

This village is home to **Cerney House Gardens**, a delightful hidden Cotswold garden, with typical Victorian features, that includes a working kitchen garden, a vast herbaceous border and a well-labelled herb garden. This mostly organic garden is open to the public from April to September.

YANWORTH
8 miles NE of Cirencester off the A429

Situated just off the Roman thoroughfare, Fosse Way, and to the west of the village lies **Chedworth Roman Villa** (National Trust), a large and well preserved Roman villa that was discovered, by chance, in 1864. Found in a beautifully wooded combe in the valley of the River Coln, it is the existence of a natural spring at the head of the combe that was probably the reason for the villa being sited on this pleasant spot. Beginning life as three separate buildings in around AD120, the villa, over the following 300 years, developed into a grand 4th century mansion that was built along three sides of a rectangle. Excavations here have revealed that this was a very grand residence as it possessed two bath houses, two large dining rooms, two kitchens and, in total, over 30 rooms. Also found here are some wonderful mosaics, on display to the public, which include one depicting the four seasons and another showing nymphs and satyrs. The villa remains are open between March and November.

Chedworth Roman Villa

NORTHLEACH
9½ miles NE of Cirencester off the A429

This traditional market town was once a major wool trading centre that rivalled Cirencester in importance and, as a consequence, it boasts many fine buildings including the magnificent **Church of St Peter and St Paul** that, as with the church at Cirencester, can claim to the a 'Cathedral of the Cotswolds'. Built in the 15th century and standing just off the market place, the treasures inside include an ornately carved fond and some of the best wool merchant's brasses in the country of which rubbings can be made (after a permit has been obtained). Meanwhile, along the entire length of the High Street, where some timber-framed buildings still remain although most of the buildings here are of Cotswold stone, the medieval property boundaries, dating back to the 13th century, can still be traced. Also of interest here is the old county prison that is now home to the **Cotswold Heritage Centre**, where there are displays and exhibits detailing the social history and the rural life of the region, whilst, in a 17th century merchant's house is **Keith Harding's World of Mechanical Music** (see panel). A living museum of antique self-playing musical instruments, music boxes, automata and clocks, all the exhibits here are maintained in perfect working order in the world famous workshops found on the premises.

UPPER AND LOWER SLAUGHTER
15 miles NE of Cirencester off the B4068

The Slaughters – the name means nothing more sinister than 'muddy place' – are typical Cotswolds villages set a mile apart on the little River Eye and both are

Upper Slaughter

much visited by tourists and they remain much as they have always been since virtually no building work has been carried out since 1904. Francis Edward Witts, author of the *Diary of a Cotswold Parson*, was the rector here between 1808 and 1854.

At Lower Slaughter, the **Old Mill**, with its tall chimney and giant waterwheel, is a prominent feature by the river. This restored 19th century flour mill is open to visitors and has a tearoom and ice cream parlour.

STOW-ON-THE-WOLD
18 miles NE of Cirencester on the A429

At some 800 feet above sea level, this is the highest town in the Cotswolds and the effects of the elements, particularly the sometime strong winds, have encouraged the townsfolk to create an enclosed town square. First settled during the Iron Age, there is evidence of earlier settlers in the area and both Stone Age and Bronze Age

burial mounds are common around Stow. The town's main source of wealth, in earlier times, was wool and, at one time, there were twice yearly sheep fairs held in the Market Square and, at one such fair, Daniel Defoe recorded that over 20,000 sheep were sold. Those days are remembered now in the names **Sheep Street** and **Shepherd's Way** whilst the square holds another reminder of the past in the town stocks that were used to punish minor offenders.

The Battle of Stow, in 1646, was the final conflict of the Civil War and, after it, some of the defeated Royalist forces made their way to St Edward's church whilst others were cut down in the market square. The church, which suffered considerable damage at this time, has been restored several times over the centuries but one treasure has managed to remain in place – a painting of the Crucifixion in the south aisle that is thought to be the work of the 17th century Flemish artist Gaspard de

THE WHITE HART INN
The Square, Stow-on-the-Wold, Gloucestershire GL54 1AF
Tel: 01451 830674 Fax: 01451 830090
website: www.whiteharthotel@tablesir.com

Old-world charm and modern amenity combine in fine style at the **White Hart Inn**, which has graced the market square in the centre of Stow for many centuries.

Much of the old look has been retained, and the cosy bars are friendly, inviting and full of character. Mandy Moore and her staff offer an excellent selection of real ales, lagers, ciders and

a stout on tap. The White Hart is the choice of many for some of the best pub food in the region offering an extensive menu, lighter chouce, daily specials and childrens menu.

The White Hart also offers 5 recently refurbished en-suite guest rooms including a family room. All rooms have colour TV, clock radio, guest information and tea and coffee making facilities, and the family room boasts a play station. The inn is an ideal base for touring the Cotswolds.

Stow-on-the-Wold

Nursery Room and a Textile room. The museum is open throughout the year (except in May).

Until 1937, when mains water was finally laid in Stow, women and children, for centuries, carried water from the spring on Well Lane. Later, water carts carried the water to the town centre where it was sold to the townsfolk and, whilst several systems were tried to force the water up the hill, it was not until 1871 that the boring of a deep well alleviated the problem.

Craeyer. The year before the Battle of Stow, Charles I stayed in the town, possibly at the Royalist Hotel (said to be the oldest inn in England) during the time of the Battle of Naseby.

Other buildings of note in the town are the 15th century **Crooked House** and the 19th century **St Edward's Hall** that was built using unclaimed funds placed in the Town Saving Bank. Also here is the **Toy and Collectors Museum**, in Park House, which displays one of the best private collections of toys from the Victorian and Edwardian eras onwards. Along with children's books, lead soldiers and animals, trains, boats and Pelham puppets there is a

BOURTON-ON-THE-WATER
14½ miles NE of Cirencester off the A429

Probably the most popular of all the Cotswold villages, Bourton-on-the-Water is often referred to as the 'Venice of the Cotswolds' as the River Windrush flows through its centre and is crossed by several delightful low-arched pedestrian bridges, two of which date from the late 18th century. The golden stone cottages add to the attraction of the village and, though the oldest only dates back to the 17th century, the large village church of St

THE GOLDEN BALL

Lower Swell, Nr Stow-on-the-Wold, Gloucestershire GL54 1LF
Tel/Fax: 01451 830247
e-mail: maureen@goldenball.fsnet.co.uk

The Golden Ball is a distinguished Cotswold stone coaching inn, in the picturesque village of Lower Swell. The interior retains many of its original features, including exposed stone walls and black beams - a delightful setting for relaxing with a glass of Donnington's real ale. Maureen Heath, who runs the inn with her husband Steve, keeps visitors happy with her fine home cooking, which she offers on printed and blackboard menus every lunchtime and evening. The inn also has three en suite guest rooms, one of them in an adjacent building with its own entrance. A quiz takes place on one Sunday each month, and in summer Aunt Sally is played on Thursday evenings. The inn has a beer garden and ample off-road parking.

Lawrence has a 14th century chancel as well as a rare domed Georgian tower. An attractive place in its own right, Bourton also has plenty of interest to offer visitors and, in particular, there is the famous **Model Village** where a replica, to one ninth scale, of the village can be seen complete with the River Windrush and its picturesque bridges and, of course, a model of the Model Village. The Model Village is open daily all year round. Meanwhile, the **Bourton Model Railway** has over 40 British and Continental trains running on three main displays and, open daily between April and

Bourton-on-the-Water

September and at weekends for the rest of the year, this is one of the finest indoor model railways in the country. Found in an 18th century water mill is the fascinating **Cotswold Motor Museum and Toy Collection** with its toys, motoring memorabilia and a huge collection of enamel advertising signs. Bourton is also home to Europe's only perfumery, the **Cotswold Perfumery**, where visitors not only have the opportunity to wander around the beautiful laid out Perfume Garden but also to test their noses in the Perfume Quiz whilst the **Dragonfly Maze**, laid out by Kit Williams, is not just an ordinary maze but one that tests the brain as there is a Rebus Puzzle that has to be solved on the way to the centre. Both the Perfumery and the Maze are open daily throughout the year. Finally, there is

THE DUKE OF WELLINGTON INN

Sherborne Street, Bourton-on-the-Water,
Gloucestershire GL54 2BY
Tel: 01451 820539 Fax: 01451 810919
e-mail: dukeofwellington@traditionalfreehouses.com

Once the premises of millers and tanners, the **Duke of Wellington** now offers the best in hospitality, good food and drink, and a comfortable bed for the night. The 16th century inn serves a good range of real ales and draught beers, and an outstanding choice of food. The printed menu is supplemented by an impressive list of blackboard specials typified by broccoli and stilton soup, tuna steak, barbecued spare ribs and duck breast with roasted peppers and a plum sauce. The Duke of Wellington has three comfortable en suite letting bedrooms, making it a perfect base for exploring the Cotswolds.

Birdland, a peaceful and tranquil place that is home to numerous tropical birds as well as penguins.

SHERBORNE
12 miles NE of Cirencester off the A40

This village is part of the **Sherborne Park Estate**, a traditional working Cotswold estate that was bequeathed, along with Lodge Park, to the National Trust by Charles Button, 7th Lord Sherborne in 1982. The eastern end of the village was built in the mid 19th century as a model estate village and here there are some 70 cottages carefully preserved by the Trust whilst the western end of the village is older. Along with this exceptionally pleasant village, complete with shop, post office and school, there are the **Pleasure Grounds**, a long neglected ornamental shrubbery with miniature hills and winding footpaths that is now being restored, an **Ice House** that dates from the 1820s and was used to store ice cut in the winter from nearby ponds for use in the house and the dairy during the summer, and the **Water Meadows**. These fields were purposefully flooded by means of sluices so that the silt would enrich the soil and encourage growth and this method of fertilization was used at Sherborne right up until the early 20th century. Today, the meadows are a haven for wildlife and are home to heron, kingfishers, mute swans, otters, badgers and hares.

Finally, there is **Lodge Park**, a unique example of a deer course, deer park and grandstand that was built in the 17th century by John 'Crump' Dutton, a hunchback, influential landowner and crafty politician who managed to remain on both sides during the Civil War. Crump was also a gambler, who enjoyed banqueting, and he built Lodge Park as a venue to indulge these two loves. Over the years, the building changed dramatically but today the National Trust has returned it to its former glory. The sport that was followed here was deer coursing, a form of 17th century greyhound racing with a mile long straight and where the dogs chased a live stag. The stag was released into the course and then two greyhounds were sent in pursuit. At the end of the course, beyond the grandstand, were two ditches: the first was the finishing line and this was jumped by all three animals whilst the second ditch was larger and only the stag could negotiate this obstacle and so escape the pursuing dogs and return to the deer park.

BIBURY
6½ miles NE of Cirencester on the B4425

Described by William Morris, founder of the Arts and Crafts Movement, as "the most beautiful village in England", Bibury has lost none of its charm and character over the years. The Church of St Mary, which displays parts from the Saxon, Norman and medieval eras, is well worth a visit but the most photographed building here is **Arlington Row**, a superb terrace of

Arlington Row

HARTWELL FARM COTTAGES

Ready Token, Near Bibury, Cirencester, Gloucestershire GL7 5SY
Tel/Fax: 01285 740210
e-mail: cottages@hartwell89.freeseve.co.uk
website: www.selfcateringcotswolds.co.uk

Hartwell Farm Cottages are two traditionally built properties in
a lovely peaceful setting with far-reaching views over open
countryside. Lilac Cottage has one double and one single room,
Lavender Cottage has one double and one small twin room, both have room for an extra bed or cot and
both are fully equipped for a pleasant and comfortable self-catering holiday. The kitchens have smart
modern units, the bedrooms have fitted carpets and colour co-ordinated fabrics and decorations, the
sitting rooms are bright and spacious, and there are large enclosed gardens with trees and shrubs. Owner
Caroline Mann has thoughtfully provided local maps and guide books to help guests plan outings.
Weekly lets commencing Fridays. (Other arrangements may be possible - please phone)

medieval stone cottages that were built as a
wool store in the 14th century and were
converted 300 years later into weavers'
cottages and workshops. Fabric produced
here was supplied to nearby **Arlington
Mill** for fulling, a process in which the
material was cleaned in water and then
beaten with mechanically operated
hammers. Today, the mill, which stands
on the site of a corn mill mentioned in the
Domesday Book, is a museum holding a
collection of industrial artefacts, crafts and
furniture, including pieces made in the
William Morris workshops.

BARNSLEY
4 miles NE of
Cirencester on the
B4425

This village is home to
**Barnsley House
Garden**, a mature
family garden that was
created in the 1950s by
the well known writer
and gardener
Rosemary Verey. The
clever mix of planting
provides interest
throughout the
seasons and, now run
by her son Charles,
this intimate garden is

open all year except from mid December to
the end of January.

FAIRFORD
8 miles E of Cirencester on the A417

Situated on a lovely stretch of the River
Coln, this little town, which was once an
important staging post on the route
between London and Gloucester, has some
fine buildings dating from the 17th and
18th centuries. There is also an abundance
of inns that originally catered for the stage
coach traffic but the town's earlier
prosperity was built on wool, as was typical
of the Cotswolds, and it was endowments
by wool merchants John and Edmund

Fairford

Tame that helped to build the superb **St Mary's Church** in the late 15th and early 16th centuries. The magnificent medieval stained glass windows inside, which depict the Christian faith in picture book style, were a gift from John Tame and they have, over the centuries, remained here in their entirety. Some local stories suggest that Tame was a part time pirate and that the stained glass for the windows came from a looted Flemish ship but the truth is less fanciful and Tame probably imported Flemish craftsmen to make the glass.

Lechlade upon Thames

LECHLADE UPON THAMES
12 miles SE of Cirencester on the A417

This historic market town lies at the point where the River Thames meets the Cotswolds and **Ha'penny Bridge**, which dates from 1792, marks the end of the navigable Thames for boat users. The bridge takes its unusual name from the sum that was collected at the toll house here. Hard though it may seem to today's visitors, Lechlade was once one of the busiest inland ports in the country and the wharves here were crowded with barges using the River Thames and the canal (sadly now in disuse) that connected this main waterway to the River Severn. Now the town, as part of the **Cotswold Water Park**, is a place of leisure where there are facilities for all manner of watersports. Meanwhile, beside St John's Lock, the first lock on the River Thames and found close to its source near Cirencester, is a sculpture of **Father Thames**, which was originally created for the Great Exhibition of 1851.

THE DANEWAY INN

Daneway, Sapperton, Cirencester,
Gloucestershire GL7 6LN
Tel: 01285 760297
e-mail: goodfellow@daneway-inn.freeserve.co.uk

The Daneway Inn, created from a row of 18th century cottages, enjoys a secluded, picturesque setting in great walking country. Walkers and others will find a warm welcome from long-time owners Richard and Elizabeth Goodfellow, who engender a very cosy, homely ambience in the beamed bar, which features a wonderfully ornate carved wooden fireplace with a copper-hooded coal-burning stove. Elizabeth cooks a selection of simple, wholesome dishes served in generous portions at very kind prices. The Daneway has gardens to the front and is on the path of several popular walks. Wednesday is quiz night.

MISERDEN
7 miles NW of Cirencester off the A417

To the southeast of the village lies **Miserden Park Gardens**, a glorious formal garden created in the 17th century and situated overlooking the Golden Valley. Along with an arboretum, there is a walled garden with a long double herbaceous border, a yew walk, climbing roses and a newly planted parterre. The gardens are open from Easter to the end of September from Tuesdays to Thursdays.

2 Wiltshire

Along with being a county rich in prehistoric remains, Wiltshire also has one of the highest concentrations of historic houses and gardens in the country as well as some fine downland and woodland that is ideal for walking or cycling. The industrial heritage of the county takes many forms. In the northeastern corner of the Wiltshire lies Swindon, the county's largest town and one that developed quickly after Isambard Kingdom Brunel established the locomotive works for the recently built Great Western Railway here in the mid 19th century. To the south of Swindon lies the fertile Vale of Pewsey and the charming town of Marlborough that has acted as a centre for the surrounding farming communities for centuries as has the ancient town of Devizes to the west.

Salisbury High Street

The northwestern region of the county borders on the Cotswold hills and here there are an abundance of towns and villages that prospered, particularly in the Middle Ages, with the woollen trade. Chippenham, Malmesbury and Bradford-on-Avon all date back to Saxon times and many of the buildings in these charming places were built using the wealth from wool although they all prospered as more general market centres. Each too has its share of ancient ecclesiastical buildings and whilst Malmesbury has an abbey that was founded in the 7th century, Bradford is home to a superb 14th century Tithe Barn that once belonged to Shaftesbury Abbey in Dorset.

To the south of the county lies Salisbury, a glorious medieval city that grew up around its Cathedral that is, undoubtedly, one of the most beautiful buildings in the world. However, Salisbury's roots go back way beyond Norman times and there is a massive Iron Age hill fort close to the city that was later inhabited by the Romans and the Saxons.

To the north of the city lies Salisbury Plain, a huge area of chalkland with few settlements that is ringed by towns and villages. Inhabited since prehistoric times, the Plain was ploughed during World War I and, today, much of its vast landscape is

Stourhead Gardens

used for army training. However, Salisbury Plain is most famous as being the home of Stonehenge, a World Heritage Site, whose massive stone blocks are one of the greatest mysteries of the prehistoric world and, close by, is the even more ancient monument that is often overlooked – Woodhenge.

Another famous prehistoric site, and again also a World Heritage Site, can be found at Avebury, to the north of the plain, where not only are there stone circles but also an avenue

Avebury Stone Circles

of stones that lead to an early Bronze Age monument at West Overton and nearby is one of the country's largest Neolithic burial tombs at West Kennet. Finally, Wiltshire is also famous for its White Horses, a series of symbolic cuttings made into the chalk downland that, whilst some of them have been made relatively recently, have a history that dates back well over a 1,000 years.

PLACES TO STAY, EAT, DRINK AND SHOP

50	Portquin Guest House, Broadbush	Bed and Breakfast	page 60
51	Great Western Railway Museum, Swindon	Museum	page 61
52	The White Hart, Lyneham	Pub, Restaurant & Accommodation	page 62
53	The Pelican Inn, Froxfield, nr Marlborough	Pub, Restaurant & Accommodation	page 65
54	The Bell @ Ramsbury, Ramsbury	Pub and Restaurant	page 66
55	The Barleycorn Inn, Collingbourne Kingston	Pub and Restaurant	page 68
56	The French Horn, Pewsey	Pub and Restaurant	page 69
57	Wharfside Restaurant, Devizes	Restaurant and Shop	page 70
58	The Wiltshire Yeoman, Chirton, nr Devizes	Pub and Restaurant	page 71
59	Avebury Stone Circles, Avebury	Place of Interest	page 73
60	Manor Farm, Calstone Wellington, nr Calne	B&B and Riding School	page 74
61	The Wig and Quill , Salisbury	Pub with Food	page 76
62	The Royal Gloucestershire, Berkshire And Wiltshire Regiment Museum, Salisbury	Museum	page 77
63	The Old Ale House, Salisbury	Pub with Food	page 77
64	The Pheasant Inn, Salisbury	Pub with Food	page 78
65	The Retreat Inn, Salisbury	Pub, Restaurant & Accommodation	page 78
66	Old Sarum, Salisbury	Hill Fort	page 79
67	The Bridge at Woodford, Upper Woodford	Pub and Restaurant	page 80
68	The Old Bakery, Netton, nr Salisbury	Bed and Breakfast	page 80
69	Stonehenge Inn, Dorrington, nr Amesbury	Pub, Restaurant & Accommodation	page 81
70	The Old Inn, Allington, nr Salisbury	Pub with Food	page 82
71	The Old Inn, The Ridge, nr Woodfalls	Pub with Food	page 83
72	Apple Tree Inn, Morgan Vale, nr Salisbury	Pub with Food	page 83
73	The Cuckoo Inn, Hamptworth, nr Salisbury	Pub with Food	page 83
74	Old Wardour Castle, Ansty	Castle	page 86
75	The Bell & Crown, Zeals	Pub with Food	page 86
76	The Seymour Arms, East Knoyle	Pub, Restaurant & Accommodation	page 87
77	Stourhead House and Gardens, Stourton	Gardens	page 87
78	River Barn, Fonthill Bishop, nr Salisbury	Café and Tea Shop	page 88

WILTSHIRE

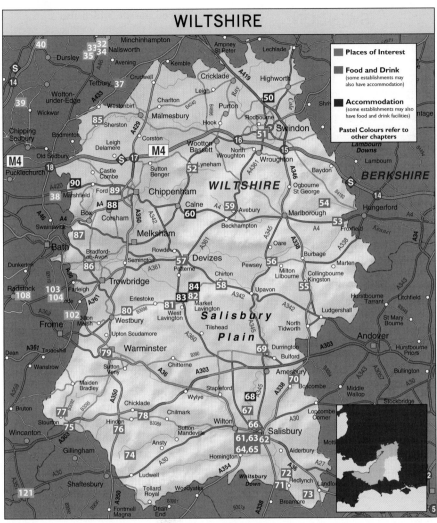

Places of Interest

Food and Drink
(some establishments may also have accommodation)

Accommodation
(some establishments may also have food and drink facilities)

Pastel Colours refer to other chapters

© MAPS IN MINUTES ™ 2002   © Crown Copyright, Ordnance Survey 2002

79	The Masons Arms, Warminster	Pub with Food	page 89
80	The Duke at Bratton, Bratton, nr Westbury	Pub and Restaurant	page 91
81	The Owl, Little Cheverill, nr Devizes	Pub, Restaurant & Accommodation	page 91
82	The Drummer Boy, Market Lavington	Pub with Food	page 92
83	West Park Farm, Market Lavington, nr Devizes	Bed and Breakfast	page 92
84	Eastcott Manor, Easterton	Bed and Breakfast	page 93
85	The Carpenters Arms, Easton Town	Pub and Restaurant	page 94
86	The Dandy Lion, Bradford-upon-Avon	Pub and Restaurant	page 97
87	The Kings Arms, Monkton Farleigh	Pub and Restaurant	page 98
88	Wadswick Barns, Wadswick, nr Corsham	Self Catering	page 99
89	Biddestone Arms, Biddestone, nr Chippenham	Pub and Restaurant	page 100
90	Court Close House B&B, North Wraxall	Bed and Breakfast	page 100

SWINDON

Until the 1840s, this was a small market town in the northeast corner of the county, between the Cotswolds and the Marlborough Downs, which served the local agricultural communities. However, in 1835, the railway line between London and Bristol was completed and, in the same year, Swindon Station was opened. It was the arrival of the railway that was to see Swindon expand, rapidly, into what is now Wiltshire's largest industrial town. In 1843, Isambard Kingdom Brunel, the Great Western Railway's principal engineer, decided that Swindon was the place to build his locomotive works and, choosing a site down the hill from the old town, the works were constructed along with cottages for the workforce, a church and public houses. However, the choice of location for the new works is said to have been made on the toss of a sandwich when, in 1833, Brunel and fellow engineer, Daniel Gooch, were surveying the proposed route of the railway line and stopped for a sandwich lunch below the old town. So impressed were they with the area laid out before them that they decided to throw a sandwich and wherever it landed would become the site of their new works.

Within a few years, the locomotive works had grown to be one of the largest in the world, with as many as 12,000

working on the site, which also incorporated the Railway Village; a model development of 300 workmen's houses built of limestone extracted from the construction of Box Tunnel. Today, this unique example of early Victorian town planning can be explored at the **Railway Village Museum** that, found in the heart of the famous village, is housed in a cottage that has been refurbished to recreate a late Victorian railway worker's home. Along with the original fittings and features, such as a range and a copper in the kitchen, the house is still lit by gas and the museum is open daily from Easter to mid October.

Meanwhile, housed in a beautifully restored railway building in the heart of the Swindon Works, is the **STEAM**, the **Museum of the Great Western Railway** (see panel opposite) that focuses on many aspects of the story of 'God's Wonderful Railway'. Through reconstructions and life-like characters, the lives of the men and women who built and repaired the locomotives is explored whilst there is a vast collection of locomotives, nameplates, signalling equipment and an exhibition of the life and achievements of Brunel.

There is, however, more to Swindon than railways and, today, this bustling and successful commercial town, which is now part of the south of England's Silicon Valley, has ample scope for shopping and leisure with plenty of open countryside

PORTQUIN GUEST HOUSE

Broadbush, Blunsdon, Swindon, Wiltshire SN26 7DH
Tel/Fax: 01793 721261
e-mail: portquin@msn.com
website: portquinguesthouse.com

Portquin Guest House is a traditional stone-built house on the northern outskirts of Swindon (B4019). Open all year, Karen and Ian Jankinson's guest house comprises nine en suite letting bedrooms, including two large family rooms; all have tv, telephone and tea/coffee making facilities. All are non-smoking rooms . A full English breakfast makes an excellent start to the day at Portquin, which combines a quiet country setting with quick and easy access to all the business and leisure amenities of Swindon, Wiltshire and the Cotswolds.

nearby. Also, housed in an elegant early 19th century house is the **Swindon Museum and Art Gallery**, which features displays on the history, archaeology and geology of the town and surrounding area whilst the gallery has an outstanding collection of 20th century British Art. The museum and art gallery are open daily all year round except for Bank Holiday Mondays.

AROUND SWINDON

HIGHWORTH
5½ miles NE of Swindon on the A361

This village's name is, indeed, appropriate as it stands at the top of a 400 foot incline and the view from **Highworth Hill** takes in the neighbouring counties of Gloucestershire and Oxfordshire as well as the countryside of Wiltshire. There are some very fine 17th and 18th century buildings around the village's old square and, close by, is the parish church. Built in the 15th century, it was fortified during the Civil War and was attacked soon after by Parliamentarian forces under General Fairfax and one of the cannon balls that struck it can be seen on display outside. The church also contains a memorial to Lieutenant Warneford, who was awarded the VC for destroying the first enemy Zeppelin in 1915.

STEAM - MUSEUM OF THE GREAT WESTERN RAILWAY
Kemble Drive, Swindon, Wiltshire SN2 2TA
Tel: 01793 466646 Fax: 01793 466615
website: www.steam-museum.org.uk

The award-winning **STEAM, the Museum of the Great Western Railway**, is located in a beautifully restored building at the heart of Swindon Railway Works, where for nearly 150 years thousands of men and women worked for the Great Western Railway. The

main activity was the building of great steam locomotives, the last being 92220 *Evening Star*, one of a fleet of powerful 2-10-0 freight engines which were destined to have all too short a working life. The star of the show in the Museum is 6000 *King George V*, which stands in a platform at the head of the 'Bristolian' express. Visitors can climb aboard the footplate of this marvellous thoroughbred and relive the glory days of 'God's Wonderful Railway'. Another of the great GWR locomotives was the Castle class, and here visitors can actually walk underneath *Caerphilly Castle* as it stands in its inspection pit.

The sounds, sights and smells of the railway works live on in the workshops, where locomotives and carriages are restored, and one section of this fascinating place contains GWR accessories and road vehicles, including the famous Scammell 'mechanical horse', which could turn on a sixpence but sometimes had a mind of its own. The great figure of early railway days was the engineer Isambard Kingdom Brunel, whose story is told together with that of the thousands of less famous workers, from the navvies to drivers, signalmen and station masters, who built and operated the railway. There are many hands-on opportunities to relive the action, from building bridges to working the signals, shunting the wagons and driving the steam trains, and special events and family activities are held regularly throughout the year.

All areas of the museum are accessible to wheelchairs, and visitors who run out of steam can relax awhile in the stylish balcony café.

WROUGHTON
3 miles SW of Swindon on the A4361

Recently, this village has expanded due to its proximity to Swindon but, to the south, remains one of the numerous airfields that were created during World War II and

THE WHITE HART

Chippenham Road, Lyneham, Wiltshire SN15 4PB
Tel: 01249 890243
e-mail: andy.daviesfive@virgin.net

The doors open at 11 o'clock at the **White Hart**, a classic 18th century pub on the outskirts of Lyneham, an easy drive from Junction 16 of the M4. Managed by experienced licensees Andy and Tricia Davies, the pub has plenty of space for enjoying a drink in the bar or lounge, and in the dining area good food at sensible prices is served lunchtime and evening seven days a week: steaks are the house speciality. The White Hart also offers overnight accommodation in four en suite bedrooms with their own entrance; all have tv and tea/coffee makers. The pub has a pool table, a beer garden and a play area for children.

Wroughton Airfield still has its historic hangars from those days. Today, the hangars are home to the **Science Museum Wroughton** and here large items from the National Collections of aircraft, land transport and agriculture are stored along with radar, fire fighting equipment and many other objects. The museum is open on selected weekends throughout the year.

Close to the airfield is **Clouts Wood Nature Reserve**, a lovely place for a ramble, whilst, just a short drive southeastwards, is the site of **Barbury Castle**, one of the most spectacular Iron Age hill forts in southern England. This open hillside was the scene of a bloody battle between the Britons and the Saxons in the 6th century, which the Britons lost, and after which the Saxon kingdom of Wessex was established under King Cealwin. The land around the castle is a now a country park.

BROAD HINTON
6 miles SW of Swindon off the A4361

Found in the village's medieval parish church is a 16th century monument dedicated to the Wroughton family that shows Sir Thomas Wroughton and his wife Anne kneeling in prayer surrounded by their children. According to legend, Sir Thomas returned home one day from hunting to find that his wife was reading the Bible and had not prepared his dinner.

In a rage, Sir Thomas grabbed the Book from her and threw it on to the fire. Anne managed to rescue her Bible but, in so doing, she badly burnt her hands and, as a punishment for his blasphemy, Sir Thomas's hands, and those of their four children, are said to have withered away. On the monument in the church, Sir Thomas and the children are depicted without hands whilst the Bible has a corner missing to illustrate where it was damaged by the flames.

Just to the north of the village, near **Broad Town**, lies the county's most northerly **White Horse** that was carved into the downland here in 1863.

LYDIARD TREGOZE
3 miles W of Swindon off the A3102

On the western outskirts of Swindon lies **Lydiard House and Park**, the ancestral home of the Viscounts Bolingbroke that was saved from dereliction and has been beautifully restored. Described by Sir Hugh Casson as "a gentle Georgian house, sunning itself as serenely as an old grey cat" and certainly one of Wiltshire's most delightful, though smaller, stately homes, the interior of the house contains fine furniture and family picture collections whilst the little blue Dressing Room is devoted to the 18th century society artist, Lady Diana Spencer, who became the 2nd Viscountess Bolingbroke. Adjacent to the house is **St Mary's Church**, which contains several fine 17ᵗʰ century memorials to the St John family who lived at the house from Elizabethan times – the most striking is the Golden Cavalier, a life-size gilded effigy of Edward St John in full battledress who was killed at the 2ⁿᵈ Battle of Newbury during the Civil War in 1645. The house and extensive parkland (where there is an adventure playground) are open throughout the year.

WOOTTON BASSETT
5 miles W of Swindon on the A3102

This small town has served the surrounding agricultural communities since Saxon times and records here date back to the 7ᵗʰ century whilst, in 1219, Henry III granted Wootton Bassett a market charter and the wide High Street was once the venue for livestock markets and hiring fairs. The first known mayor of Wootton Bassett was John Woolmonger, who was appointed in 1408, while another holder of the office, some years later, was acting as the town magistrate when a drunk was brought before him after an overnight drinking spree. When asked by the mayor whether he pleaded guilty to drunkenness, the man reminded the mayor that he too had been on the same drinking spree and was, therefore, not as sober as a judge. "Ah well", said the mayor, "that was different. Now, I am the mayor and I am going to fine you five shillings."

The most remarkable building in Wootton is the **Old Town Hall**, which stands on a series of stone pillars and leaves an open-sided ground floor area that once served as a covered market. Today this half-timbered 17ᵗʰ century building is home to the **Wootton Bassett Museum** that holds an extensive photographic collection that illustrates life

in the town during the 19ᵗʰ and 20ᵗʰ centuries. Also on display are a rare, late 17ᵗʰ century ducking stool, a whipping post, silver maces and a mayoral sword of office. The museum is open all year on Saturday mornings only.

A section of the **Wiltshire and Berkshire Canal** has been restored at nearby **Templars Fir** and the mile section is not only home to a biennial Boat Fair but also a wealth of wildlife inhabit the banks.

PURTON
4½ miles NW of Swindon off the B4553

A large, scattered village, which was originally several ancient hamlets, **St Mary's Church**, at the heart of Purton, is unique among English churches in that it has both a central tower, a western tower and a spire. Local legend explains that the church was built by two sisters and, unable to agree on a design, they reached this unusual compromise. However, this charming tale is inaccurate as the spire was built in around 1325 and the western tower was added some 150 years later. The history of the village, from Neolithic times to the present day, can be explored at **Purton Museum**, found in the public library, where there is also a comprehensive collection of agricultural tools and dairy equipment that act as a reminder of the area's long reliance on farming. The museum is open in the afternoon on Tuesdays, Wednesdays and Fridays and the Mini Museum Detective is on hand to introduce the museum's younger visitors to the exhibits and displays.

To the north of Purton, on the road to Purton Stoke, is **Watkins' Corner** that is said to be haunted by the ghost of a man, Watkins, who was hanged for a murder here to which, later, his father confessed.

CRICKLADE
6½ miles NW of Swindon on the B4040

The only town in Wiltshire on the River Thames, Cricklade was an important Roman military post on Ermin Street, the route that continued northwards to Cirencester. Later, the Saxons built a defensive tower here against the Danes and it was important enough at that time to have its own mint. There are several buildings of interest here, especially down the wide High Street, where there is a Victorian Jubilee Clock, the famous school founded by London goldsmith Robert Jenner in 1652 and the magnificent **St Sampson's Church**. Dating from the 13th century, this is a magnificent church with a cathedral-like four-spired tower and it plays host to a festival of music each September. The **Cricklade Museum** holds an interesting collection of local history artefacts that covers the town's heritage from the times of the Roman occupation through the Saxon era to the 20th century. The museum has limited opening throughout the year.

The **Thames Path National Trail** passes through Cricklade and, nearby, is the **North Meadow**, a National Nature Reserve where, in spring, the country's largest area of the rare Snakeshead fritillary can be seen in bloom. Also close by, at Blunsdon Station, is the **Swindon and Cricklade Railway**, the only standard gauge railway in the county that restores and runs both steam and diesel locomotives along with having several historic signal boxes and buildings.

LATTON
8 miles NW of Swindon off the A419

This lovely old village has some delightful 17th century Cotswold stone cottages and larger Victorian houses and it was once an important junction of the **Wiltshire and Berkshire** and **Thames and Severn Canals**.

ASHTON KEYNES
9 miles NW of Swindon off the B4696

Situated on the upper reaches of the River Thames, this village is surrounded by some 133 lakes that were formed by gravel extraction and that are now the **Cotswold Water Park**. Along with a wide variety of watersports, including sailing, wind surfing, canoeing and water skiing, visitors also have the opportunity to explore **Keynes Country Park** in which the water park is set. Open all year round, the country park has its own nature reserve and visitor centre along with picnic sites, children's beach and play area, walks and trails and facilities for coarse fishing.

MARLBOROUGH

Situated in the rural eastern region of Wiltshire in the upland valley of the River Kennet, which flows through the town, Marlborough borders the Marlborough Downs to the north and this area has been settled for centuries. Home to the Romans, whose settlement of Cunetio gave rise to the name of the River Kennet, the land around Marlborough shows evidence of earlier inhabitants including those from Neolithic, Bronze and Iron Age tribes. The town is, naturally, steeped in history and legend and, until the 14th century, it was believed that Merlin, King Arthur's magician, was buried under a mound here and it was this, 'Merle Barrow' or Merlin's Tomb, which gave the town its name. This mound is thought to have its origins in prehistoric times and it was here that the Normans built Marlborough's Royal Castle, which stood for several centuries. The borough was granted its charter in 1204 by King John and it was in the castle's Great Hall, in 1267, that Henry III initiated the famous 'Statutes of Marlborough'.

Marlborough's main street is one of the finest, and widest, in the country and it is lined by many fine Tudor houses and some handsome Georgian buildings. At each end of the High Street there is a splendid church: at the west end is 15th century St Peter's Church (now redundant) whilst at the east end lies the parish **Church of St Mary**. Dating from Norman times, the church was severely damaged by the fire of 1653 that ravaged the town and the flat ceiling and single arcade date from the time of its rebuilding during the Cromwellian period. St Mary's stands in **Patten Alley** that is so named because pedestrians had to wear pattens (an overshoe with a metal sole) to negotiate their way through the mud on rainy days and the church has a ledge in its porch where churchgoers would leave their pattens before entering.

Also along the High Street is the **Merchant's House** that was built in 1656 for a rich silk merchant and his wealth is reflected in the lavish decoration that includes a rare painted balustrade in the Staircase Hall and the floor to ceiling oak panelling and stone fireplace with decorative wooden panel in the Great Panelled chamber. Other buildings of interest include those clustered around **The Green**, the site of a Saxon community,

Marlborough High Street

and although many of the cottages were rebuilt after a devastating fire destroyed much of the town some of their cellars have Saxon origins.

However, Marlborough's most famous building is undoubtedly **Marlborough College**, which was founded in 1843 primarily for the sons of the clergy but that is now co-educational. Close to the mound, which can be found in the college grounds, the Seymour family built a family mansion that was, in the early 18th century, replaced by the present building that became the Castle Inn and is now C House, the oldest part of the school. Famous old boys include William Morris, founder of the Arts and Crafts Movement, and the poet John Betjeman and it was also boys from the college who, in 1804, cut the **Marlborough White Horse**.

THE BELL @ RAMSBURY

The Square, Ramsbury, Nr Marlborough,
Wiltshire SN8 2PE
Tel: 01672 520230 Fax: 01672 521476

In the heart of the peaceful riverside village of Ramsbury, the **Bell** is one of the leading pub restaurants in the region, rightly earning its motto as 'the epitome of fine dining and wines'. The pleasing black and white building dates back some 300 years, and the interior has a splendidly traditional atmosphere assisted by such features as old church pews.

A regularly changing à la carte menu that is outstanding in its variety and quality. Fresh fish is a speciality, exemplified by superb grilled red mullet on a roasted pepper and almond parfait dressed with a pesto oil, or whole baked gilthead bream anointed with top-quality olive oil. But everything else on the menu tastes as good as it sounds, coming from a kitchen that combines classic technique with a good measure of inventiveness and

takes its inspiration from around the world: tomato, coconut and coriander soup garnished with lemon grass oil; stuffed Lebanese peppers with a spicy tomato coulis; roasted fillet of pork with caramelised apple and a sweet stem ginger jus; medallions of venison and haggis stack napped with a red wine reduction.

Food as good as this deserves fine wines, and the Bell's list is selected with care from the best of Old and New World vintages. In the bar, a good range of ales and snacks is served. The Bell has ample parking and a beer garden. Ramsbury is signposted off the B4192, about four miles from the A4 at Hungerford.

AROUND MARLBOROUGH

SAVERNAKE FOREST
2 miles SE of Marlborough off the A346

The ancient Savernake Forest is a magnificent expanse of unbroken woodland, open glades and bridle paths that has been in the wardenship of descendents of the same family since the Norman Conquest in 1066. Henry VIII hunted wild deer here and married Jane Seymour, whose family lived nearby, and, for a while Jane's brother Edward owned both the Forest and the ruins of Marlborough Castle. Designated a Site of Special Scientific Interest, the forest is home to an abundance of wildlife, including a small herd of roe and fallow deer and some 25 species of butterflies.

Savernake Forest

GREAT BEDWYN
6 miles SE of Marlborough off the A4

Though a village today, Great Bedwyn was, in medieval times, a town and this is why the Church of St Mary the Virgin, built in the 12th and 13th centuries appears to be much larger than today's needs would

Kennet and Avon Canal, Little Bedwyn

suggest. The tomb of Sir John Seymour, the father of Henry VIII's third wife Jane, is in the Chancel.

The aptly named Mason's Yard is open to a **Stone Museum**. The museum is run by the seventh generation of a family of stonemasons and includes an assortment of tombstones and a stone aeroplane with an 11foot wingspan.

CROFTON
6 miles SE of Marlborough off the A338

The eastern end of the Vale of Pewsey carries the London Penzance railway line and the Kennet & Avon Canal, which reaches its highest point near Crofton. The site is marked by a handsome Georgian pumping station which houses the **Crofton Beam Engines**. These engines - the 1812 Boulton & Watt and the 1845 Harvey of Hayle - have been superbly restored under the guidance of the Kennet & Avon Canal Trust and the 1812 engine is the oldest working beam engine in the world, still in its original building and still doing its original job of pumping water to the summit level of the canal. Both engines are steamed from a hand-stoked, coal-fired Lancashire boiler. The separate brick chimney has also been restored, to its original height of 82 feet.

WILTON
8 miles SE of Marlborough off the A338

A footpath of about a mile links the Crofton Beam Engines with Wilton. This is the smaller of the two Wiltshire Wiltons, best known as the site of the **Wilton Windmill**. This traditional working windmill, the only one operating in the county, was built in 1821 after the **Kennet & Avon Canal** Company had taken the water out of the River Bedwyn for their canal, thereby depriving the water millers of the power to drive their mills. The mill worked until 1920, when the availability of steam power and electricity literally took the wind out of its sails. After standing derelict for 50 years it was restored at a cost of £25,000 and is now looked after by the Wilton Windmill Society. This superb mill is floodlit from dusk until 10pm, making a wonderful sight on a chalk ridge 550 feet above sea level.

WOOTTON RIVERS
3½ miles S of Marlborough off the A338

This attractive village is home to a real curiosity – a highly unusual church clock – the **Jack Sprat Clock** that was built by a local man from an assortment of scrap metal including old bicycles, prams and farm tools. Constructed to mark the coronation of George V in 1911, the clock has 24 different chimes and its face has letters instead of numbers.

PEWSEY
6 miles S of Marlborough on the A345

Situated in the heart of this beautiful valley, the **Vale of Pewsey**, this is a charming village of thatched, half-timbered cottages and Georgian houses through which the Kennet and Avon Canal runs. It was once the property of Alfred the Great and his statue stands at the central crossroads whilst the parish church, built on a foundation of sarsen stones, has an unusual altar rail made from timbers taken from the *San Josef*, a ship captured by Nelson in 1797.

Attractions for visitors here include the old wharf area along the canal and the **Pewsey Heritage Centre**, housed in an 1870 foundry building, which contains an interesting collection of old and unusual tools and farming machinery.

The original **Pewsey White Horse**, to the south of the village on Pewsey Down, was cut in 1785 and it apparently included a rider but the horse was redesigned by Mr George Marples and cut by the Pewsey Fire Brigade to celebrate the coronation of George VI in 1937.

A minor road runs past the White Horse across Pewsey Down to the isolated village of **Everleigh**, where the Church of St Peter

THE BARLEYCORN INN

Collingbourne Kingston, Nr Marlborough,
Wiltshire SN8 3SD
Tel/Fax: 01264 850368

The Barleycorn Inn is a handsome 18th century redbrick building situated on the busy A338 midway between Marlborough and Andover. Neat, cosy and inviting within, it has a beer garden that offers pleasant views. Heather and David Wheeler attract a loyal, mature clientele with their ready welcome, a superb range of real ales and good home cooking on a menu that includes excellent pies. Visitors on Sunday evening should arrive with wits sharpened, for this is quiz night at the Barleycorn.

THE FRENCH HORN

Marlborough Road, Pewsey, Wiltshire SN9 5NT
Tel: 01672 562443 Fax: 01672 562785
e-mail: info@french-horn-pewsey.co.uk
website: www.french-horn-pewsey.co.uk

Situated in the Vale of Pewsey, **The French Horn** dates back to early 19th century when it was built as a roadside house for the French prisoners of war who were digging the final stretch of the Kennet and Avon Canal. Today, this is a wonderful hidden treasure, a charming country inn that is highly regarded for the excellence of both its cuisine and its cellar. In the summer of 2001 partners Andrew Cannon and Lauren Daniels first moved here and, in this short space of time, they have gained a very enviable reputation for their hospitality. Warmed by two log fires in the winter, the bar area and lounge are just the places to relax over a quiet drink and there are several real ales here from which to choose whilst there is also a good bar menu for the peckish.

However, it is for its restaurant that The French Horn is becoming particularly popular. Cosy and attractive, with crisp white table linen, here diners are treated to a wonderful menu of imaginative dishes that are freshly prepared and cooked to order. A renowned chef, Andrew's constantly changing menu includes such delights as Grilled sea bass on fresh vegetable ratatouille and Barbary duck with plum chutney and orange sauce and there are some equally mouth-watering desserts to round off the meal. The wine list provides the final complement to a meal here and children have their own special menu.

is of unusual iron-framed construction. Rebuilt on a new site in 1813, the church has a short chancel and narrow nave, an elegant west gallery and a neo-medieval hammerbeam roof.

ALTON BARNES AND ALTON PRIORS
7 miles SW of Marlborough off the A345

Found in the Vale of Pewsey, these two villages lies adjacent to each other and their two small, ancient churches stand just a few hundred yards apart. To the north of the villages lies **Alton Barnes White Horse** that was cut in 1812 and is said to be visible from Old Sarum Castle, which lies some 20 miles away. Close by are several prehistoric remains including Knap Hill and Adam's Grave, a Neolithic long barrow.

DEVIZES
12 miles SW of Marlborough on the A361

At the western edge of the Vale of Pewsey, Devizes is the central market town of Wiltshire and it was founded in 1080 by

Devizes Market Place

Devizes Castle

Bishop Osmund, nephew of William the Conqueror and its name is thought to come from the Latin, 'ad divisas', meaning 'at the boundaries', because it grew up at a point where the manors of Cannings, Rowde and Potterne once met. Bishop Osmund was responsible for building a timber castle and, after the wooden structure burnt down, Roger, Bishop of Sarum, built a stone castle in 1138 that survived until the end of the Civil War when, in 1646, it was demolished following a Parliamentary order. All that can be seen today of **Devizes Castle** are the original mound, traces of the moat and remains of the foundations of the Great

Hall. Bishop Roger also built two churches in Devizes: **St John's**, whose chancel and transepts represent some of the finest examples of the Norman style in England, and, as it is only a short distance from the castle mound was undoubtedly the castle church whilst **St Mary's**, though not as fine, has an imposing nave and a tower containing six bells.

Meanwhile, Devizes' **Market Place** is one of the country's largest and here there is an unusual market cross inscribed with the story of Ruth Pierce, a market stall holder who stood accused, in 1753, of swindling her customers when she and two other women agreed to divide the cost of a sack of corn between them. However, their payment was found to be three pence short and all three women protested their innocence saying that they had given the correct share. Ruth Pierce went further and declared that if she had cheated she wished to fall down dead on the spot and this she did and the missing three pennies were found clutched in her grasp.

Another local legend concerns a smuggling gang from the 17th century who fooled excise men when they were caught recovering brandy kegs they had hidden in the pond. Pretending to be simple, the smugglers said that they thought that the moon's reflection on the surface of the pond was a large round cheese and that

WHARFSIDE RESTAURANT & PINS AND NEEDLES

13 Couch Lane, Devizes, Wiltshire SN10 1EB
Tel: 01380 726051

Judy Podger owns and runs two delightful outlets in a Bath stone building close to the Kennet & Avon Canal. The 60-cover **Wharfside Restaurant** is open for tea and coffee from 8.30 in the morning and serves good wholesome fare such as jacket potatoes, quiche, lasagne and salads for lunch, with a roast on Sunday. On the other side of the archway is **Pins and Needles**, a little retail shop selling wools, ribbons, buttons and bows - and, of course, pins and needles.

they were attempting to rake it in. This story gave rise to the name Moonraker for the local area.

For a greater insight into the history of the town there is **Devizes Visitor Centre**, which, through an interactive exhibition, allows visitors to explore the early medieval town whilst the **Wiltshire Heritage Museum** contains a prehistoric collection of international importance of artefacts found during archaeological excavations undertaken within the county. These include the Stonehenge barrow finds and there are also galleries of Roman, Saxon and medieval finds along with displays on local natural history. The museum is open all year except Sundays. Meanwhile, the art gallery, which is open daily, is home to a John Piper window and hosts several changing exhibitions throughout the year.

Kennet and Avon Canal

Devizes stands at a key point on the **Kennet and Avon Canal**, one of the country's most beautiful waterways, and, along with being home to, in July, the Canalfest that takes place at the town's Wharf, the canal's towpath is now open as a public footpath. The **Wharf**, once a busy port area, has been restored and here visitors can take a boat trip, see the start of the famous Devizes to Westminster Canoe

Race that takes place each Good Friday, attend the theatre and also learn more about the waterway at the **Kennet and Avon Museum**. Dedicated to the waterway, the exhibition tells the story of the creation and restoration of this waterway link between London and Bristol. The museum is open from Easter to Christmas.

To the north of the town lies **Roundway Hill**, the site of a Civil War battle and where, from its summit, there are breathtaking views over the Vale of Pewsey, Devizes and beyond. The hill, too, is home

to **Devizes Millennium White Horse**, the county's most recently created white horse that was cut to celebrate the millennium and also where, on New Year's Eve 1999, a time capsule was buried.

WEST OVERTON
3½ miles W of Marlborough off the A4

The area between Marlborough and Avebury sees the biggest concentration of prehistoric remains in the country and the scattered community of West Overton stands at the foot of **Overton Hill**, the site of an early Bronze Age monument called **The Sanctuary**. These giant standing stones are at the southeastern end of West Kennet Avenue, an ancient pathway that once connected them to the main megalithic circles at nearby Avebury. Overton Hill is also the start point of the **Ridgeway** long-distance path that runs for 80 miles to the Chilterns. Just off this path is **Fyfield Down**, now a nature reserve, where quarries once provided many of the great stones that are such a feature of the area. **Devil's Den** long barrow lies within the reserve and local legend says that Satan sometimes appears here at midnight attempting to pull down the stones with a team of white oxen.

WEST KENNET
5 miles W of Marlborough on the A4

This hamlet is home to **West Kennet Long Barrow**, one of Britain's largest Neolithic burial tombs, which is situated just a gentle stroll away from here and from its twin hamlet, East Kennet. The tomb is of impressive proportions – some 330 feet long, 80 feet wide and 10 feet high – and it is reached by squeezing past some massive stones in the semicircular forecourt.

AVEBURY
6 miles W of Marlborough on the A4361

This tiny village lies at the centre of a 28 acre World Heritage Site, a concentration of prehistoric sites, which has, at its heart, the **Avebury Stone Circles** (see panel opposite), the most remarkable ritual megalithic monuments in Europe and much of which is under the protection of the National Trust. Archaeologists working on the site have recently found the remains of a long-vanished **West Kennet Avenue of Stones** leading southeastwards to The Sanctuary at West Overton.

However, Avebury is not all prehistoric stone circles and here can also be found **Avebury Manor** (National Trust), a gem from the Elizabethan era, which stands on the site of a 12th century priory. Noted for its Queen Anne alterations and renovation work undertaken by Colonel Jenner in the early 20th century, the manor house has a walled garden that features topiary, flower gardens and numerous themed areas or 'rooms'.

West Kennet Long Barrow

AVEBURY STONE CIRCLES

Avebury, Wiltshire

A 28-acre World Heritage Site is the centre of the **Avebury Stone Circles**, the most remarkable ritual megalithic monuments in Europe. A massive bank and ditch enclose an outer circle and two inner circles of stones. The outer circle of almost 100 sarsen stones (sand and silica) enclose two rings with about 40 stones still standing. Archaeologists working on the site found the remains of a long-vanished avenue of stones leading south towards Beckhampton.

This discovery seems to vindicate the theory of the 18th century antiquary William Stukeley, who made drawings of the stone circles with this avenue marked. The stones in the avenue had disappeared so completely (perhaps destroyed out of some superstition in the Middle Ages) that few believed Stukeley. The research team from Southampton, Leicester and Newport Universities uncovered a series of subterranean features which appear to be buried stones and the sockets in which they were set. Two large stones, known as Adam and Eve, had always been known about on this route, but there were no further traces until the team's discoveries in 1999.

The **Avebury Stones** bear testimony to the enormous human effort that went into their construction: some of the individual stones weigh 40 tons and all had to dragged from Marlborough Downs. The Avebury stones are in two basic shapes, which have been equated with male and female and have led to the theory that the site was used for the observance of fertility rites.

Built by Celtic farmers and shepherds in around 1800 BC, the size of the monuments suggest that there was a well organized community here and one that was probably led by priests. In the Middle Ages, the Christian Church became concerned with the revival in pagan rites and, as Avebury certainly had such a meaning, the clergy gave orders for the stones to be buried. Excavations in the 1930s revealed the skeleton of a man, along with various coins and surgical tools, beneath one of the megaliths and, identified as a surgeon-barber who died in around 1320, it is thought that he was killed when the stone that he was helping to bury fell on him.

During the 17th and 18th centuries many of the stones were used locally for building purposes but a massive restoration programme in the 20th century, led by the archaeologist Alexander Keiller, saw them re-erected in their rightful places. Many of the archaeological finds from the site are displayed in Avebury's **Alexander Keiller Museum**, which also describes the reconstruction of the site by Keiller in the 1930s. The museum is open from March to Christmas.

SILBURY HILL
6 miles W of Marlborough off the A4

The largest man-made prehistoric mound in Europe, Silbury Hill was built in around 2800 BC, stands 130 feet high, covers five acres and, whilst excavation in the late 1960s revealed some details of how it was constructed, little light has been shed on its purpose. Theories include a burial place for an otherwise forgotten King Sil and the

Silbury Hill

burial place of a solid gold horse and rider. Stories, too, link the creation of the mound with the Devil who is said to have been going to empty a sack of earth on Marlborough but was forced, by the power of the priests at Avebury, to drop it here.

CALNE
12 miles W of Marlborough on the A4

This former weaving centre in the valley of the River Marden gained fame in the Middle Ages for its woollen broadcloth and its prominent wool church reflects the prosperity of those earlier times and the wealth of the prosperous clothiers who provided funds for its construction. One of the memorials in the church is to Dr Ingenhousz, who is widely credited with creating a smallpox vaccination before

Edward Jenner, whilst Dr Joseph Priestly, who discovered oxygen in 1774, lived in the town.

To the west of Calne lies **Bowood House and Gardens**, the magnificent family home of the Marquis and Marchioness of Lansdowne, which was built in 1625 and is now a treasury for the heirlooms of the Shelborne family. The splendid rooms house a remarkable collection of furniture, porcelain, ivory, costumes, silver and miniatures from Georgian times through to the era of the Indian Raj. Among the numerous and varied exhibits are Napoleon's death mask and Lord Bryon's Albanian costume whilst the Robert Adam's Orangery, originally designed as a conservatory, is now a superb art gallery housing important 18th and 19th century

---

Manor Farm

Calstone Wellington, Nr Calne, Wiltshire SN11 8PY
Tel: 01249 816804   e-mail: calstonebandb@farmersweekly.net
Fax: 01249 817966   website: www.calstone.co.uk

Comfort, peace and relaxation in a scenic location - that's the promise of **Manor Farm**, a fifth generation family home with two en suite guest bedrooms. These rooms are tastefully decorated, very spacious and comfortable; one is furnished with antiques including a splendid Victorian four-poster bed, and the other is a double or twin suite.
Top-quality ingredients highlighted by local and home-made produce ensure that the multi-choice breakfast served at the family table makes a memorable start to the day at Patrick and Sandra Maundrell's working sheep and arable farm, which also has an indoor riding school. Though quiet and secluded, Manor Farm is only minutes from the A4, so it's an excellent base for touring the region.

works as well as those by Old Masters. The mausoleum at the house was commissioned in 1761 by the Dowager Countess of Shelborne as a memorial to her husband and it was Adam's first work for the family. Meanwhile, it was in the Bowood Laboratory that Dr Joseph Priestly, tutor to the 1st Marquis of Lansdowne's son, conducted his experiments that led to the identification of oxygen. The house and grounds are set within one of Britain's most beautiful parklands, designed by Capability Brown, and along with sloping lawns, a tranquil lake and a terraced rose garden, there is an arboretum, a pinetum, a Doric temple and a cascade waterfall. There is also the Rhododendron Walk, some three miles from the house, and this woodland garden is considered one of the most exciting gardens of its type in the country.

Just outside Calne, to the southeast, lies **Atwell-Wilson Motor Museum**, home to a collection of 100 vintage and classic cars, motorcycles and vehicles that span the 1920s through to the 1980s. The majority

Waterfall, Bowood House

of vehicles on display here are still in working order and as well as the grand Rolls Royces, there are more humble Singers and a Model 'T' Ford. The museum is open all year from Sunday to Thursday and on Good Friday.

To the east of Calne lies **Cherhill Down** (National Trust), an area of ancient downland that overlooks the Vale of Pewsey and where, on the chalk ridge summit, there is the Iron Age hill fort of **Oldbury Castle** along with the **Lansdowne Monument**, which was built in 1845 by the 3rd Marquis of Lansdowne in memory of the economist Sir William Petty. Carved into the hillside, and not owned by the Trust, is another Wiltshire **White Horse** and there are Bronze Age barrows and other prehistoric earthworks nearby.

White Horse, Cherhill

SALISBURY

The glorious medieval city of Salisbury stands at the confluence of four rivers, the Avon, Wylye, Bourne and Nadder, and, originally called New Sarum, it grew around the present Cathedral, which was built between 1220 and 1258 in a sheltered position two miles south of the site of its windswept Norman predecessor at Old Sarum. Over the years the townspeople followed the clergy into the new settlement, creating a flourishing religious and market centre whose two main aspects flourish to this day.

One of the most beautiful buildings in the world, **Salisbury Cathedral** is the only medieval cathedral in England to be built in the same Early English style – apart from the spire, the tallest in England, which was added a generation later and, rising to an awesome

Salisbury Cathedral

404 feet, it is a significant local landmark. The Chapter House opens out of the cloisters and contains, among other treasures, one of the four surviving

The Wig and Quill

1 New Street, Salisbury, Wiltshire SP1 2PH
Tel: 01722 335665

Found in the shadow of Salisbury's famous cathedral and dating from the 16th century the two cottages that now house **The Wig and Quill** were originally homes for the cathedral servants. This traditional town centre inn, which is well known for its friendly village pub atmosphere, has been managed by Vanessa and Ken since 1999 and, in this short time, they have made The Wig and Quill one of the town's most popular inns. A cosy and comfortable place

inside, where there are areas for playing pool and

darts, the inn is unique in having a viewable working cellar and customers can see the original wooden casks that dispense such delicious brews as Wadworth's 6X and Henry's IPA bitters.

A winner of the Cask Marque award and also listed in the Good Beer Guide, this inn certainly has a reputation for serving high quality ales but it is also a popular place for its food. The classic pub dishes served here at lunchtime are all created by Vanessa and her home-made specialities include lasagne, steak and ale pie and paté. The Sunday roast lunches are also well worth sampling. Finally, The Wig and Quill also has a walled garden that backs on to the cathedral close.

originals of 1215 Magna Carta along with a unique medieval biblical frieze. The oldest working clock in Britain, and possibly in the world, is situated in the fan-vaulted north transept; it was built in 1386 to strike the hour and has no clock face. The cathedral is said to contain a door for each month, a window for each day and a column for each hour of the year. A small statue inside the west door is of Salisbury's 17th century **Boy Bishop**. In those times it was a custom for choristers to elect one of their number to be bishop for a period lasting from St Nicholas Day to Holy Innocents Day (6-28 December). One year the boy bishop was, apparently, literally tickled to death by the other choristers and, since he died in office, his statue shows him in full bishop's regalia.

The **Close** at Salisbury, the precinct of the ecclesiastical community serving the cathedral, is the largest in England and contains a number of museums and houses open to the public. The **Salisbury and South Wiltshire Museum**, in the 17th century King's House, is home of the Stonehenge Gallery and the winner of many awards for excellence. The displays here go back to prehistoric times and continue through Roman and Saxon remains to the history of Old Sarum and

THE ROYAL GLOUCESTERSHIRE, BERKSHIRE AND WILTSHIRE REGIMENT (SALISBURY) MUSEUM

58 The Close, Salisbury, Wiltshire SP1 2EX
Tel:01722 414536 Fax:01722 421626
e-mail: curator@thewardrobe.org.uk
website: www.thewardrobe.org.uk

The Museum of the Royal Gloucestershire Berkshire and Wiltshire Regiment is housed in the Wardrobe. The original house was first built in 1254 probably as a Canon's residence. In the 14th Century the Bishop took possession and used it as a store for his clothes. The 18th Century additions include papier mache wall decoration, Rococo Fire places and stucco work. The garden has been attractively landscaped and leads down to the river Avon with views of the Water Meadows. Telling the story of a soldier's life over 250 years, the museum collection includes uniforms, weapons, medals and silverware.

the development of the city today. Also to be seen here is the **Anglo-Saxon Jewel** that is said to have connections with Alfred the Great. The museum is open all year round, from Monday to Saturday, and on Sunday afternoons in July and August.

THE OLD ALE HOUSE

80 Crane Street, Salisbury, Wiltshire SP1 2QD
Tel: 01722 333113

The Old Ale House could hardly have a more apt name, as it has been dispensing hospitality and good cheer since as far back as 1411. Behind its cream-painted frontage among the little streets of Salisbury, the pub has old oak floors and exposed beams that create character aplenty, and in the husband-and-wife team of Sarah and Patrick Barker it has landlords who know how to look after their customers. Sarah cooks a range of wholesome no-frills dishes served lunchtime and evening every day, and when the sun shines the beer garden is a pleasant spot to enjoy a drink and a snack. Live music is performed on Thursday nights, and major sporting events are shown on tv in the bar. Open 11-11 (Sunday 12-10.30).

Originally known as the **Wardrobe** and dating from 1254, the building that once was used as a clothing and document store by the 13th and 14th century bishops is now home to the **Museum of the Royal Gloucestershire, Berkshire and Wiltshire Regiment** (see panel on page 75) and the collection here tells the story of this English county regiment from 1743 onwards. Among the exhibits is Bobbie the Dog, the hero of Maiwand, and many other artefacts from foreign campaigns. Open daily from April to October and less so during February, March, November and December, the museum has landscaped gardens that lead down to the River Avon.

Other wonderful buildings in the cathedral close include the **Medieval Hall**, a magnificent banqueting hall that dates from the 13th century that is now home to a presentation that provides an essential guide to this historic city. Whilst, **Mompesson House** (National Trust) is an

Gateway to Cathedral Close

THE PHEASANT INN

Salt Lane, Salisbury, Wiltshire SP1 1DT
Tel: 01722 320675

The date 1435 displayed on an outside wall tells one and all that the **Pheasant Inn** is one of the oldest hostelries in the region. The attractive exterior, half-timbered under a stone-tiled roof, promises much, and the inside certainly does not disappoint, with oak featuring strongly in the beams, the bar counter and the splendid tables. In this delightful setting Graham and Beverley Jenkins share the cooking, producing high-quality dishes at very reasonable prices lunchtime and evening. Regular weekly entertainment is provided by karaoke on Tuesday and a quiz on Wednesday, and darts and pool are available throughout opening hours, which are 12-11 Monday to Saturday, 12-10.30 Sunday.

THE RETREAT INN

33 Milford Street, Salisbury, Wiltshire SP1 2AP
Tel: 01722 338686
website: www.theretreatinn.co.uk

Dating back to the 15th century and a former coaching inn, **The Retreat Inn**, in the heart of Salisbury, is a charming and traditional place that has a wonderfully comfortable lounge bar, complete with large Chesterfield sofas, and an equally attractive restaurant where customers can enjoy an excellent lunch or dinner. The inn also provides accommodation in a choice of 11 en suite guest rooms that have been, like the rest of the inn, recently refurbished to this high standard.

OLD SARUM

Tel: 01722 335398
website: www.english-heritage.org.uk

Situated high above Salisbury Plain, **Old Sarum**, the site of the ancient city of Salisbury, was first settled in the Iron Age when a massive hill fort was created here. Later occupied by the Romans (several Roman roads converge here), the town grew in Saxon times within its prehistoric ramparts until, by the time of the Norman Conquest, there were two palaces here along with Salisbury's first great cathedral.

People continued to live at Sarum until the 16th century, although a new town grew up around the 13th century cathedral, and in the 19th century Old Sarum was one of the country's most notorious 'rotten boroughs'. Today, the massive earth ditches and ramparts remain intact and there are spectacular views across the Salisbury plain and the surrounding countryside.

elegant and spacious 18th century house, a perfect example of Queen Anne architecture, which has some superb plasterwork, an elegant carved oak staircase, fine period furniture and the important Turnbull Collection of 18th century drinking glasses. Outside there is a delightful walled garden with a pergola and traditional herbaceous borders and it is not surprising that this glorious house was used as a location for the award winning film of Jane Austen's *Sense and Sensibility*.

Away from Salisbury's ecclesiastical centre there is the Market Place and here can be found the **John Creasey Museum and the Creasey Collection of Contemporary Art**, a permanent collection of books, manuscripts, objects and art that relate to the late John Creasey. Whilst the museum is open by appointment the Creasey Collection of Contemporary Art is on show throughout the year. Also in the Market Place, in the library, is the **Edwin Young Collection** of 19th and early 20th century oil paintings of Salisbury and its surrounding landscape.

There are many other areas of Salisbury to explore on foot and a short drive takes visitors to the ruins of **Old Sarum**, abandoned when the bishopric moved into the city, and here, too, can be found **Old Sarum Castle** (English Heritage - see panel above), a massive hill fort that was subsequently also used by the Romans, Saxons and Normans. Traces of the original cathedral and palace are visible on the huge uninhabited mound, which dates back to the Iron Age, and today there are glorious views from the site out over the surrounding landscape. Old Sarum became the most notorious of the 'rotten boroughs', returning two Members of Parliament, despite having no voters, until the 1832 Reform Act stopped the cheating. A plaque on the site commemorates Old Sarum's most illustrious MP, William Pitt the Elder.

To the west of the city lies **Salisbury Racecourse**, one of the country's oldest and where racing has been taking place since the 16th century. Today, race meetings are held here throughout the summer months.

AROUND SALISBURY

MIDDLE WOODFORD
4 miles N of Salisbury off the A360

To the east of this village lies **Heale Garden**, a beautiful garden of 8 acres that shows a varied collection of plants and shrubs that are all grown within a formal setting of clipped hedges and mellow stonework. Offering colour and interest throughout the seasons, from the snowdrops and aconites in January to the water garden in the autumn, this is a must for every garden enthusiast. The garden and its plant centre are open throughout the year, although Heale House is not open to the public.

AMESBURY
7 miles N of Salisbury on the A345

This attractive small town, on a loop of the River Avon, was established by Queen Elfrida when she founded an abbey here in

THE BRIDGE AT WOODFORD

Upper Woodford, near Salisbury, Wiltshire SP4 6NU
Tel: 01722 782323
website: www.thebridge@woodford.net

Found in the famous Woodford valley, which is renowned for its glorious, unspoilt countryside, **The Bridge at Woodford** is a charming country inn set in an idyllic location. Overlooking the River Avon and with a large and attractive beer garden that runs down to the water's edge, this early 20th century inn has much to offer visitors along with its scenic situation. The traditional and informal interior of The Bridge at Woodford helps to create the friendly and welcoming atmosphere that is one of the inn's trademarks.

Landlord, Andrew Sargent, and his family have only been here for a short time but, with a background that includes working with Terence Conran in London, Andrew has used his expertise to make The Bridge the 'in pub' in the area. As well as serving an excellent range of real cask ales from the bar, this inn has an enviable reputation for the high standard of its food. The mouth-watering menu is complemented by the ever-changing daily specials list and throughout only the very best of local produce is used. Ranging from Tomato tart and Crab and prawn risotto starters to Calves' liver and a superb Fish and chips, there is plenty here to whet the appetite and, for those with a sweet tooth, there is an equally tempting menu of home-made puddings.

THE OLD BAKERY

Netton, Nr Salisbury, Wiltshire SP4 6AW
Tel: 01722 782351
e-mail: valahen@aol.com

In a pleasantly modernised former village bakery in the scenic Woodford Valley, Val and Henry Dunlop offer quiet, comfortable Bed & Breakfast accommodation all year round. **The Old Bakery** has two double rooms with showers en suite, and one twin with bath en suite. All three rooms have tv, radio-alarm and hospitality tray, and the house enjoys lovely views of the surrounding fields and meadows. Fishing, golf and excellent walking are all available nearby, and Stonehenge is only five miles away.

979 in atonement for her part in the murder of her son-in-law, Edward the Martyr, at Corfe Castle. However, **Amesbury Abbey** is believed to stand on the site of an earlier abbey that was said to be where Queen Guinevere stayed after the death of King Arthur. Henry II rebuilt the abbey's great Church of St Mary and St Melor, whose tall central tower is the only structure to survive from the pre-Norman monastery.

Stonehenge

However, Amesbury is most famous for the **Stonehenge**, which stands just a couple of miles to the west, and that is, perhaps, the greatest mystery of the prehistoric world as well as being one of the wonders of the world and a monument of unique importance. The great stone blocks of the main ring are truly massive and it seems certain that the stones in the outer rings – rare bluestones from the Preseli Hills of west Wales – had to be transported over 200 miles. Stonehenge's orientation on the rising and setting of the sun has always been one of its most remarkable features, leading to theories

STONEHENGE INN

Stonehenge Road, Dorrington, near Amesbury, Wiltshire SP4 8BN Tel: 01980 655205
e-mail: paul@stonehengeinn.co.uk
website: www.stonehengeinn.co.uk

Situated in the edge of the village, the **Stonehenge Inn** is the closest pub to the famous ancient monument from which it takes its name and, so, is popular with visitors coming to marvel at the giant stones. However, this delightful inn is worth a visit in its own right. Managed by the experience couple, Paul and Doreen Banks, this late Victorian building has plenty to offer visitors including an excellent selection of cask real ales and fine wines. The food served here too is delicious and the comprehensive menu, which ranges from light snacks and sandwiches to full three course meals, is complimented by the daily special's list.

Where ever possible, locally grown meat and vegetables and fish from the nearby coast is used to

create the mouth-watering array of home-made dishes. Although Paul and Doreen have only been here since 2000 they have undertaken a refurbishment programme that included redecorating the attractive en suite guest rooms to provide comfortable and spacious accommodation. Meanwhile, to the rear of the building Paul has created a new patio style beer garden and also a traditional skittle alley. A convenient stopover, particularly at lunchtime, when visiting Stonehenge, this inn is also an ideal base from which to explore the Avon Valley that lies to the south and is, at this point, called the Woodford Valley.

that the builders were from a sun-worshipping culture or that the whole structure is part of a huge astronomical calendar – or both. The mystery remains, and will probably remain forever. In the 12th century the chronicler, Geoffrey of Monmouth, suggested that the massive stones had been brought firstly from Africa to Ireland by a race of giants and then to Wiltshire, in the 6th century by Merlin at the request of Ambrosius Aurelianus, King of the Britons who wanted them as a war memorial to those slain near Amesbury by Hengist the Saxon.

Stonehenge Down (National Trust), surrounds this World Heritage Site, and this area of downland contains many other prehistoric remains of ceremonial and domestic purpose including some fine Bronze Age barrows and the Cursus, which is thought to be either an ancient racecourse or a processional way.

A mile to the north of Amesbury, lies **Woodhenge**, a ceremonial monument that is even older than Stonehenge. This was the first major prehistoric site to be discovered by aerial photography and its six concentric rings of post holes were spotted as crop marks by Squadron Leader Insall in 1925. Like Stonehenge, Woodhenge seems to have been used as an astronomical calendar and, when major excavation work was carried out here in the 1920s, a number of Neolithic tools and other artefacts were

found, along with the skeleton of a three-year-old child whose fractured skull suggested some kind of ritual sacrifice.

BULFORD
8½ miles N of Salisbury on the A3028

Best known for its army camp that was established during World War I, this village was the scene of a macabre suicide that is alleged to have taken place here in the early 18th century. The local cobbler, who treated his apprentices badly, angered the villagers so much that they paraded an effigy of him through the streets and then hanged it from a mock gallows. This ceremony was repeated each day until, in despair, the cobbler turned to his best friend for advice and he was told that the only thing to do was to bow to the will of the people. So the cobbler committed suicide by hanging himself.

CHOLDERTON
9 miles NE of Salisbury on the A338

This small village is home to **Cholderton Rare Breeds Farm**, which is set in superbly landscaped gardens, water gardens and woodland and is home to endangered breeds of British farm animals. A delight for all the family, there are over 50 breeds of rabbits here along with a toddlers' and an adventure play ground, pig races and much more. The farm is open from March to November.

THE OLD INN
Tidworth Road, Allington, Nr Salisbury, Wiltshire SP5 6LS
Tel: 01980 610421

The Old Inn, located in the pretty Bourne Valley seven miles north of Salisbury, lies on the main A338, making it a magnet for both local and passing trade. Inside, all is spick and span, thanks to a top-to-toe redecoration programme carried out by the new landlords when they took over early in 2002. They offer traditional pub cuisine at very kind prices, served lunchtime and evening and all day in the summer. Lasagne and meat pies come near the top of the popularity stakes. A quiz takes place on the first Sunday of each month, and the pub fields darts teams and a pool team in the local leagues. The Old Inn has a beer garden and off-road parking. Opening times are 11-3 and 6-11; open all day Friday, Saturday and Sunday.

THE OLD INN

The Ridge, Woodfalls, Wiltshire SP5 2LH
Tel: 01725 510422 Fax: 01725 513474

The Old Inn is a substantial redbrick building set on the main road from Downton to Cadnam, and is an easy drive south from Salisbury. Landlords Marion Goodchild and her husband have built up a loyal, mature clientele, and the spacious bars are well provided with comfortable and easy chairs for enjoying a chat and a drink, the sports bar has most pub games available. Good-value home-cooked dishes are served lunchtime Wednesday to Sunday, and live music is performed every Saturday night. Opening hours are 11-2.30 and 5-11pm; all day Saturday and Sunday, and all day every day in high season. Limited B&B accommodation is available.

DOWNTON

5½ miles SE of Salisbury on the B3080

Situated on the River Avon, this ancient settlement has links with the Romans, Saxons and Normans and, its New Town, dates from the 13th century and has thatched cottages on either side of the main street. The village's Cuckoo Moot, held on the first Bank Holiday Saturday of May, has been a feature of life here since the 16th century whilst the **Moot** is an ancient monument that is believed to be a Saxon meeting place and the site of a long ago parliament. In the 18th century it was converted into ornamental gardens from where walkers can stroll down to the river.

LOVER

7 miles SE of Salisbury off the B3080

In the vicinity of this charmingly named village is the National Trust's **Pepperbox Hill** topped by an early 17th century

APPLE TREE INN

Morgan Vale, Nr Salisbury, Wiltshire SP5 2JF
Tel: 01725 510403 Fax: 01725 514740

On the B3080 four miles south of Salisbury, the **Apple Tree Inn** is a distinguished 16th century thatched building which started life as a cider house. Transformed down the years into today's exquisite village pub, it is now in the caring hands of Mary and John Trussler, who fell for the inn when they first saw it - the apple of their eye, as it were. In the bars, sturdy stone walls, exposed beams, splendid little oak tables and lots of intimate corners add up to a charming, traditional setting for enjoying a drink and something from the menu of beautifully presented home-cooked dishes served every session except Sunday evening and Monday. The inn has a beer garden where children can play. Sunday is quiz night.

THE CUCKOO INN

Hamptworth, near Salisbury, Wiltshire SP5 2DU
Tel: 01794 390302

A charming early 18th century thatched building, **The Cuckoo Inn** is a quintessential English country inn with a cosy and friendly atmosphere that is warmed by wood burning stoves in winter. Along with the superb range of real ales, including Cuckoo Ale, the inn, which is owned and personally run by Janet and Tim Bacon, has a delicious menu of simple, home-made dishes and traditional English puddings, such as cauliflower cheese, cottage pie and treacle sponge, which is served throughout the week except on Sunday and Monday evenings.

octagonal tower known as **Eyre's Folly**. From here not only are there great panoramic views but also some good walks.

BERWICK ST JOHN
13 miles SW of Salisbury off the A30

To the south of this village lies **Cranbourne Chase**, an area of rolling chalk downland that is said to have been a hunting ground of King John. Right in the heart of the chase, at **Tollard Royal**, is **Larmer Tree**

Wilton House

Gardens, which were created by Genergy Pitt Rivers in 1880 and where restoration work began in the early 1990s. A charming and attractive garden, it contains an open air theatre, a Roman temple and it is inhabited by ornamental pheasants and peacocks. Open daily (except Saturdays) from Easter to the end of October, the gardens also play host to regular concerts and festivals throughout the high season.

LUDWELL
15 miles SW of Salisbury on the A30

Near to this village is the National Trust owned **Win Green Hill**, the highest point in Wiltshire, which is crowned by a copse of beech trees set around an ancient bowl barrow. From the summit there are wonderful views as far as the Quantock Hills to the northwest and the Isle of Wight to the southeast.

WILTON
4 miles W of Salisbury on the A30

The third oldest borough in England and once a capital of Saxon Wessex, this quintessential English market town is best known for its carpets and the **Wilton Carpet Factory**, on the River Wylye, continues to produce top quality Wilton

and Axminster carpets. Visitors can tour the carpet-making exhibition in the historic courtyard then go into the modern factory to see the carpets made on up-to-date machinery using traditional skills and techniques. Alongside the factory is the Wilton Shopping Village offering high-quality factory shopping in a traditional rural setting.

Wilton House is the stately home of the Earls of Pembroke and also one of the country's great mansions. When the original house was destroyed by fire in 1647, Inigo Jones was commissioned to build its replacement and he designed both the exterior and the interior, including the amazing Double Cube Room, although the house was later remodelled by James Wyatt. However, it is what the house contains that makes it so important and its art collection is one of the very finest, with works by Rembrandt, Van Dyke, Rubens and Tintoretto, whilst the furniture includes pieces by Chippendale and Kent. There is also plenty to keep children busy and happy, notably the Wareham Bears (a collection of 200 miniature costumed teddy bears), a treasure hunt quiz and a huge adventure playground. There's a Tudor kitchen, a Victorian laundry and 21 acres of landscaped grounds with parkland as well as cedar trees, water and rose gardens and an elegant Palladian bridge. During World War II the house was used as an operations centre for Southern Command and it is believed that the Normandy landings were planned here. Wilton House is open between April and October.

FOVANT
8 miles W of Salisbury on the A30

The **Fovant Badges** are badges carved in the chalk hillside by troops during the First World War. They include the Australian Imperial Force, the Devonshire Regiment, 6th City of London Regiment, the London Rifle Brigade, the Post Office Rifles, the Royal Corps of Signals, the Royal Wiltshire Yeomanry, the Wiltshire Regiment and the YMCA. The badges can be seen from the A30.

The Fovant Badges

DINTON
8 miles W of Salisbury off the B3089

This lovely hillside village is home to two National Trust properties: **Little Clarendon**, a Tudor manor house that was altered in the 17th century and has a 20th century Catholic chapel; and **Philipps House and Dinton Park**, a neo-Grecian house that was built by Jeffry Wyatville in the early 17th century for William Wyndham. The main rooms on the ground floor of Philipps House display some fine Regency furniture whilst the surrounding parkland, where there are pleasant walks, has been restored. The house is open from the end of March to the end of October.

TEFFONT MAGNA
9½ miles W of Salisbury on the B3089

To the west of the village and set in attractive Wiltshire countryside is **Farmer Giles Farmstead**, a working dairy farm where visitors can watch the cows being milked and help to feed the other animals here that include pigs, Shetland ponies, donkeys, sheep, rabbits and chipmunks. Along with the Pet's Corner and the adventure playground, other attractions that will interest the family, both young and old, are the walks through the Beech Belt, the tractor rides and the gift shop. Open from mid March to early November, and at weekends throughout the rest of the year, Farmer Giles Farmstead also has a licensed restaurant serving home-cooked food.

TISBURY
12½ miles W of Salisbury off the A30

This village, found on a steep slope beside the River Nadder, seems more like a little town with its meandering main street, large church and stone buildings. Just to the west lies the severely classical early 19th century **Pyhouse**, which has limited opening, whilst, to the south, is **Old Wardour Castle** (English Heritage - see panel) with its bloodthirsty past. Set beside a lake and surrounded by acres of woodland, the tranquil location for the unusual hexagonal ruins of this castle make it a place well worth visiting today. However, it was here, in 1643, that a terrible battle was fought when Cromwell's forces besieged the castle for weeks and, by the time the Royalist occupants had surrendered, the damage to the fortification was extensive. The castle and its grounds are open daily and, between November and March, from Wednesday to Sunday.

OLD WARDOUR CASTLE

Tel: 01747 870487
website: www.english-heritage.org.uk

One of the most romantic ruins in England (15 miles west of Salisbury), **Old Wardour Castle** was built in the late 14th century for John, 5th Lord Lovel and its six-sided design, with many suites of rooms for guests, is unique in this country. Lord Lovel had been inspired by the castles then being built in France and he was determined to copy the style for his new home. As well as providing security, the castle was a place for luxurious living and was also designed to impress. Besieged twice during the Civil War, the castle was badly damaged in the second siege, in 1644, and was never restored. When Wardour New Castle was built in the 1770s, the old castle was left as an ornamental feature, deliberately integrated into the landscaped gardens to be admired as a romantic ruin. It has featured in the film, *Robin Hood, Prince of Thieves* and is a venue for regular special events during the summer.

MERE
20 miles W of Salisbury on the B3095

This pretty small town, nestling beneath the chalk downlands, played host to Charles II, in 1651, when he rested here after being defeated at the Battle of Worcester. Housed in the public library, **Mere Museum** has a local history collection, with a good photographic archive, whilst displays are changed regularly and also include temporary exhibitions on a range of subjects. However, the museum's large and detailed map of Mere, drawn by local artists, is permanently on display. The museum is open each week day afternoon and also on Tuesday mornings.

STOURTON
23 miles W of Salisbury off the B3092

This beautiful village lies at the bottom of a steep wooded valley and it is a particularly glorious sight in the daffodil season. The main attraction is, of course, **Stourhead** (National Trust), one of the most famous examples of the early 18th century English

THE BELL & CROWN

New Road, Zeals, Wiltshire BA12 6NY
Tel/Fax: 01747 840227 e-mail: markdaustin@aol.com

Mark Austin took over the **Bell & Crown** in the autumn of 2001, inheriting a long tradition of hospitality. Off the A303 at the junction with the B3092, this is a very substantial pub with plenty of space both inside and out. Four real ales - two residents and two guests - are usually on tap, and straightforward, good-value food is served every lunchtime and evening, with a traditional roast lunch on Sunday. Entertainment and diversions include live music on Friday, regular karaoke sessions, skittles, pool and darts. In the beer garden are a boules pitch and a children's play area. The Bell & Crown is open from 11 to 11 (till 10.30 on Sunday).

THE SEYMOUR ARMS

The Street, East Knoyle, Wiltshire SP3 6AJ
Tel: 01747 830374

On the main street of the village where Sir Christopher Wren was born, the **Seymour Arms** is in the capable hands of Bruno Fellmann and Terena Burgess. It's a handsome and substantial building in red brick, but you might not be aware of the brick as virtually the whole facade is covered in a luxuriant growth of ivy. In the 60-cover restaurant high-quality dishes include daily specials and an evening à la carte. A good selection of wines accompanies the food, which is cooked by Swiss-born Bruno. Special children's dishes are available, and a 40-cover function room is a popular venue for private parties. The Seymour Arms has a beer garden and a children's play area, and for guests staying overnight there are two en suite rooms with tv and tea/coffee-making facilities.

landscape movement (see panel).

On the very edge of the estate, some three miles by road from the house, the imposing **King Alfred's Tower** stands at the top of the 790 foot Kingsettle Hill. This 160 foot high triangular redbrick folly was built in 1772 to commemorate the king, who reputedly raised his standard here against the Danes in 878.

STAPLEFORD
6½ miles NW of Salisbury on the B3083

This is one of a number of delightful unspoilt villages that includes the three Langfords and **Berwick St James**, where the grid of the medieval board game Nine Men's Morris can be seen on a stone bench in the church porch. At Stapleford there was once a castle belonging to Waleran, the chief huntsman of William the Conqueror.

WYLYE
9½ miles NW of Salisbury off the A36

Peace and quiet finally arrived

STOURHEAD HOUSE AND GARDENS

Stourton,
Warminster BA12 6QD
Tel: 01747 841152

Stourhead (National Trust), one of the most famous examples of the early 18th century English landscape movement . The lakes, the trees, the classical temples (including the Pantheon and the Temple of Apollo), a grotto and a classical bridge make the grounds a paradise in the finest tradition and the gardens are renowned for their striking vistas and woodland walks as well as a stunning selection of rare trees and specimen shrubs, including tulip trees, azaleas and rhododendrons. These splendid gardens were designed by Henry Hoare II and they were laid out between 1741 and 1780.

The house itself, a classical masterpiece built in the 1720s in Palladian style by Colen Campbell for a Bristol banker, contains a wealth of Grand Tour paintings and works of art along with furniture by Chippendale the Younger and wood carvings by Grinling Gibbons. The house is open from April to October whilst the gardens are open daily throughout the year.

RIVER BARN

Fonthill Bishop, Salisbury, Wiltshire SP3 5SF
Tel: 01747 820232 Fax: 01747 820105

Found opposite the River Fonthill in this charming village is **River Barn**, the village post office, which is now, under the direction of partners Jo Denby, Sarah Caldecott and Joanna Kozubska, a wonderful café as well as much, much more. Open throughout the day for morning coffee and afternoon tea, this is also the ideal place for a relaxing bistro style lunch or supper. In these distinctive surroundings customers can also view the contemporary art exhibitions and browse around the distinctive and stylish gift shop that stocks objects d'art by both local and international artists and craftspeople. Finally, River Barn has three charming bed and breakfast guest rooms – an idyllic place for a tranquil break away.

in Wylye in 1977 when a bypass was opened to divert traffic away from the village although, earlier, it had been an important junction and staging post on the London to Exeter coaching routes. A statue near the bridge of the River Wylye (from which the village, Wilton and, indeed, the county of Wiltshire take their name) commemorates a brave post boy who drowned here after falling into the water from a stage coach.

Above the village is the little known **Yarnbury Castle**, an Iron Age hill fort surrounded by two banks and an outer bank whilst, to the west, is a triangular enclosure from Roman times that could have held cattle or sheep. From the 18th century right up to the outbreak of World War I Yarnbury was the venue of an annual sheep fair.

CODFORD ST PETER & CODFORD ST MARY
13 miles NW of Salisbury off the A36

These sister villages lie beneath the prehistoric remains of **Codford Circle**, an ancient hilltop meeting place which stands some 617 feet up on Salisbury Plain. The church in Codford St Peter has one of Wiltshire's finest treasures – an exceptional 9th century Saxon stone carving of a man holding a branch and dancing.

Close by, and to the east of Malmpit Hill, is a rising sun emblem carved by Australian soldiers during World War I whilst in the

military cemetery at Codford St Mary are the graves of Anzac troops who were housed in a camp in the village.

WARMINSTER
19½ miles NW of Salisbury on the B3414

Found to the southwest of Salisbury Plain, amid chalk downlands, Warminster dates back to Saxon times although the surrounding area has been occupied by both Stone Age and Iron Age communities who have left their mark in the numerous long barrows and earthworks found locally as well as **Battlesbury Camp**, one of Britain's major Iron Age hill forts. Meanwhile, to the west of the town is 800 foot high **Cley Hill**, another Iron Age hill fort with two Bronze Age barrows. Once owned by the Marquis of Bath, the hill was given to the National Trust in the 1950s and is now a renowned sighting place for UFOs whilst the region is also noted for the appearance of crop circles and some have linked the two phenomena. Reports of unknown flying objects began to be recorded here in the 1960s, though sceptical locals suggest that the strange bright lights seen crossing the night sky probably originate from the Army's School of Infantry, which is based in the town, or from the various military camps on the nearby Plain. An important military base today, the **Warminster Training Centre** holds a comprehensive **Weapons Collection** that can be visited by prior

THE MASONS ARMS

East Street, Warminster, Wiltshire BA12 9BN
Tel: 01985 212894

The Masons Arms is a delightful old coaching inn with a history
tracing back to 1678. Owned and run for 18 years by Robin Clifford,
the inn has a strong local following built up by a combination of
friendly staff and a relaxed, unpretentious ambience. Snacks such as
filled rolls and pasties are available during the week, but the main
eating event is the popular Sunday lunch served from noon to 3
o'clock. Open all day, every day.

arrangement.

A prosperous wool town in the Middle
Ages, Warminster also became a major
corn trading centre for the whole of
southern England and buildings that date
from those days include the 14th century
Minster Church of St Denys, surrounded
by trees that include a yew that is over 600
years old, and that has, inside, an organ
that was originally built for Salisbury
Cathedral. In the High Street is another
place of worship, the early 13th century
Chapel of St Lawrence, which was
founded by the Maudit family, Lords of
the Manor at the time, as a chapel of ease.
The town is also famous for being the
home of **Warminster School**, a leading
public school dating from 1707 whose
doorway was originally designed by Sir
Christopher Wren for Longleat
House but was later moved to
this present site.

Housed in the public library,
the **Warminster Dewey
Museum** holds a wide range of
local history exhibits that
range from the Iron Age to the
present day along with the
Victor Manley geology
collection. The museum is
open all year from Monday to
Saturday but is closed on Bank
Holiday Mondays and
Wednesday afternoons.

On the northern edge of

Warminster is **Arn Hill Nature Reserve**
that has waymarked footpaths that form a
circular walk of two miles through
woodland and open downland.

LONGLEAT

22 miles NW of Salisbury off the A362

The magnificent home of the Marquis of
Bath was built by an ancestor, Sir John
Thynne, in a largely symmetrical style in
the 1570s and, in 1999, **Longleat House**
celebrated its 50th anniversary of its being
open to the public. Inside, there are many
treasures including Old Masters, Flemish
tapestries, beautiful furniture, rare books
and, of course, Lord Bath's famous murals.
This ancient house is not without its
legends and, in the 18th century, Thomas
Thynne, the 2nd Viscount Weymouth, is

Longleat House

Longleat Safari Park

said to have murdered his wife's lover in a duel that took place in a top floor corridor of the house and the lover's body was buried in the cellar. The Viscount's grief stricken wife, Lady Louisa is said to walk the corridor at night, now called the Green Lady's Walk, whilst, in the early 20th century, a man's skeleton, wearing 18th century boots, was found under the flagstone floor in the house's cellar.

The superb grounds of Longleat House were landscaped by Capability Brown and they are one of the country's best venues for a marvellous day out. Meanwhile, in the famous **Longleat Safari Park**, the Lions of Longleat, first introduced in 1966, have been followed by a wealth of exotic creatures including elephants, rhinos, zebras and white tigers. The park also features safari boat rides, a narrow gauge railway, a children's amusement area and the largest hedge maze in the world.

WESTBURY
21 miles NW of Salisbury on the A350

Westbury, at the western edge of the chalk downlands of **Salisbury Plain**, was a major

player in the medieval cloth and wool trades, and still retains many fine buildings from those days of great prosperity, including some cloth works and mills that continued to produce textiles through to the Victorian age. Worth seeking out is **All Saints' Church**, a 14th century building constructed on much earlier foundations that has many unusual and interesting features including a stone reredos, a copy of the Erasmus Bible and a clock with no face that was made by a local blacksmith in 1604. The church also boasts the third heaviest peal of bells in the world. On the southern edge of town is another church well worth a visit and, behind the simple, rustic exterior of St Mary's, Old Dilton, are a three-decker pulpit and panelled pew boxes with original fittings and individual fireplaces.

Westbury was formerly a rotten borough and the town's 62 burgesses returned two Members of Parliament from medieval times through to 1832. Scandal and corruption were rife and the **Old Town Hall**, in the market place, is evidence of such goings-on and it was a gift to Westbury from a grateful victorious

Westbury White Horse

candidate in 1815. This was Sir Manasseh Massey Lopes, a Portuguese financier and slave-trader who 'bought' the borough to advance his political career. Today, the parliamentary constituency, which includes four of the five West Wiltshire towns, is known simply as Westbury.

Following the arrival of the railway in 1848, large deposits of iron ore were found in the area but today the extraction industry takes the shape of chalk and clay and, from the nearby clay pits, two full skeletons of prehistoric dinosaurs have been unearthed.

However, Westbury's best known feature, by far, is the famous **Westbury White Horse**, a chalk carving measuring 182 feet in length and 108 feet high, which was originally carved in 878 to celebrate King Alfred's victory over the Danes at nearby

THE DUKE AT BRATTON

Bratton, near Westbury, Wiltshire BA13 4RW
Tel: 01380 830242 Fax: 01380 831239

Found in the heart of this pretty village at the foot of the famous White Horse is **The Duke at Bratton**, a charming 18th century village inn that has, since 1994, been under the successful management of Marion and Ian Overend. Though large, this is a truly friendly inn and in the time that they have been here this charming and enterprising couple have not only made many friends but also put the inn very much on the local map. Along with their superb selection of real ales, which has earned the inn a mention in the CAMRA's Good Beer Guide, Ian and Marion have won numerous awards for the outstanding meals that they serve here, including being the national winner of the Pub Food Best Sunday Roast award. In the attractive surroundings of the recently refurbished restaurant customers are treated to a superb range of dishes, from light snacks to a full à la carte, and of course there are their delicious Sunday lunches, which are also served throughout the week.

Along with the large beer garden that is an ideal place to while away a day in the summer, The Duke at Bratton, which is named after the Duke of Wellington, has four delightful cottage style bedrooms and the inn is also the proud winner of the Loo of the Year award for the whole of the southwest of England. A wonderful inn offering the very best in English pub hospitality, The Duke has also had one of its more unusual features recently restored – a whale's giant jawbone has been re-erected over the gateway to the inn. It is advisable to book a table for this busy restaurant.

THE OWL, LOW ROAD

Little Cheverill, Nr Devizes, Wiltshire SN10 4JS
Tel: 01380 812263
e-mail: paul@theowl.info

The Owl is a grand old redbrick inn set in attractive rural surroundings on the B3098 seven miles south of Devizes. Paul Green and Jamie Carter, who took over towards the end of 2001, are quickly making their mark at this delightfully unpretentious pub, adding to its amenities by bringing on stream three en suite letting bedrooms. Jamie prepares a wide-ranging selection of dishes served every day from 12 to 3 and from 7 to 10. Families are very welcome, and children even have their own special dishes. A new attraction is the 65 ft decked area with dining benches, overlooking the garden. The pub hosts an annual beer festival.

Ethandune (Edington). The present horse, facing the opposite way from the original, was cut by Mr Gee in 1770 and, at one time, there were stories of the horse walking down to a brook close to Bratton to take a drink of water each Midsummer's Eve. A major landmark of the area and from which there are extensive views across Wiltshire and Somerset, Westbury's White Horse is the oldest in Wiltshire and, above its head, are the ruins of **Bratton Castle**, an Iron Age hill fort covering some 25 acres.

Just northwest of Westbury, is **Woodland Park and Heritage Centre**, 80 acres of ancient broadleaf woodland with a wide range of trees, plants and animals, nature trails, a lake with fishing, a picnic and barbecue area, a tea room and gift shop, a museum, a play area and a narrow-gauge railway.

EDINGTON
20 miles NW of Salisbury off the B3098

Found on the northern edges of Salisbury Plain, **Edington Priory**, on which work was begun in 1352, represents an excellent example of Monasterial architecture despite, over the years, it being extended and altered. Each August, this small village plays host to people from all over the world who come here for its annual Music Festival.

MARKET LAVINGTON
17 miles NW of Salisbury on the B3098

Found in the old schoolmaster's cottage, behind the old village school, is **Market Lavington Museum** whose displays include a Victorian kitchen and a superb collection of local photographs that go back over 100 years. This fascinating village museum is open from May to the

---

THE DRUMMER BOY

Church Street, Market Lavington, Wiltshire SN10 4DU
Tel: 01380 812329

Found opposite the village church, **The Drummer Boy** is a cosy and traditional inn that, during the winter, is warmed by coal fires whilst, in the summer, the exterior is bedecked with hanging baskets and window boxes. Friendly and welcoming, this is just the place to enjoy a refreshing drink and landlords, Mary Ann and Michael Hoban, also offer a delicious menu of tasty home-cooked dishes such as Gammon and egg, Liver and bacon and Michael's home-made curries

---

WEST PARK FARM

Market Lavington, near Devizes, Wiltshire SN10 4NW
Tel: 01380 813314

A rambling early Victorian farm house, the home of Jennie Sharp, provides relaxed and comfortable bed and breakfast accommodation in a choice of three en suite guest rooms that have their own televisions and drinks making facilities. The cosy dining room was once part of the dairy and guests can enjoy a delicious home-cooked breakfast that includes local preserves and honey and fresh fruit. **West Park Farm** has been in the family for three generations and this peaceful setting is an idyllic place for a short break away.

EASTCOTT MANOR

Easterton, Wiltshire SN10 4PH
Tel: 01380 813313

Located off the A360 six miles south of Devizes, **Eastcott Manor** is a handsome country house set in 20 acres of well-kept gardens and grounds. Owner Janet Firth provides a very comfortable and civilised ambience for a rural break in four Bed & Breakfast rooms - two singles with private facilities and a twin and a double both en suite. The house is decorated and furnished in a style in keeping with its ancient origins and is ideally placed either for a complete getaway or as a base for touring West Wiltshire and the Somerset borders.

end of October on Wednesday, Saturday, Sunday and Bank Holiday Monday afternoons.

CHIPPENHAM

This historic settlement on the banks of the River Avon was founded in around 600 by the Saxon king Cyppa and it was chosen by King Alfred as the location for his hunting lodge. By then it was an important administrative centre and it was here, in 878, that Alfred the Great forged a treaty with invading Danes to withdraw from Wessex. Chippenham, later, came to prominence as a wool trading centre, along with holding large corn and cheese markets, and its importance was further enhanced by its location: as a major stopping point on the London to Bristol coaching runs and, later, with the opening of the Great Western Railway that ran between the same two cities.

There are several buildings of note here including the 15th century **Church of St Andrew**, a half-timbered hall that was used by the burgesses and bailiffs of the Chippenham Hundred, and, on the edge of the town, **Hardenhuish Hall** where John Wood the Younger built the Church of St Nicholas. Completed in 1779, the church has a domed steeple and elegant Venetian windows. Today, Chippenham remains a market town and street markets

are still held every Friday and Saturday.

For an insight into the history of this ancient market town the **Chippenham Museum and Heritage Centre** has an interesting and fascinating range of displays from prehistoric times through to the 20th century. Open all year round from Monday to Saturday, the museum and centre, focus in particular, on the Saxon town and its links with Alfred the Great, the cheese market, Brunel's Great Western Railway and Victorian life in the town.

AROUND CHIPPENHAM

MALMESBURY
8½ miles N of Chippenham on the A429

Situated on the banks of the River Avon, Malmesbury is England's oldest borough and also one of its most attractive and it is dominated by the impressive remains of the Benedictine **Malmesbury Abbey**, which was founded in the 7th century by St Aldhelm. In the 10th century, King Athelstan, Alfred the Great's grandson and the first Saxon king of All England, granted 500 acres of land to the townspeople in gratitude for their help in resisting a Norse invasion. These acres are still known as **King's Heath** and are owned by 200 residents who are descended from those far-off heroes. Both Athelstan, who made Malmesbury his capital, and St

Aldhelm were buried at the abbey and it became, for a period, a place of pilgrimage.

The abbey tower was the scene of an early attempt at human-powered flight when, in 1010, Brother Elmer strapped a pair of wings to his arms and, jumping from the tower, plummeted to the ground breaking both his legs. However, the monk survived, though a cripple, and went on to live a long life. The flight of this intrepid cleric, who reputedly foretold of the Norman invasion following a sighting of Halley's Comet, is commemorated in a stained glass window. Meanwhile, the **Abbey House Gardens**, in the town centre, hold the country's largest private collection of roses as well as having spring bulbs, herbaceous borders, fruit trees and herbs. Open daily from March to October, there are also woodland and riverside walks that take in ancient monastic fish ponds, fountains and topiary.

Malmesbury was also, once, an important centre for the production of woollen cloth, and later the production of fine lace and silk, whilst it was, too, a market centre and its 15th century octagonal **Market Cross**, in the town square, is one of the finest in the country. Found close to the historic abbey and housed in the Town Hall is the **Malmesbury Athelstan Museum** where there are numerous displays and exhibits covering the town's lace-making, costume, rural life, early cycles, a manually operated

fire engine and local photographs and maps. Meanwhile, there is also a display of noted local philosopher, Thomas Hobbes.

A more recent piece of local history concerns the **Tamworth Two**, a pair of pigs who made the headlines with their dash for freedom and their trail is one of the many that can be followed in and around the town.

EASTON GREY
9 miles N of Chippenham on the B4040

Here the southern branch of the River Avon is spanned by a handsome 16th century bridge with five stone arches whilst a manor house has overlooked the village since the 13th century and the present house, with a classical facade and an elegant covered portico, dates from the 18th century. Used as a summer retreat by Herbert Asquith, British Prime Minister from 1908 to 1916, it was at this manor house that the Prince of Wales stayed in 1923 whilst attending the Duke of Beaufort's hunting season at Badminton.

LANGLEY BURRELL
1½ miles NE of Chippenham off the B4069

Nearby Steinbrook Hill is said to be haunted by the ghost of Reginald de Cobham, a young lord of the manor of Langley Burrell who became a follower of the anti-papist John Wycliffe. Wycliffe's teachings were believed to be heretical and Reginald was burnt at the stake in 1413.

THE CARPENTERS ARMS
Easton Town, Sherston, Wiltshire SN16 0LS
Tel: 01666 840665

The Carpenters Arms is a 300-year-old roadside inn on the B4040 four miles west of Malmesbury. Karen Myers and Keith Britton, who took over the reins in the summer of 2001, are very welcoming hosts, and the conservatory restaurant, lounge and bar are all pleasant places to linger. A new chef is doing great work in the kitchen, producing a good choice of dishes for both lunch and dinner, including the very popular pies, which come with a variety of fillings. The pub has a beer garden with a barbecue area and is the venue for the local boules league - not a surprise, as Sherston hosts the annual European boules championship. Monday is quiz night at the Carpenters.

On moonlit nights, Reginald's ghost, with his head carried under his arm, walks naked around the hill.

BREMHILL
4 miles E of Chippenham off the A4

In the flood plain to the east of Chippenham stands a 4½ mile elevated footpath known as **Maud Heath's Causeway**. This remarkable and ingenious walkway, consisting of 64 brick and stone arches, was built at the end of the 15th century at the bequest of Maud Heath, who spent most of her life as a poor pedlar trudging her often muddy way between her village of Bremhill and the market at Chippenham. However, she died a relatively wealthy woman and the land and property she left in her will provided sufficient funds for the upkeep of the causeway. On nearby Wick Hill is a stone inscribed: "From this Wick Hill begins the praise, Of Maud Heath's gift to these Highways," whilst, close by, is **Maud Heath's Monument**, a statue of the lady on a high column with basket in hand and dressed in the costume of the period of Edward IV, which was erected in 1838 and overlooks the flood plain.

LACOCK
3 miles S of Chippenham off the A350

This National Trust village is one of England's real treasures, a quadrangle of streets that hold a delightful assortment of mellow stone building and, with no intrusive power-cables or other modern day eyesores, Lacock, with its period look, is in great demand as a film location. Dating back to the 13th century and with many limewashed half-timbered and stone houses and cottages it has starred in such productions as *Pride and Prejudice*, *Moll Flanders* and *Emma*. Overlooking this beautifully preserved gem is **Lacock Abbey** that was founded in 1232 by Ela, Countess

of Salisbury in memory of her husband, William Longsword, stepbrother to Richard the Lionheart. After the Dissolution of the Monasteries in 1539, the abbey was converted into a country house and, over the years, a brewery, Great Hall and Gothic archway were added although the original medieval cloisters, chapter house and sacristy still remain.

The impressive country house seen today, with its elegant octagonal tower that overlooks the River Avon, was chiefly the work of Sir William Sharrington and, after being held by the Talbot family for 350 years, the estate passed into the hands of the National Trust in 1944. During the 1570s, Olive Sharrington, the owner's daughter, became engaged to John Talbot of Worcestershire very much against her parents' wishes and, despairing that she would never be allowed to marry her lover, she jumped off the abbey battlements.

Lacock Abbey Cloisters

Lacock Village

However, as she fell to the ground, her petticoats billowed out, slowing her descent and she landed on top of but not killing John. After John's recovery, Olive's father, impressed by his daughter's resolve to remain faithful to her betrothed, allowed them to marry.

However, the most distinguished member of the Talbot family was undoubtedly William Fox Talbot, the pioneering photographer, who carried out his photographic experiments here in the 1830s and his negative of the oriel window, produced in 1835, is the oldest in existence. The **Fox Talbot Museum** holds a permanent exhibition commemorating the live and achievements of William who lived at the abbey for 50 years and who was not only a photographer but also a mathematician, physicist, classicist, philologist and transcriber of Syrian and Chaldean cuneiform. William also remodelled the south elevation of the abbey and added three new oriel windows. Meanwhile, the museum, which is open daily from March to the end of

October (except Good Friday) and at weekends during November and December, plays hosts to several exhibitions a year by both 19th century and contemporary master photographers.

Just to the north of Lacock and surrounded by beautiful Wiltshire countryside lies Lackham College and the **Lackham Museum of Agriculture and Rural Life**. The various thatched and traditional buildings found here contain several collections that feature the local trades and crafts, the farming year and village domestic life whilst the adjacent woodland and historic gardens provide further interest. The museum is open from Easter to the end of August on Sundays and Bank Holiday Mondays and also has several child friendly activities.

MELKSHAM
6 miles S of Chippenham on the A3102

This small town on the banks of the River Avon, where there is good coarse fishing available, was one of Wiltshire's weaving towns of the past and this previous

Melksham

prosperity has left a legacy of stone built 17th and 18th century houses. Most of the older buildings are clustered around the sizeable 15th century church whilst there are also some Regency residences that date from a brief time in the early 19th century when Melksham was developed as a small spa.

HOLT
8 miles SW of Chippenham on the B3107

During the 18th century, this village was developed as a small spa and the old natural mineral well can still be seen in a factory in the village. Meanwhile, right at the heart of the village is **The Courts Garden** (National Trust), an English country garden and one of Wiltshire's best kept secrets, which, in particular, features unusual topiary, water gardens, an apple orchard, a herb garden and an arboretum. The house, where local weavers came to settle disputes until the end of the 18th century, is not open to the public.

Just to the north of Holt lies **Great Chalfield Manor** (National Trust), a charming manor house with a moat and a gatehouse that dates from 1480 and was restored in the early 20th century by Major R Fuller. Similarly, the garden, which was designed by Alfred Parson and that compliments the house, has also been restored and replanted.

TROWBRIDGE
11 miles SW of Chippenham on the A361

The county town of Wiltshire, Trowbridge was, from medieval times to the Victorian age, an important weaving centre and, along with the 19th century mill buildings, there are many fine Georgian stone houses still to be seen here. Housed in the town's last working woollen mill, the **Trowbridge Museum** tells the fascinating story of the town, its people and its past. Among the exhibits here are a reconstruction of the medieval castle, tableaux of a weaver's cottage, a drapery shop and working textile looms. The museum, which also hosts a series of temporary exhibitions, is open from Tuesdays to Saturdays.

The parish Church of St James, crowned by one of the finest spires in the county, contains the tomb of the poet and former rector George Crabbe, who wrote the work on which Benjamin Britten based his opera *Peter Grimes*. Trowbridge's most famous son was Isaac Pitman, the shorthand man, who was born in Nash Yard in 1813.

BRADFORD-ON-AVON
10 miles SW of Chippenham on the A363

This historic market town, at an ancient crossing point of the River Avon (its name is derived from 'broad ford'), has managed to retain several buildings of interest but, undoubtedly, the most fascinating is the

THE DANDY LION

35 Market Street, Bradford-upon-Avon, Wiltshire BA15 1LL
Tel: 01225 863433 Fax: 01225 869169

Once a shop, the **Dandy Lion** is now a very popular and successful pub with an excellent upstairs restaurant. Behind the inviting red and cream facade, the pub retains some features from its 17th century origins, and partners Jenny Joseph and Phil Taylor fully deserve the success the pub has gained through a combination of period charm, a warm, relaxed ambience and good home cooking that ranges from bar snacks to a full à la carte choice. Booking is advisable at the weekend and Friday evening for a table in the restaurant.

tiny **Church of St Laurence** that is believed to have been founded by St Aldhelm in around 700. It disappeared for over 1,000 years, when it was used, variously, as a school, a charnel house for storing the bones of the dead, and a residential dwelling, and was rediscovered by a keen-eyed clergyman, in 1871, who looked down from a hill and noticed the cruciform shape of a church. The surrounding buildings were gradually removed to reveal the little gem seen today. One of the most complete and extraordinary survivors from those far off times, the interior of the church is exceptional with its tall, stone built nave and fragmented Saxon cross and flying angels on the walls. In 1001, the estate of Bradford-on-Avon was given, by Aethelred,

Kennet and Avon Canal, Bradford on Avon

to the Shaftesbury Abbey in Dorset, where his dead brother's body was also moved, and it remained an important part of the nuns' estate for several centuries. Meanwhile, the town's Norman church, which was restored in the 19th century, has an interesting memorial to Lieutenant-

THE KINGS ARMS

Monkton Farleigh, Bradford-on-Avon, Wiltshire BA15 2QH
Tel: 01225 858705 Fax: 01225 858999
e-mail: *enquiries@kingsarms-bath.org.uk*
website: www.kingsarms-bath.org.uk

Dating back to 11th century, this former monks' retreat was converted into an inn in the 17th century and, today, **The Kings Arms** blends together beautifully the ancient and modern by offering a wonderful historic setting with the very best in 21st century hospitality. In the traditional surroundings, which include the largest inglenook fireplace in the county that was only discovered during recent renovations, customers can enjoy a selection of real ales before tucking into a delicious lunch or dinner from the appetising bar menu. Meanwhile, in the sumptuous surroundings of the inn's Chancel Restaurant, appropriately named after a chair used by the French monks, visitors are treated to a superb à la carte menu that features both classic and

contemporary dishes including such mouth-watering feasts as Pork with lemon and coriander potato crust, Chicken Kiev and Mushroom ragout.

Whether eating formally or in the relaxed surroundings of the bar diners can rest assured that the dishes are all prepared to order from the very best of local produce including, in season, game. Whilst the interior of The Kings Arms is certainly special, the beauty of this ancient building can best be viewed from the sheltered courtyard or from the inn's charming gardens where, not only are there plenty of tables and chairs, but also two aviaries that house Spook, the inn's resident African Eagle Owl, pairs of love birds, Golden Pheasant and Italian Quail.

General Henry Shrapnel, the army officer who, in 1785, invented the shrapnel shell.

Another of the town's outstanding buildings is the mighty **Tithe Barn** that was once used to store the grain from local farms that was destined for Shaftesbury Abbey. A stunning stone building, the barn was erected in 1341 and its cathedral like proportions – it is 168 feet long and has a massive timbered roof – are as impressive today as when it was first built.

Along with ecclesiastical influences Bradford was, for six centuries, a wool and cloth producing town and the river bank is lined with 19th century former cloth mills whilst the town is littered with simple weavers' cottages and the more elaborate houses of the clothiers. At the **Bradford-on-Avon Museum**, opened in 1990, there are numerous displays on the natural and historical heritage of the town and the surrounding villages that once formed the Bradford Hundred. However, the centrepiece of the museum is a pharmacy shop that stood in the town for 120 years and that was carefully moved, medicine bottles and all, to this new site where it was rebuilt. The museum is open from Easter to October from Wednesday to Sunday and, for the rest of the year, on Wednesday to Sunday afternoons.

The River Avon here is now spanned by the ancient **Barton Packhorse Bridge**, which is now closed to traffic but open to foot passengers, and it leads to **Barton**

Farm Country Park, which offers delightful walks in lovely countryside beside the river and the Kennet and Avon Canal on the western edge of the town. Once a medieval farm serving Shaftesbury Abbey the bridge was originally built to assist in the transportation of grain from the farm to the abbey's tithe barn.

A little further away, to the west of the town, is the charming 15th century **Westwood Manor** (National Trust), a stone manor house, altered in the early 17th century, which has some late Gothic and Jacobean windows and ornate plasterwork. The house, with its modern topiary garden, is open from the end of March to the end of September.

Just to the south of Bradford, by the River Frome is the Italian-style **Peto Garden** at **Iford Manor**. Famous for its romantic, tranquil beauty, its steps and terraces, statues, colonnades and ponds, the garden was laid out by the architect and landscape gardener Harold Ainsworth Peto between 1899 and 1933. He was inspired by the works of Lutyens and Jekyll to turn a difficult hillside site into "a haunt of ancient peace."

CORSHAM
4 miles SW of Chippenham on the A4

Believed to be the most picturesque town in Wiltshire, Corsham, which owes its prosperity to the wool trade and the

---

WADSWICK BARNS

Manor Farm, Wadswick, Corsham, Wiltshire SN13 8JB
Tel: 01225 810733 Fax: 01225 810307
e-mail: barns@wadswick.co.uk website: www.wadswick.co.uk

In a peaceful rural hamlet, three old Cotswold stone barns have been sensitively converted by Carolyn Barton to provide beautifully appointed self-catering accommodation. In a courtyard that was once part of a 16th century farm, Hayward's, The Granary and The Dairy have a wealth of original features, lawned gardens and absolutely everything for a luxurious, carefree holiday. Hayward's has four bedrooms, the others two each; all have modern farmhouse-style kitchens and spacious beamed living rooms. Fine walking and cycling are on the doorstep, and the barns are situated close to an Area of Outstanding Natural Beauty.

quarrying of Bath Stone, has a host of beautiful buildings that date from the 16th century onwards. Of particular interest here is **Corsham Court** that was based on an Elizabethan house of 1582 and that stands on the site of a former Saxon royal manor. Bought by Paul Methuen in 1745 and still owned by the family, this now stately mansion houses an internationally famous collection of Old Masters along with rooms furnished by Robert Adam and Chippendale that also contain collections of 17th and 18th century English and Continental furniture. Meanwhile, the grounds, laid out by Capability Brown and Repton, contain an 18th century Bath House. The mansion, which is open daily from Good Friday to the end of September

BIDDESTONE ARMS

Biddestone, near Chippenham,
Wiltshire SN14 7DG
Tel: 01249 714377

Found just beyond the duck pond in this pretty village, the **Biddestone Arms** is a charming country pub that was, until 1875, the local police station. There is little inside to remind customers of the building's past life as the Biddestone Arms has a wonderful, traditional décor of exposed stone walls, stripped beams decorated with brasses and other artefacts and scrubbed pine tables. Meanwhile, outside there is an attractive lawned beer garden that is perfect for lazy summer days. Well known for stocking a superb range of real ales, including some from the local area, the Biddestone Arms is fast gaining a fine reputation for the high standard and excellent value of its cuisine.

The restaurant, with its à la carte menu, is open for both lunch and dinner and customers are treated to an imaginative and extensive menu of both classic and contemporary dishes. Along with home-made soups and Tortellini with sundried tomatoes, there are such delights as Beef bourguignon and Lasagne al forno con pollo. However, it is for its excellent home-made pies that the inn is famous and, in particular, there is the house game pie that is stuffed with a mouth-watering mixture of venison, wild boar, snipe and woodcock. For less formal dining there is also an equally superb bar menu that is served in the early evening and, again, customers can enjoy the house speciality pies. A popular place with a strong following that is increasing daily, it is advisable to book a table here to avoid disappointment

COURT CLOSE HOUSE BED AND BREAKFAST

North Wraxall, Chippenham, Wiltshire SN14 7AD
Tel: 01225 891930 Fax: 01225 891907
e-mail: vickyosborne@delomosne.co.uk

The delightful 18th century **Court Close House** is situated in a beautiful corner of Wiltshire that is ideal for both walkers and naturalists and this friendly bed and breakfast establishment is the perfect place from which to explore the surrounding countryside. Along with superb accommodation in an attractive en suite guest room, visitors are treated to a full English breakfast that uses both organic and home-made produce wherever possible. The owners of Court Close also run a specialized antiques business that deals in the best quality 18th century glass and porcelain.

(except Mondays) and at weekends for the rest of the year, might seem familiar to visitors who have never been here before as it was used as a location for the filming of both *Northanger Abbey* and *The Remains of the Day*.

Whilst Corsham Court is indeed grand, another wonderful building here is the **Hungerford Almshouses** that were built in 1668 and that carry the arms of their founder, Dame Margaret, wife of the Commander of Cromwell's forces in Wiltshire who owned Corsham Court at that time, above the door. Meanwhile, Arnold House is now home to the **Corsham Heritage Centre**, a fascinating place that explores various aspects of the town through imaginative and exciting hands-on exhibits and interactive displays. In the Cloth Room, William Arnold, the owner of the house in the 17th century, introduces visitors to the world of textiles and explains the processes of carding, spinning, weaving and dyeing wool whilst, in the Stone Room, visitors travel back millions of years to the origins of Bath Stone, which is believed to have been discovered by St Aldhelm.

Castle Combe

CASTLE COMBE
5 miles NW of Chippenham on the B4039

Undoubtedly one of the loveliest villages in the region if not in the country, Castle Combe was once a centre of the prosperous wool trade and, in particular, it was famed for its red and white cloth. Many of the present day buildings date from the 15th and 16th centuries, including the Perpendicular **Church of St Andrew**, the covered market cross and the manor house that was built with stone from the Norman castle that gave the village its name. One of the lords of the manor in the 14th century was Sir John Fastolf, who is reputedly the inspiration for William Shakespeare's famous 'Falstaff'. **Castle Combe Museum**, whose collection of artefacts all relate to the history of the village, is open on Sunday afternoons from Easter to October.

LUCKINGTON
8½ miles NW of Chippenham on the B4040

This village, close to the county border with Gloucester and on the edge of the Cotswolds, is home to **Luckington Court Gardens**, a formal garden with a fine collection of ornamental trees and shrubs that surrounds a Queen Anne house that was used as the home of the Bennett family in the BBC television adaptation of *Pride and Prejudice*. The gardens are open on Wednesday afternoons from May to September and the house is closed to the public.

3 North and East Somerset

Elegant cities such as Bath, charming ancient market towns, the glorious countryside of the Mendip Hills, the legends of King Arthur and coastal resorts with expansive sandy beaches – this region of Somerset has much to offer the visitor whatever their interests. The most fashionable spa town in the country during the 18th century, some 1,600 years earlier Bath was equally fashionable amongst the Roman high ranking officials and soldiers. A gloriously elegant city of beautiful Georgian buildings; no one wandering through its pleasant

Sham Castle, Bath

streets and boulevards today can help but capture some of the atmosphere that inspired Jane Austen to feature Bath so heavily in her novels. Close by is Somerset's

Continued page 104

PLACES TO STAY, EAT, DRINK AND SHOP

91	The Fox & Goose, Barrow Gurney	Pub with Food	page 114
92	The Old Barn, Wraxall	Pub with Food	page 115
93	Wassells House, Cheddar	Bed and Breakfast	page 116
94	The Gordons Hotel, Cheddar	Hotel and Restaurant	page 116
95	The Gardeners Arms, Cheddar	Pub with Food	page 116
96	Bath Arms Hotel, Cheddar	Hotel and Restaurant	page 116
97	The Railway Inn, Yatton	Pub with Food	page 118
98	The Wheatsheaf Inn, Stone Allerton	Pub, Food & Accommodation	page 120
99	Penscot Hotel & Restaurant, Shipham	Hotel and Restaurant	page 121
100	Lillypool Cheese & Cider Emporium, Shipham	Restaurant	page 121
101	Hillend Holiday Cottages, Locking	Self Catering	page 123
102	The Woolpack, Beckington, nr Bath	Pub with Food	page 126
103	Bath Lodge Hotel, Norton St Philip, nr Bath	Hotel	page 126
104	Fleur-De-Lys, Norton St Philip, nr Bath	Pub with Food	page 126
105	The Kings Head, Lower Coleford, nr Radstock	Pub with Food	page 129
106	Ring o' Roses Inn, Holcombe, nr Bath	Hotel and Restaurant	page 130
107	Seven Stars, Timsbury, nr Bath	Pub with Food	page 130
108	Lamb Inn, Clandown, nr Radstock	Pub with Food	page 130
109	Franklyns Farm, Chewton Mendip, nr Bath	Bed and Breakfast	page 130
110	The Sun Inn, Wells	Pub with Food	page 132
111	Carringtons, Wells	Restaurant	page 132
112	Manor FarmDulcote, Dulcote, nr Wells	Bed and Breakfast	page 132
113	Riverside Restaurant, Coxley, nr Wells	Restaurant	page 132

NORTH AND EAST SOMERSET

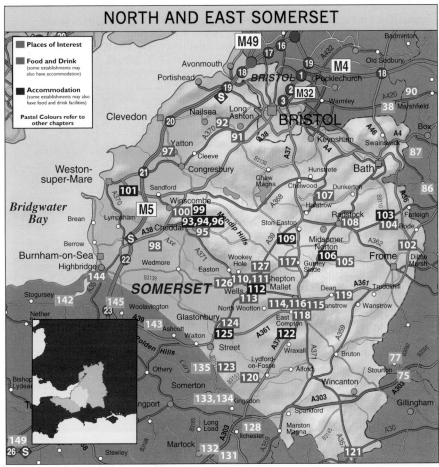

Places of Interest

Food and Drink
(some establishments may also have accommodation)

Accommodation
(some establishments may also have food and drink facilities)

Pastel Colours refer to other chapters

© MAPS IN MINUTES ™ 2002 © Crown Copyright, Ordnance Survey 2002

114	The Charlton Inn, Shepton Mallet	Pub with Food	page 134
115	East Somerset Railway, nr Shepton Mallet	Railway	page 135
116	The Kings Arms Hotel, Shepton Mallet	Pub, Restaurant & Accommodation	page 135
117	The Horse & Jockey, Binegar	Pub and Restaurant	page 136
118	The Horseshoe Inn, Bowlish	Pub, Food & Accommodation	page 136
119	The Strode Arms, West Cranmore	Pub with Food	page 136
120	Three Old Castles Inn, Keinton Mandeville	Pub with Food	page 138
121	The Fountain Inn Motel, Henstridge	Pub, Food & Accommodation	page 139
122	Pennard Hill Farmast Pennard	B&B and Self Catering	page 140
123	The Rose & Portcullis, Butleigh	Pub and Restaurant	page 141
124	Glastonbury Abbey, Glastonbury	Abbey	page 142
125	Tordown Bed & Breakfast, Glastonbury	Bed and Breakfast	page 143
126	The Pheasant Inn, Worth Wookey, nr Wells	Pub with Food	page 145
127	The Slab House Inn, West Horrington	Pub and Restaurant	page 146

largest city, Bristol, which, despite its modern appearance has its origins in Saxon times when a settlement was founded here at this strategically important crossing point of the Avon gorge. Although the castle that once protected the crossing has long since been demolished, the gorge is now spanned by one of the city's most famous features, the Clifton Suspension Bridge, which was finally opened after the death of its designer, the engineer Isambard Kingdom Brunel.

The limestone Mendip Hills, running from Weston-super-Mare to Frome, cut across this region of Somerset in spectacular fashion and, although at their highest point they only reach just over 1,000 feet, there are some magnificent panoramic views out across the flat lands of the Somerset Levels and over the Bristol Channel to South Wales. A wealth of prehistoric remains have been found here but two of the Mendips most popular and famous attractions are both natural. The cliffs of Cheddar Gorge rise up over 400 feet high on either side of the road that runs along the bottom whilst the caves at Wookey Hole, from where the River Axe emerges from beneath the hills, are famous for their echo and their fantastic stalagmite and stalactite formations. Meanwhile, to the south of the hills lies the Iron Age hill fort of Cadbury Castle that is thought to be the location of King Arthur's Camelot and, whilst excavations have confirmed that there was indeed a fortification here from that period, it is probably the remote setting that has promoted this romantic legend.

Wells Cathedral

The Mendips are also the home of the smallest city in England – Wells – and it was here, in the 12th century, that the cathedral was founded on the site of a Saxon church. A magnificent building that contains a wonderful 14th century Astronomical Clock, although Wells is dominated by its cathedral and associated ecclesiastical buildings it continues to be a busy market centre for the small towns and villages of this rural area of Somerset. However, just to the southeast is another ecclesiastical centre that is not only older but far more well known than Wells. Glastonbury and, in particular, its Abbey is said to have been founded by Joseph of Arimathea in AD 60 and, therefore, it is the earliest seat of Christianity in the British Isles and is also believed to have been the last resting place of King Arthur and Queen Guinevere. Whether true or not, it is indisputable that, in the Middle Ages, this was a place of great importance and not only did the abbey's powers of influence stretch far and wide but it was also considered such a place of learning that scholars travelled here from all over Europe. Even more ancient than the abbey is the conical shaped tor just outside the town that, from prehistoric times, has been considered a place of mystery and great spiritual power.

BATH

Since time immemorial over half a million gallons of water a day, at a constant temperature of 46°C, have bubbled to the surface at Bath and it remains Britain's only natural hot spring. These famous healing waters are believed to have been discovered by Bladud, the son of Lud Hudibras, a legendary king of England. After contracting leprosy Prince Bladud was banished from the royal court by his father but, before he left, Bladud's mother gave him a ring and remind him that, if he should ever be cured, he could return back to court and his home. Bladud became a swineherd but, unfortunately, the swine entrusted to his care also caught the disfiguring disease and, to prevent the owner finding out, Bladud drove the animals over the River Avon, crossing it at a point that is, today, still called Swineford. One lonely day, the prince left the swine unattended and, maddened by the disease, the animals stampeded up the valley and plunged into a black evil smelling bog. Bladud managed, with great difficulty, to pull the beasts from the mud but, when they had all been rescued, he realised that the swine were no longer leprous. Indeed, where the muddy water had touched his own skin the disease had disappeared. Totally immersing himself in the bog, Bladud came out cured and he joyfully set off to be reunited with his mother and father and, although he was in ragged and unkempt clothing, the ring that the Queen had given him ensured that he was quickly identified.

The ancient Celts believed the mysterious steaming spring was the domain of the goddess Sulis and they were aware of the water's healing powers long before the invasion of the Romans. However, it was the Romans who first enclosed the spring and they went on to create a spectacular health resort that became known as Aquae Sulis and, by the 3rd century, Bath had become so renowned that high ranking soldiers and officials were coming here from all over the Roman Empire. Public buildings and temples were constructed and the whole city was enclosed by a stone wall but, by AD 410, the last remaining Roman legions had left and, within a few years, the drainage systems failed and the area returned to marshland. Ironically, the ancient baths remained hidden throughout the entire period of Bath's 18th century renaissance and were only discovered in the late 19th century. The restored remains can now be seen today and they centre around the **Great Bath**, a rectangular lead-lined pool that stands at the centre of the complex system of buildings, the **Roman Baths,** which took over 200 years to complete and comprised a swimming pool, mineral baths and a series of chambers heated by under floor air ducts. The museum here houses some of the treasures that were offered to the goddess of the springs, Sulis Minerva, along with carvings, inscriptions and sculptures that reveal something of the life of the people of Aquae Sulis.

Roman Baths

The population of Bath fell during the Dark Ages until the 8th century when the Saxons founded a nunnery here that was later elevated to monastic status when King Edgar of Wessex chose to be crowned 'King of all England' here in 973. However, the joy of finally crowning a king of a unified nation was short lived as Edgar died in 975 but the event is remembered in a fine stained glass window in the present abbey. The present great church was begun in 1499, after its Norman predecessor had been destroyed by fire, but building work was halted at the time of the Dissolution and the church remained without a roof for 75 years and, indeed, it was not finally completed until 1901! However, **Bath Abbey** is now considered to be the ultimate example of English Perpendicular church architecture whilst, inside, there is a memorial to Richard 'Beau' Nash, one of the people responsible for turning Bath into a fashionable Georgian spa town. The **Vaults Museum** has displays and exhibits that tell the story of Bath Abbey over the last 1,000 years.

Bath Abbey

Prior to Nash's arrival in the early 18th century, Bath was a squalid place with farm animals roaming the streets within the confines of the walls of the old Roman town. Despite this, however, the town had continued to attract small numbers of rich and aristocratic people but, eventually, the town authorities finally took action to improve sanitation and their initiative was rewarded, in 1702, when Queen Anne paid Bath's spa a visit. The elegant and stylish Beau Nash, who had only come to the town to earn a living as a gambler, became the Master of Ceremonies and, under his leadership, the town became a relaxing place for the elegant and fashionable of the day's high society. Among the entrepreneurs and architects who shared Nash's vision was the architect John Wood who, along with his son (also John), designed many of the city's

Royal Crescent

fine neoclassical squares and terraces. Among these is the **Royal Crescent**, John Wood the Younger's Palladian masterpiece that was the first terrace in Britain to be built to an elliptical design. Meanwhile, Bath's third 18th century founding father was Ralph Allen, an entrepreneur who made his first fortune developing an efficient postal system for the provinces and who went on to make a second as the owner of the local quarries that supplied most of the honey-coloured Bath stone to the city's Georgian building sites.

Pulteney Bridge

Famed for its wealth of Georgian architecture Bath is a delightful city to wander around and marvel at the buildings. Beside the original Roman Baths is the **Pump Room**, which looks much as it did when it was completed in 1796 and that remains at the social heart of life in Bath. Visitors here today can still try a glass of the spa water that is drawn fresh from the fountain whilst also enjoying the splendid and relaxing surroundings. Meanwhile, the **Assembly Rooms** (National Trust), one of the places where polite 18th century society met to dance, play cards or just be seen, was severely damaged during World War II and was not re-opened until 1963. In the basement of the building, which too was designed by John Wood the Younger and completed in 1769, is the interesting **Museum of Costume**, which contains one of the finest collections of fashionable dress in the world.

Another fine feature found in the heart of the city is the magnificent **Pulteney Bridge**, which spans the River Avon and was designed by Robert Adam and inspired by Florence's Ponte Vecchio. Meanwhile, set in beautiful gardens is the **Holburne Museum** that is housed in one of the city's

finest examples of elegant Georgian architecture. Originally a spa hotel, it was converted into a museum in the early 20th century and it now contains the superb collection of decorative and fine art that was put together by Sir William Holburne in 19th century. Of the town's other museums there is the **Bath Museum**, which holds a fascinating collection that chronicles the city's unique architectural evolution; the **Museum of East Asian Art** where artefacts from China, Japan, Korea and Southeast Asia are on display; and the **Bath Postal Museum** with its reconstruction of a Victorian sorting office. The city, too, is synonymous with Jane Austen and her novels and, at the **Jane Austen Centre**, enthusiasts can learn more about the Bath of her time and the importance of the city to her life and works.

An ideal way to gather a general impression of this magnificent city is to take the **Bath Skyline Walk**, an eight mile footpath that runs through some superb landscaped gardens and woodland to the southeast of the city (through National Trust owned land) and from where there are extensive views out over Bath.

Meanwhile to the northwest of the town, and found in a beautiful rural setting, is **Bath Racecourse** where both visitors and local people alike can enjoy a relaxed days racing in beautiful surroundings throughout the flat season.

AROUND BATH

BATHAMPTON
1½ miles NE of Bath on the A36

Found on a bend of the River Avon and on the banks of the Kennet and Avon Canal, the village church stands beside the canal and it is the last resting place of Admiral Arthur Phillip, the first governor of New South Wales who took the initial shipload of convicts out to the colony and established the settlement of Sydney. Considered by some to be the founder of modern Australia, a chapel in the south aisle, known as the Australian Chapel, contains memorials to the admiral's family. Above the village lies **Bathampton Down**, which is crowned with an ancient hill fort that, according to some historians, was the site of the 6th century Battle of Badon in which the forces of King Arthur defeated the Saxons. A more modern series of buildings can now be found beside the down as this is the site of the campus of Bath University that was founded in 1966.

BATHFORD
3 miles NE of Bath off the A363

This residential community once belonged to Bath Abbey and among the many fine 18th century buildings to be seen here is **Eagle House**, a handsome residence that takes its name from the great stone eagle that stands with its wings outstretched on the gabled roof. Meanwhile, on the hill above Bathford, there is a tall Italianate tower known as **Brown's Folly** that was built following the Napoleonic Wars to provide local craftsmen with work during the economic depression of the 1830s.

CLAVERTON
2 miles E of Bath on the A36

Just to the west of the village lies the 16th century country mansion, **Claverton Manor** that was bought in 1764 by Ralph Allen, the quarry owning co-founder of 18th century Bath. The mansion that Allen knew has since been demolished, leaving only a series of overgrown terraces, but some of the stone from the old house was used in the construction of the new mansion on the hill above the village. It was here, in 1897, that Sir Winston Churchill is said to have given his first political speech but it is as the **American Museum and Gardens** that Claverton Manor is best known. Founded in 1961, it is the only establishment of its kind outside the United States and the rooms of the house have been furnished to show the gradual changes in American living styles from the arrival of the Pilgrim Fathers in the 17th century to New York of the 19th century.

PRISTON
4 miles SW of Bath off the B3115

Found on the outskirts of the village is **Priston Mill**, which was first mentioned in the *Domesday Book* and from then until now it has continued to supply flour to the people of Bath. Powered by a spectacular 25 foot overshot water wheel, the millstones still produce genuine stone ground flour for retail and visitors to the mill can not only learn about its history and workings but also take a trailer ride about the adjoining working farm. Moreover, the site incorporates an award winning nature trail and an adventure play area for children.

STANTON DREW
9½ miles E of Bath off the B3130

This ancient settlement stands beside a prehistoric site of some importance – a series of stone circles over half a mile across that were constructed by the Bronze Age Beaker people between 2000 and 1600 BC. This complex of **Standing Stones** consists of three circles, a lone stone known as **Hauteville's Quoit** and a large chambered burial tomb called **The Cove**. The stones are composed of three different types of rock – limestone, sandstone and conglomerate – and they are thought to have been erected for religious or possibly astronomical purposes. In common with many stone circles in southwestern Britain, the origin of this stone circle is steeped in legend and the most widespread tale tells of a foolhardy wedding party who wanted to continue dancing into the Sabbath. At midnight, the piper refused to carry on, prompting the infuriated bride to declare that if she had to, she would get a piper from hell. At that point, another piper stepped forward to volunteer his services and the party resumed its dancing. As the music got louder and louder and the tempo faster and faster, the dancers realised, too late, that the good natured piper was the Devil himself and, when his playing reached its terrifying climax, he turned the whole party to stone. To this day, this curious group of standing stone is still known as 'The Wedding'.

A couple of miles to the north of Stanton Drew, the line of the ancient **Wansdyke** runs in a roughly east-west direction around the southern fringes of Bristol. Built during the Dark Ages as a boundary line and defensive barrier against the Saxons, short sections of this great earthwork bank can still be seen, particularly, at Maes Knoll and along the ridge adjoining the Iron Age hill fort on Stantonbury Hill.

CHEW MAGNA
11 miles E of Bath on the B3130

Situated just to the north of Chew Valley Lake, this former wool village is a pleasant

place and, despite now being a commuter village for Bristol it has managed to retain its charm along with some handsome Georgian houses. The nucleus of the village is its three-sided green whose surrounding shops and pubs are linked by an unusual raised stone pavement. Found at the top of the green is the striking early 16th century **Church House** that was originally intended to be the venue for the annual Church ales and for brewing the ale and baking the bread to be sold on these occasions. The funds raised at this event were then used to maintain the parish church for the coming year and these church houses, which were usually built in the 15th or early 16th century, were mainly confined to the counties of Somerset and Devon.

Close by is the impressive parish Church of St Andrew that is a testimony to the former prosperity of this village and, inside, can be seen the interesting double effigy of Sir John Loe, a 15th century local squire who was reputed to be 7 feet tall, and his wife. Meanwhile, behind a high wall adjacent to the churchyard lies **Chew Court**, a former summer palace of the bishops of Bath and Wells.

KEYNSHAM
6 miles NW of Bath on the A4175

A former industrial centre that is also a dormitory town for Bristol, despite its modern appearance Keynsham has ancient roots and, during the excavations for a chocolate factory, the remains of two Roman villas were discovered. These remains have since been incorporated into an interesting small **Museum** near the factory entrance. The town is named after St Keyne, the daughter of a 6th century prince of Wales, who, when she arrived here to convert the locals to Christianity was given a piece of land by the then lord of the manor. However, the land was so infested by venomous snakes that she received few visitors but, undeterred, St Keyne turned the snakes into stone and, so local legend has it, the fossilised ammonites (a form of prehistoric shellfish) that are abundant in this area are the remains of those snakes.

In the late 12th century an abbey was founded here, close to the River Chew, but it seems that the medieval monks were not as pious as they should have been as, eventually, they were banned from keeping sporting dogs, going out at night, employing private washer-women and entertaining female guests in the monastery. Today, the abbey buildings lie under the bypass but the part 13th century parish church has survived and, along with being a good example of the Somerset Gothic architectural style, it contains some impressive tombs to members of the Bridges family.

Much later, two large brass mills were established at Keynsham during the town's 18th century industrial heyday – one on the River Avon and the other on the River Chew – and, though production had ceased at both mills by the late 1920s, they are still impressive industrial remains.

BRISTOL
12 miles NW of Bath on the A4

Founded in Saxon times, Bristol, which is strategically situated at an important bridging point at the head of the Avon gorge, soon became a major port and market centre. Growth was rapid and by the early 11th century, it had its own mint and was trading with other ports throughout Western Europe, Wales and Ireland. The Normans quickly realised the importance of the port and, in 1067, began to build a massive stone keep and, although the castle was all but destroyed at the end of the English Civil War, the site of the fortification remains as **Castle Park**. Situated just to the west of the castle site stands **Bristol Cathedral** that was founded

University Tower

in around 1140 by Robert Fitzhardinge as the great church of an Augustinian abbey and, whilst the abbey no longer exists, several original Norman features, such as the chapter house, gatehouse and the east side of the abbey cloisters, remain. Following the Dissolution in 1539, Henry VIII took the unusual step of elevating the abbey church to a cathedral and, soon after, the richly-carved choir stalls were added. However, the building was not fully completed until the 19th century when a new nave was built. Amongst the treasures found inside the cathedral are a pair of candlesticks that were donated to the cathedral in 1712 by the rescuers of Alexander Selkirk, the castaway on whom Daniel Defoe based his hero Robinson Crusoe.

During the Middle Ages, Bristol expanded further as a trading centre and, at one time, it was second only to London as a seaport and the trade here was built on the export of raw wool and woollen cloth from the Mendip and Cotswold Hills and the import of wines from Spain and southwest France. It was around this time that the city's first major wharf development took place when the River Frome was diverted from its original course into a wide artificial channel that is now known as **St Augustine's Reach**. A remarkable achievement for those days, the excavation created over 500 yards of new berthing and was crucial in the city's development. Later, in the early 19th century the harbour was further increased when a semi-artificial waterway, the **Floating Harbour**, was created by diverting the course of the River Avon to the south. Another huge feat of engineering, the work took over five years to complete and was largely carried out by Napoleonic prisoners of war using only picks and shovels. Today, the main docks have moved downstream to **Avonmouth** and the Floating Harbour has become home to a wide assortment of pleasure and small working craft.

Much of Bristol's waterfront has now been redeveloped for recreational and leisure use and down on the harbour side is @ **Bristol**, the home of three spectacular attractions – Explore, a hands-on centre of science and discovery where visitors explore the workings of the world, discover the complexity of human brains and senses and gain an understanding of the creation of global communications technologies; Wildscreen takes visitors on a breathtaking journey through the natural world using still, moving and three dimensional technology to present an original picture of the planet Earth; and the Imax Theatre that promises the ultimate cinematic experience. Also clustered around the old port area of the city is the **Bristol Industrial Museum**, which presents a fascinating record of the achievements of the city's industrial and commercial pioneers, including those with household names such as Harvey (wines and sherries), McAdam (road building), Wills (tobacco) and Fry (chocolate). Visitors can also find out about the port's history, view the aircraft and aero engines that have been made here since 1910 and inspect some of the many famous vehicles that have borne the Bristol name since Victorian times. Meanwhile, the city's connections with the sea are remembered at the **Maritime Heritage Centre** that is dedicated to the history of shipbuilding in Bristol and where a number of historic ships line the wharf, including Brunel's mighty *SS Great Britain*, the world's first iron-hulled passenger liner that was launched in 1843. There are boat trips past this famous old liner whilst the Bristol Harbour Railway runs steam trains along the dockside from Brunel's great ship to the Industrial Museum. Also found here is the world's oldest steam tug, *Pyronaut*, which was built in 1861 and the city's unique 35 ton capacity crane – the Fairbairn Steam Crane. The museum is open from Saturday to

The Waterfront

SS Great Britain

Wednesday between April and October and at weekends only for the rest of the year.

Beyond the old waterfront there is much to see in Bristol and, as well as being a modern city with an excellent array of facilities for both residents and visitors, there are numerous fine buildings to discover. With their increasing wealth the city's medieval merchants founded one of the most impressive parish churches in the country and the **Church of St Mary Redcliffe** was described by Queen Elizabeth I as "the fairest, goodliest and most famous Parish Church in England." Along with its wonderful exterior, the church contains monuments to John Cabot, the maritime pioneer who, in the 15th century, was the first non-Scandinavian European to set foot on Newfoundland, and Admiral Sir William Penn, whose son founded the state of Pennsylvania in the United States. The sandstone beneath the church is riddled with underground passages that are known as the **Redcliffe Caves** and there are occasional guided tours of these unusual natural subterranean caverns.

Elsewhere in the city there is **Llandoger Trow**, the striking timber framed merchant's house of 1669; **The Red Lodge**, the only remaining Tudor domestic

interior in Bristol that has a Tudor style knot garden; the elegant **Georgian House** with many original features that was originally built in 1791 for a wealthy Bristol sugar merchant and Caribbean plantation owner, John Pinney; and **John Wesley's Chapel**, the oldest Methodist chapel in the world that was constructed by the preacher in 1739. The Red Lodge and the Georgian House are open from Saturday to Wednesday between April and October whilst the Chapel is open daily all year round except on Sundays when it is closed. The city is also home to one of the oldest theatres in the country that is still is use, the **Theatre Royal** that was built in the 1760s and is the home of the famous **Bristol Old Vic** theatre company.

Meanwhile, along with the museums down by the waterfront, there is the **British Empire and Commonwealth Museum**, which traces the history of Britain's discovery and colonisation of foreign lands and the rich cultural legacy of the Commonwealth from John Cabot's journey to Newfoundland in 1497 onwards. Housed within Brunel's historic railway station, Temple Meads, the museum is open daily (except Mondays) all year round. The **City Museum and Art Gallery**, which has among its fine collections some exceptional Chinese glass, is open daily all year round.

However, for most people Bristol's most famous feature is the graceful **Clifton Suspension Bridge** that spans the Avon gorge to the west of the city centre. Opened in 1864, five years after the death of its designer, Isambard Kingdom Brunel, the bridge continues to be a major route into the city and, suspended more that 200 feet above the river, it also provides magnificent views over Bristol and the surrounding countryside. Not far from the bridge is the **Clifton Suspension Bridge Visitor Centre** where an exhibition illustrates the interesting and involved story of the construction of this famous landmark and great feat of engineering. In 1754, a Bristol wine merchant left a legacy in his will to provide funds for a bridge across the Avon gorge and, whilst the first spectacular design was produced in 1793, a competition for a wrought iron suspension bridge was held in 1829. Thomas Telford, the leading engineer of the day despite his advanced years (he was 70), was asked to judge the 22 competition entries and, having rejected them all, he submitted a design of his own. Not surprisingly, this decision was extremely unpopular and another competition was held the next year and, after fierce debate, the 24 year old Isambard Kingdom Brunel was declared the winner and appointed engineer of the project – his first major commission. The foundation stone was laid in 1831 but the intervention of the Bristol Riots, which wrecked business confidence, put pay to the project and construction eventually began again in 1836. By 1843 funds for the bridge had run out and, with only the towers built, the project was formally abandoned in 1853. However, the bridge was finally finished and it was opened in 1864 but not before the premature death of its original creator, Brunel, in 1859. The Visitor Centre, which is open daily all year round, also has on display memorabilia from the bridge's opening ceremony, a selection of picture postcards featuring the famous landmark and an intricate scale model of the construction. Meanwhile, whilst

Clifton Suspension Bridge

Brunel's bridge will always connect him with the city, it was in Bristol that many of his most famous works were created including the world's first comprehensive railway terminus for the Great Western Railway, Temple Meads; the world's first ocean going liner, the *Great Western*; and the first iron hulled steam driven ship the *SS Great Britain*.

The land just to the west of the bridge is now the **Avon Gorge Country Park** and there are some delightful walks here through Leigh Woods to the summit of an Iron Age hill fort. Whilst on the eastern side of the gorge an old snuff mill has been converted into an observatory whose attractions include a camera obscura. Once a genteel suburb, **Clifton** is now an attractive residential area with elegant Georgian terraces and **Goldney House**, which is now a university hall but is also the home of the unique subterranean folly, **Goldney Grotto**, which dates from the 1730s. A fantastic labyrinth filled with spectacular rock formations, foaming cascades and a marble statue of Neptune, the walls of the grotto are covered with thousands of seashells and 'Bristol diamonds', fragments of a rare quartz found in Avon gorge. The suburb is also home to the **Bristol Zoo Gardens** and its

300 different species of wildlife that are sympathetically housed in beautiful surroundings. The zoo, with its new Seal and Penguin enclosure and favourites such as Gorilla Island, Bug World and the Reptile House, is open daily all year round.

To the north of Clifton is the suburb of **Westbury on Trym** that is the home of **Westbury College Gatehouse**, a 15th century gatehouse to the now demolished College of Priests that was founded in the 13th century. Whilst a little further to the north is **Blaise Hamlet**, a tiny hamlet of nine detached and individual stone cottages that were designed in a romantic rustic style by John Nash in 1809. Both properties are owned by the National Trust but the cottages are not open to the public.

Finally, Bristol lies at one end of the **Severn Way**, the longest riverside walk in Britain – it is 210 miles from sea to source – that also links Wales and England. Passing through glorious Welsh and English countryside as well as historic towns, the walk from the river's source at Plynlimon takes in many other attractions along the way.

BARROW GURNEY
13½ miles NW of Bath on the B3130

Before the construction of the reservoirs at Blagdon and Chew Valley, Bristol's fresh water came from the three small reservoirs at Barrow Gurney. The first was opened in

1852 but, within two years, it developed a leak and had to be drained causing a serious disruption to the city's water supply. Like many of the villages to the southwest of Bristol, Barrow Gurney has undergone considerable change since World War II and is now becoming a dormitory settlement for the city's commuters.

HENBURY
14½ miles NW of Bath on the B4057

This now suburb of Bristol is home to **Blaise Castle House Museum**, an 18th century house that contains a varied collection of toys, model trains, costumes and domestic equipment that illustrate everyday life in days gone by. The museum is open from Saturday to Wednesday between April and October.

WRAXALL
17 miles NW of Bath on the B3130

This village, which dates back to medieval times, is home to **Noah's Ark Farm Centre** that is set in beautiful countryside and has plenty to entertain the family. Along with the indoor adventure play areas there are tractor rides over the 300 acre farm, stunning views and a wide range of animals to feed and hold. Other attractions include the demonstration bee hive, the llamas, buffalo, wallabies and rheas. The farm and its café are open from the end of March to the end of October

THE FOX & GOOSE
Barrow Gurney, Nr Bristol BS48 3SL
Tel: 01275 472202 Fax: 01275 476556
website: www.thefoxandgoose.com e-mail: info@thefoxandgoose.com

A lovely old inn with eaves, an outside staircase and small-paned windows, the **Fox & Goose** is located on the A38 a mile from Bristol Airport. Peter Wilson heads the family partnership running this super pub, whose interior features heavy pile carpets and sturdy furnishings, lots of brass and plenty of space to enjoy a drink and a meal in comfort. Food is big business here, and the mouthwatering menu is highlighted by superb fish dishes with all the main courses and sweets being home made. They also have a 'Special' and 'Fox's 2 course menu' that change daily. A major development for 2003 will be the bringing on stream of 14 en suite letting bedrooms. The Fox & Goose is open 11 to 3 and 5 to 11 Monday to Friday, 11 to 11 Saturday and 12 to 10.30 Sunday.

THE OLD BARN

Wraxall, Somerset BS48 1BU
Tel: 01275 819011

Old stone barns have been converted into a most unusual and atmospheric public house. **The Old Barn** retains its original stone-tiled roof, and inside, the period charm continues with flagstone floors, exposed stone walls, interesting old tables and chairs, and a fascinating assortment of prints, books, ornaments and bric-a-brac. Food is served only on Wednesday, Thursday and Friday and takes the form of ploughman's-style lunches and buffet platters. Proprietors Tony and Lisa Fey also own the nearby Tickenham Farm Brewery, which produces 1,000 barrels a year. Tickenham Tipple and Old Farmer Durstons are two of the home brews sold in the pub and in other local outlets. The Old Barn stands in its own grounds back from the B3130 just outside Nailsea.

from Tuesdays to Saturdays and Bank Holiday Mondays.

PORTISHEAD
19½ miles NW of Bath off the A369

The early development of this old coastal town has much in common with its neighbour further down the coast, Clevedon, as it too started to build villas, hotels, a pier and bath houses in the 1820s and 30s. However, Portishead changed abruptly in 1867 when the railway arrived here and transformed the resort into a busy port and industrial area. A flourishing residential area today, Portishead's most impressive feature is undoubtedly **Portishead Point**, a wooded viewpoint that overlooks the Severn estuary.

National Trust and it is also a Site of Special Scientific Interest. Numerous rare plants grow here and it is also a haven for butterflies whilst there is a circular walk through the area that takes in plantations, natural woodland and rough downland. A place that draws rock climbers, the less ambitious may like to take the 322 steps of **Jacob's Ladder** that lead up the side of the

CHEDDAR

This sprawling village is best known for its dramatic limestone gorge, **Cheddar Gorge**, which is one of the most famous and most often visited of Britain's many natural attractions. Characterised by its high vertical cliffs, from which there are outstanding views out over the Somerset Levels, the Quantock hills and across the Bristol Channel to south Wales (on a clear day), most of the land around this magnificent ravine is owned by the

Cheddar Gorge

WASSELLS HOUSE

Upper New Road, Cheddar, Somerset BS37 2DW
Tel: 01934 744317
e-mail: aflinders@wassells99.freeserve.co.uk

Wassells House is a handsome modern residence where Kath White and Alan Flinders offer very comfortable and stylish Bed & Breakfast accommodation. The decor is superb throughout, from the cosy dining room to the three splendidly furnished bedrooms. These comprise two doubles and a single or twin; two have en suite facilities, the third a private bathroom not en suite, and all have tv and a tea/coffee tray with sparkling water and biscuits. One of the rooms looks out over the garden, where a brick patio and an ornamental pond with koi carp lead to a beautifully manicured lawn - a perfect spot for enjoying a cream tea in the summer sun.

THE GORDONS HOTEL

Cliff Street, Cheddar, Somerset BS27 3PT
Tel: 01934 742497 Fax: 01934 742511
e-mail: gordons.hotel@virgin.net website: www.gordonshotel.co.uk

The **Gordons Hotel** is situated at the foot of the famous Cheddar Gorge in an ideal location for touring the delightful Somerset countryside. Sue Barker offers hospitality in a comfortable, relaxed atmosphere, and guests can unwind in a pleasant lounge and browse through information about the local places of interest. The hotel has 14 well-appointed bedrooms, most fully en suite, all with tv and teamaking facilities. A full English breakfast is served in the charming dining room, where an evening meal is available for party bookings. The heated outdoor swimming pool is a boon for hot summer days, and guests have the use of the pleasant garden that surrounds it.

THE GARDENERS ARMS

Silver Street, Cheddar, Somerset BS27 3LE
Tel: 01934 742235

A row of cottages dating from early 19th century was converted early in its life to this classic country inn. **The Gardeners Arms** has many attractive features, including exposed black beams and an old bread oven over the fireplace in the main bar. But the main attraction is the food, and owner Ian King's chalkboard menu offers something for everyone. His dishes are served every session except Sunday evening, and among the favourites is the superb trio of venison sausages with sweet potato mash and a red wine sauce. The inn has a beer garden with a barbecue and a children's play area. Quiz night is every second Sunday. Opening hours are 12-3 and 6.30-11 (Sunday 7-10.30).

BATH ARMS HOTEL

Bath Street, Cheddar, Somerset BS27 2AA
Tel: 01934 742425 Fax: 01934 744569
website: www.batharmshotel.co.uk

The **Bath Arms** has, since the 18th century, been a favourite with both local residents and tourists. Owned and run by James Paul Low, it combines the best aspects of pub, restaurant and hotel, and in the spotless, spacious day rooms visitors can relax and unwind with a drink and a superb meal. The Bath Arms Cheese Platter has long been recommended by the British Cheese Board. The oak-panelled restaurant (non-smoking) is open from 8 o'clock for breakfast, and the wide-ranging main menu is served daily from noon to 10 pm. There are nine well-appointed en suite bedrooms with tv and tea-makers. The hotel has ample off-road parking and a garden with play equipment for children.

gorge to the site of **Pavey's Lookout Tower**, a novel vantage point that offers yet more spectacular views of the surrounding area.

Whilst the gorge is undoubtedly everyone's idea of Cheddar, the village is also renowned for its caves and, of course, its cheese. Although much embellished by modern tourist paraphernalia, its two main show caves, **Gough's Cave** and **Cox's Cave**, are worth seeing for their sheer scale and spectacular calcite formations. In 1903 an almost complete skeleton, named 'Cheddar Man', was discovered in Gough's Cave and this can now be seen in a nearby **Museum** along with further evidence of early human occupation of the caves that includes flint and bone tools dating from the last Ice Age and artefacts from the Iron Age and the Roman occupation of Britain.

The term 'Cheddar cheese' refers to a recipe that was developed in the mid 19th century by Joseph Harding, a farmer and pioneer food scientist from near Bath who made the first scientific investigation into cheese-making. As the name refers to a recipe and not a place, the cheese can be made anywhere in the world, however, north Somerset is dotted with cheese manufacturers of various sizes, from single farmhouses to large scale dairies, all making Cheddar cheese. A number of these places supplement their income by offering guided tours, craft demonstrations and catering facilities.

AROUND CHEDDAR

CONGRESBURY
6½ miles N of Cheddar on the A370

Seemingly just another commuter town today, this sizable village has a long and eventful history that goes back to Roman times. Around 2000 years ago a settlement stood here at the end of a spur of the Somerset marshes and fragments of Roman and pre-Saxon pottery have been found on the site of the ancient hill that overlooks the present village.

The early Celtic missionary, St Congar, is believed to have founded an early wattle chapel at Congresbury in the 6th century and a tree bound by an iron hoop, on the eastern side of the church, is still referred to as 'St Congar's Walking Stick'. This is reputed to have grown from the saint's staff that miraculously sprouted leaves after he had thrust it into the ground outside the chapel.

CHARTERHOUSE
3 miles NE of Cheddar off the B3134

Rising, in some places, to over 1,000 feet above sea level, the **Mendips** form a landscape

Gough's Cave

THE RAILWAY INN

6 Station Road, Yatton, Somerset BS49 4AJ
Tel: 01934 832119

The Railway Inn is an eyecatching 18th century stone building with a main door that would not look out of place in a castle. Inside, all is spacious and spotless, kept that way by Keith Conliffe and Amanda Dyer, who arrived here early in 2002. They attract a wide cross-section of local residents and tourists with a warm welcome, well-kept real ales, an excellent draught cider and good, straightforward food served from 11 o'clock to 9.

Weekends bring live music or karaoke. Open 11 to 11 (Sunday 12 to 10.30), the inn stands opposite the station in the small town of Yatton between Bristol and Weston-super-Mare.

that is like no other in Somerset and, although hard to imagine today, lead and silver were once mined from these picturesque uplands. The Mendip lead-mining activity was centred around the remote village of Charterhouse and the last mine in the district, at Priddy, closed in 1908. This range of limestone hills runs from the sea at Weston-super-Mare across Somerset to Frome in the east and there are several Bronze Age barrows and Iron Age hill forts to be found here. Today's visitors will, however, find a typical area of limestone countryside with upland divided into fields separated by drystone walls, pretty villages and picturesque gorges. Another feature of this limestone landscape are the caves, particularly those at Cheddar and Wookey, where the rock has been eroded by underground streams and rivers.

Charterhouse takes its name from a Carthusian monastery, **Witham Priory**, which owned one of the four Mendip mining sectors, or liberties. This area has been known for its mineral deposits since the Iron Age and such was its importance that the Romans declared the mines here state property within just six years of their arrival in Britain. Under their influence, silver and lead ingots, or pigs, were exported to France and to Rome and the settlement grew into a sizable town with its own fort and amphitheatre (the remains of

which can still be seen today). Centuries later, improved technology allowed the original seams to be reworked and the area is now littered with abandoned mine buildings and smelting houses.

A footpath from Charterhouse church leads up onto **Black Down** that is, at 1,067 feet, the highest point in the Mendips and from here, to the northwest, the land descends down into **Burrington Combe**, a deep cleft that is said to have inspired the Rev Augustus Toplady to write the hymn *Rock of Ages*.

BLAGDON

4½ miles NE of Cheddar on the A368

To the north and northeast of Blagdon, which lies on the lower slopes of Blagdon Hill on the edge of the Mendips, are the two reservoirs that were constructed to supply Bristol with fresh water but that also provide a first class recreational amenity: the smaller **Blagdon Lake** was completed in 1899 and **Chew Valley Lake** in 1956. Together they have around 15 miles of shoreline and attract visitors from a wide area who come to fish, take part in watersports and observe the wide variety of waterfowl and other bird life that is drawn to this appealing habitat.

The Holman Clavel Inn near the Blagdon is said to contain a hearth spirit, called Chimbley Charlie, who sits on the beam over the fireplace that is made of 'holman', the local name for holly. One local story tells how a dinner party was prepared at the inn for a local farmer who had scoffed at Charlie and, after setting out the tables, the maids shut the doors ready for the party to arrive. Just before the guests were due to enter the dining room, the maids went in to see that all was ready and, inside, they found that the table was bare, the tankards were hanging up empty, the silver had been put away and the table linen neatly folded. Charlie had shown his dislike of the farmer and the dinner party was cancelled.

WEDMORE
4 miles S of Cheddar on the B3151

The ancient capital of the Somerset Marshes, in 878 King Alfred is said to have brought the newly baptised Danish King Guthrum to this remote village to sign the Peace of Wedmore, a treaty that left Wessex in Alfred's hands but gave East Anglia, East Mercia and the Kingdom of York to the Danes. The village's main street, the Borough, is lined with fine stone buildings, including a lovely old coaching inn, and the parish church's spectacular Norman south doorway is thought to have been carved by the same craftsmen who built Wells Cathedral.

BURNHAM-ON-SEA
9½ miles SW of Cheddar on the B3140

In the late 18th century, mineral springs were discovered here and an attempt was made to turn Burnham-on-Sea into a spa town to rival the spas at Cheltenham and Bath but the efficacious effects of its waters were never properly realised and, in the end, the town fell back on to its wide sandy beach to attract visitors. A large and popular seaside resort today with, particularly at low tide, a vast expanse of beach, Burnham's most distinctive landmark is the **Low Lighthouse**, a

curious square structure that is raised above the beach on tall stilts. Meanwhile, another of the town's buildings that has fared less well on its sandy foundations is the church and, in particular, its 80 foot tower, which leans some three feet from the vertical. Whilst not as dramatic as the famous leaning Tower of Pisa, the structure is quite stable and has not moved for many decades. Inside the church there are some reredos that were designed by Inigo Jones and made by Grinling Gibbons that were originally intended for the chapel at Whitehall Palace but, in 1820, they were presented to the vicar of Burnham by George IV.

To the southeast of Burnham is the small town of **Highbridge** that was once a busy coastal port on the Glastonbury Canal whilst, to the northeast, lies **Brent Knoll**, a conspicuous landmark that can be seen from as far away as South Wales. Before the Somerset Levels were drained, this isolated hill would almost certainly have been an island and, like many other natural features that appear out of place in the landscape, there are several stories that suggest that the knoll owes its existence to the Devil. The 445 foot summit is crowned with the remains of an Iron Age hill fort and, several hundred years later, Brent Knoll's southern slopes are said to have been the site of a battle that King Alfred fought and won against the Danes. The summit, which can be reached by footpaths that begin near the churches at East Brent and Brent Knoll, offers walkers a spectacular view out over the Bristol Channel, the Mendips and the Somerset Levels.

AXBRIDGE
1½ miles W of Cheddar off the A371

This fortified market town had its own mint during Saxon times and by the late medieval period Axbridge had developed

THE WHEATSHEAF INN

Stone Allerton, Axbridge, Somerset BS26 2NH
Tel/Fax: 01934 712494
e-mail: wheatsheafinnwil371@supanet.com

The Wheatsheaf is a fine old country inn in a pleasant rural setting, run in fine style by Keith and Lorraine Williams. A stone-faced fireplace is a feature in the cosily rustic public bar. Keith is a very accomplished chef, and since his arrival, the Wheatsheaf has built up a strong following from Bristol and beyond with its excellent food, served lunchtime and evening every day. Freshness is paramount, and the choice is supplemented by daily blackboard specials. In the summer, the beer garden is a very popular spot. For visitors staying overnight the inn has two bedrooms with tv, tea-makers and a shared bathroom. Pub hours are 12-3 and 6-11 (10.30 Sunday).

into a prosperous wool centre that made its living processing the Mendip fleeces into woven cloth. A small town today with a delightful centre, the old market square is home to an exceptional example of a half-timbered merchant's house that dates from around 1500. Although it has nothing to do with King John or hunting (but its name is a reminder that the Mendip hills were once a royal hunting ground), **King John's Hunting Lodge** (National Trust) was extensively restored in the early 1970s and it is home to an excellent **Local History Museum**. Elsewhere in the centre of Axbridge there are an unusual number of handsome Georgian shops and town houses.

To the east of the town is Cheddar's curious circular reservoir whilst, to the west, lies the hamlet of **Webbington Loxton** that is home to the **Wheelwright's Working Museum** and the **Gypsy Folklore Collection**.

BLEADON
7½ miles W of Cheddar off the A370

Local legend says that Bleadon was originally called 'Bleed Down' in memory of a bloody battle between the local inhabitants and Danish raiders. One morning around the 7th century, six Danish longboats came up the River Severn on a strong spring tide and the local fishermen, having seen the invaders, hurried to nearby Uphill to rouse the

farming people but they left behind an old and lame woman who was by the riverside gathering rushes. Hidden by the tall reeds, the old lady watched the invaders land and rush off in search of plunder leaving their boats unattended. The tide began to turn and the old woman hobbled from boat to boat cutting the mooring ropes as she went whilst the Uphill men had rallied and driven the Danes, hampered by their loot, back to their landing place. With no boats left to aid their escape not one of the invaders survived.

BREAN
10 miles W of Cheddar off the A370

This elongated, mainly modern resort village is sheltered, to the north, by the 320 foot high **Brean Down**, an imposing remnant of the Mendip hills that projects out into the Bristol Channel – another fragment can be seen in the form of the offshore island **Steep Holm**. A site of settlement, ritual and defence for thousands of years, the remains of an Iron Age coastal fort and a Roman temple have both been found on the down along with some medieval 'pillow' mounds. However, the tip of the promontory is dominated by the Palmerston fort of 1867, which was built as part of the defences to protect the Bristol Channel, and there are also some 20th century gun emplacements. Along with being of interest to archaeologists and geologists, this peninsula has been designated a Site of Special Scientific Interest: oystercatcher and dunlin can be seen along the foreshore and estuary; the scrubland is an important habitat for migrating birds such as redstart, redpoll and reed bunting; rare plants take root in the shallow and exposed soil; and the south-facing slopes are home to a variety of butterflies. With one of the widest tidal ranges in Europe, the currents around the headland can be as dramatic as they are dangerous.

BANWELL
5½ miles NW of Cheddar on the A368

This pleasant village was once the site of a Saxon monastery but, whilst the parish church here is certainly ancient, **Banwell Castle** is a relatively recent addition to the village and is, in fact, a Victorian mansion house. Just to the west of the village, on Banwell Hill, a remarkable discovery was made in 1821 when a series of caverns were found that contained the remains of prehistoric animals including bison, bear and reindeer. Known as the **Bone Caves**, some years after the discovery the local bishop created an extravagant romantic park, around the caves' entrance, which he filled with pyramids, a monk's cell, fairy cottages and other fanciful buildings. Meanwhile, there is the prehistoric earthwork of **Banwell Camp** where there is a great cross constructed out of turf. Rising some two feet above the enclosed ground and with its four points following the lines of the compass, the origin of the cross remains a mystery. However, local stories suggest that the Devil blew down each upright arm of the cross that the villagers erected so they finally laid a cross on the ground to defy the Devil.

A couple of miles north of Banwell is the village of **Puxton** that is noted for its eccentric church tower that leans at such an angle that it looks as if it might topple at any moment, causing its weathercock to nose dive into the churchyard.

PENSCOT HOTEL & RESTAURANT

The Square, Shipham, Nr Cheddar, Somerset BS25 1TW
Tel: 01934 842659   Fax: 01934 842576

Penscot Hotel & Restaurant is a delightful 15th century building overlooking the green in the village of Shipham. Terry White fell in love with the place on a visit and has put in an immense amount of work into refurbishing and upgrading the inn since buying it in the autumn of 2001. Twelve comfortably furnished en suite bedrooms with tv and tea-makers provide excellent guest accommodation, and stone-flagged floors, wooden beams and an inglenook fireplace create an inviting ambience for enjoying a drink and a snack in the bar. In the oak-beamed restaurant an extensive menu based on fresh local produce is served Monday to Saturday evenings and Sunday lunchtime. Close to the A38, the inn is a convenient and pleasant base for touring the local attractions.

LILLYPOOL CHEESE & CIDER EMPORIUM

Shipham Hill, Shipham, Winscombe, Somerset BS25 1RQ
Tel: 01934 743994

Lillypool Cheese & Cider Emporium is a delightful roadside farm shop and restaurant selling those two products at their very best. Open every day from 8 o'clock until 5, the restaurant is open for breakfasts, teas, lunches and a splendid Sunday roast; inside there are seats for 30, and when the weather is kind 20 more can sit out in the garden. Owner Edward Bliss welcomes visitors of all ages, and children can romp in an adventure playground beside the car park. Behind the emporium is a 20-acre campsite in the rolling Somerset countryside, where campers can do it the old-fashioned way, lighting camp fires and going back to nature - assisted perhaps by a chunk of Cheddar and a billycan or two of cider.

WESTON-SUPER-MARE
10 miles NW of Cheddar on the A370

A popular seaside resort that has, in recent years, also developed as a centre of light industry, Weston-super-Mare was, as late as 1811, just a fishing hamlet with only 170 residents but, within 100 years, it grew to become the second largest town in Somerset. Despite its relatively modern appearance, this area has been inhabited since prehistoric times and the wooded promontory at the northern end of Weston Bay was the site of a sizable Iron Age hill settlement known as **Worlebury Camp**. In the 1st century AD this is said to have been captured by the Romans after a bloody battle and recent excavations,

Weston-super-Mare Pier

which revealed a number of skeletons showing the effects of sword damage, provide confirmation. A pleasant walk from the town centre now leads up through attractive woodland to this ancient hill top site from where there are magnificent views out across the mouth of the River Severn to Wales. Meanwhile, at the southern end of Weston Bay another spectacular view can be found from the clifftop site of the semi-ruined church at **Uphill**. This village also lies at the start (or the finish) of the **Mendip Way**, a 50 mile long footpath that takes in the whole length of the Mendip Hills, including the broad vale of the Western Mendips, the high plateau of the central part and the wooded valleys in the eastern region. Ending at Frome, walkers thinking of tackling the entire route should note that the footpath includes some steep climbs.

The development of Weston began in the 1830s around the Knightstone, an islet joined to the shore at the northern end of the bay, and here was eventually built a large theatre and swimming baths. The arrival of the railway in 1841 saw the town's expansion increase rapidly and, in 1867, a pier was built on the headland below Worlebury Camp that connected the offshore Birnbeck Island with the mainland. Intended as a berth for steamer

Weston-super-Mare Beach

traffic, the pier was found to be slightly off the tourist track and, later, a more impressive pier was built nearer the town centre that, prior to serious fires in the 1930s and during World War II, was approximately twice its current length. The **Grand Pier** now stands at the centre of an area that is crammed with souvenir shops, ice cream parlours, cafés and assorted attractions that are part and parcel of a British seaside resort. There are also the indoor attractions of the **Winter Gardens**, along the seafront, and the fascinating **Time Machine Museum**.

For anyone wishing to explore Weston on foot there is the Museum Trail that begins on the seafront and, following a trail of carved stones created by artist Michael Fairfax, leads visitors to the **Woodspring Museum**, who sponsor the trail. Meanwhile, the **Sea Life Aquarium** has over 30 fascinating marine displays, along with feeding times and demonstrations, to amuse the whole family and the **Weston Miniature Railway** provides a leisurely way to see Weston's seafront.

To the north of the resort, whose greatest asset is undoubtedly its vast expanse of sandy beach, is **Sand Point**, a ridge overlooking a lonely salt marsh that is home to a wide variety of wading birds and that also provides an excellent viewpoint. Just back from the headland is **Woodspring Priory**, a surprisingly intact

medieval monastery that was founded in the early 13th century by a grandson of one of Thomas à Becket's murderers, William de Courtenay. The priory fell into disrepair following the Dissolution when the buildings were given over to agricultural use but the church, tower, refectory and tithe barn have all survived and the outline of the cloister can also still be made out.

Just to the southeast of the town lies Weston Airport that is home to the world's largest collection of helicopters and autogyros. The only museum in Britain dedicated to rotary wing aircraft, the International **Helicopter Museum** has over 40 exhibits that range from single-seater autogyros to multi-passenger helicopters and here visitors can see displays on the history and development of these flying machines and a conservation hangar where the aircraft are restored. The museum is open from Wednesday to Sunday and daily at Easter and during the summer holiday period.

CLEVEDON
11 miles NW of Cheddar on the B3133

Developed in the late 18th and early 19th century as a resort, the lack of a railway prevented the town from expanding further and so it was overtaken by Weston-super-Mare as the leading seaside town along this stretch of coast. As a result there are few of the attractions that are normally associated with a holiday resort although the exception is **Clevedon Pier**, a remarkably slim and elegant structure that was built in the 1860s from iron rails that were intended for Brunel's ill-considered South Wales railway. When part of the pier collapsed in the 1970s, its long term future looked bleak but, following an extensive restoration programme, the pier is now the landing stage, during the summer, for large pleasure steamers such as the *Balmoral* and the *Waverley*, the only surviving sea-going paddle steamers in the world. Unusually for a holiday resort Clevedon has a **Market Hall** that was built in 1869 to provide a place for local market gardeners to sell their produce.

Beginning at Clevedon promenade and leading up to Church and Wain's Hills is the **Poet's Walk**, a flower-lined footpath that is said to have been popular with Victorian poets and, on the top of Wain's Hill, are the remains of an Iron Age coastal fort and this is an excellent place from which to look out over the town, the Somerset Levels and the Severn Estuary.

However, it is **Clevedon Court**, an outstanding 14th century manor house that brings most people to this town. One of the earliest surviving country houses in Britain, this house not only displays many of its original 14th century features still intact but it also incorporates a massive 12th century tower and a 13th century great hall. Once partly fortified, this imposing manor house has been the home of the Elton family since 1709 and, as longstanding patrons of the arts, the family invited many of the country's finest poets and writers to Clevedon in the early 19th century. Those to visit the house included Coleridge, Tennyson and Thackeray. It was whilst staying here that Thackeray fell in love with one of his host's daughters, Mrs Brookfield, and he was to spend some time here seeing her and also writing *Vanity Fair*. Another

member of the Elton family was Arthur Hallam, a student friend of Lord Tennyson who showed great promise as a poet but who died at a young age. Tennyson never got over his friend's untimely death and, in 1850, he visited his grave whilst on honeymoon – the same year that his poem, *In Memoriam, AHH*, was published.

Although the Elton family is closely associated with the arts, one member of the family in the Victorian era invented a special technique for making the type of brightly coloured pottery that was to become known as Eltonware. Particularly popular in the United States, there are many fine examples on display in the house, along with a collection of rare glass from the works at Nailsea. Now owned by the National Trust, Clevedon Court is not only an impressive place that houses some fine treasures but it is surrounded by beautiful 18th century terraced gardens and, from here, a footpath leads through nearby woodland on to a ridge overlooking the low and once marshy Gordano valley.

Just to the east of Clevedon lies the tiny village of **Walton-in-Gordano** and here can be found the wonderful gardens of the **Manor House** that are planted with rare shrubs, trees and herbaceous plants.

FROME

This large town grew up beside the river from which it takes its name and the first permanent settlement here was founded in around 685 when St Aldhelm, the Abbot of Malmesbury, set up a mission station on the river banks. Then on the edge of Selwood Forest, this was a suitable river crossing and it was also close to the tracks that used the Mendip Hills and the Salisbury Plain gap. Such was the expansion around St Aldhelm's stone Church of St John that, by the time of the

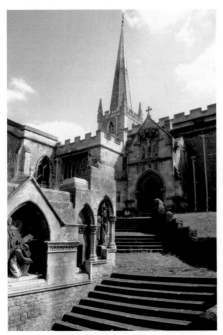

Church of St John

Domesday Book, the settlement had a market, which suggests that it had become a place of some importance.

Frome continued to prosper during the Middle Ages on the back of its cloth industry and, before the hot springs at Bath were discovered, Frome was the larger and more important of the two. Indeed, after the Dissolution of the Monasteries in the 16th century, the church lands were bought by the local Thynne family, who established their Longleat estate just over the county border in Wiltshire. Competition from the northern woollen towns in the 19th century saw Frome's textile industry begin to decline although the trade did not vanish from the town completely until the 1960s. Since then other industries, and in particular printing, have flourished and, fortunately, this new growth has not spoilt the charm of the town's old centre. Still with a flourishing

weekly market, Frome is home to the largest one day agricultural show in the southwest of England – the **Frome Cheese Show** – held each September whilst its annual late summer St Catherine's Medieval Fair draws stallholders, buskers and entertainers from all over the country.

Best explored on foot the town's old quarter is an attractive conservation area and here, amidst the interesting shops, cafés and restaurants, can be found the **Blue House** that was built in 1726 as an almshouse and a boy's school and is one of the town's numerous listed buildings. In fact, Frome has more listed buildings that any other town in Somerset and many date from the elegant Georgian era. Elsewhere, across the River Frome, there is the **Bridge**, a contemporary of Bath's Pulteney Bridge that dates from 1667 and that has buildings along its length.

Surprisingly, this charming place is the fourth largest town in Somerset and, along with its steep cobbled streets, wealth of architecture and its lively market, visitors should also take time to discover the local history collections at **Frome Museum** (limited opening).

AROUND FROME

LULLINGTON
2½ miles N of Frome off the B3090

A footpath leads southwards from this peaceful village beside the River Frome to **Orchardleigh Park**, an imposing Victorian mansion that was built in the mid 19th century. In the grounds of the house is a lake with an island that is home to a small church whose churchyard contains the grave of Sir Henry Newbolt, the author of *Drake's Drum*.

Meanwhile, to the northeast of Lullington and, again on the banks of the river, is the famous **Rode Bird Gardens,** an impressive park of some 17 acres that is home to over 200 different species of exotic bird from around the world, many of which are allowed to fly freely. The grounds incorporate a miniature woodland steam railway, a pets' corner and a series of lakes that are inhabited by flamingos, penguins and other species of waterfowl.

NORTON ST PHILIP
5 miles N of Frome on the A366

A former wool village that was recorded in the *Domesday Book,* in the 13th century the Carthusian monks were given some land here and they founded a priory near the village that was completed in 1232. The monks were also responsible for building the village's most famous landmark – the splendid **George Inn** – that was originally

THE WOOLPACK

Beckington, near Bath, Somerset BA11 6SP
Tel: 01373 831244 e-mail: info@thewoolpackinn.co.uk
Fax: 01373 831223 website: www.thewoolpackinn.co.uk

Dating back to the 16th century, **The Woolpack** is a former coaching inn that has been stylishly refurbished and renovated without loosing any of its original charm as a quaint rural pub. Here, visitors can enjoy a drink in the stone floored bar before moving on to one of the inn's two very different dining rooms, where a mouth-watering menu of dishes, including fish and game, is served daily. Meanwhile, those visiting the area will also have the opportunity to make use of the inn's eleven individually and charmingly styled en suite guest rooms where the excellent hospitality offered by this exceptional inn continues.

BATH LODGE HOTEL

Norton St Philip, near Bath, Somerset BA2 7NH
Tel: 01225 723040 Fax: 01225 723737
e-mail: info@bathlodge.com website: www.bathlodge.com

Despite its castle like appearance, the **Bath Lodge Hotel** was originally the gatehouse to the Farleigh estate but, today, it a superb country hotel that offers guests fabulous hospitality in superbly decorated and furnished, romantic surroundings. Situated just 7 miles from Bath, it provides the ideal location for visiting local attractions such as Longleat, Stonehenge, Wells and Glastonbury without the problems of parking and access associated with staying in the town. From the cosy lounge with its roaring log fire to the sumptuous en suite bedrooms, guests here will certainly have a relaxing stay. Owned and personally run by Richard and Sue Warren, the couple match these delightful surroundings by offering guests a magnificent breakfast each morning that is fit for a king.

FLEUR-DE-LYS

Norton St Philip, Nr Bath, Somerset BA2 7LQ
Tel/Fax: 01373 834333

The **Fleur-de-Lys** is a fine 15th century coaching inn on a corner site in the attractive village of Norton St Philip, just off the A36 Frome-Bath road. The interior is as pleasing as the Cotswold stone facade, with flagstone floors and lots of intimate little nooks. Owner Simon Shannon, who bought the Fleur-de-Lys in the autumn of 2001, is host to a wide cross-section of locals, who come here for the good company, the well-kept ales and the excellent home-cooked food served every lunchtime and evening - the fish specials are not to be missed. The inn is open 11-3 and 5-11 Monday to Friday and all day Saturday.

established as a house of hospitality for those visiting the priory and it is still a hostelry today. The timber framed upper floors were added in the 15th century when the inn doubled as a warehouse for storing the locally produced woollen cloth and, in 1668, the diarist Samuel Pepys stayed whilst on his way to Bath with his family and noted that he "Dined well. 10 shillings." Just a short while later, the inn played host to the Duke of Monmouth

Farleigh Hungerford Castle

who made the George his headquarters shortly before his defeat at the Battle of Sedgemoor in 1685. According to a local story, 12 men implicated in the uprising were imprisoned here after the battle, in what is now the Dungeon Bar, and later they were taken away to be hanged, drawn and quartered at the local market place. Virtually unaltered today, this ancient inn is a wonderful fusion of medieval stonework, oriel windows and timber framing.

FARLEIGH HUNGERFORD
6 miles N of Frome on the A366

The first recorded mention of 'Farnleah' was made in a charter granted by King Ethelred in 987 and, by the time of the *Domesday Book*, it had become 'Ferelege', a manor owned by the great Norman Baron, Roger de Coureulles. An old fortified settlement, Farleigh Hungerford (it was Farleigh by the 12th century and the Hungerford was added later when the manor was sold to Sir Thomas Hungerford) is still overlooked by the impressive remains of **Farleigh Hungerford Castle** (English Heritage) that stands on a rise above the River Frome to the northeast of the village. Built by Sir Thomas, the first Speaker of the House of Commons, on the site of an old manor house that he

acquired in the late 14th century, legend has it that he failed to gain the proper permission for his fortification from the Crown and this oversight led to his downfall. The Hungerford family remained at the castle until 1686 when it was sold following the bankruptcy of Sir Edward Hungerford who is said to have wasted a £14,000 annuity along with a capital amount of £80,000! The castle changed hands in the early 18th century and the incoming family saw it as a quarry for building stone rather than as a place to live and much of the castle was left to ruin whilst the family built a new mansion on the other side of the village. Nevertheless, an impressive shell of towers and perimeter walls has survived intact, along with the castle's **Chapel of St Leonard**. This contains a striking 15th century mural of St George, some fine stained glass and a number of interesting monuments, including the tomb of Sir Thomas Hungerford himself. The castle's glorious setting in the picturesque rolling valley of the River Frome makes it a pleasant place to visit and, open daily all year round (except between November and March when it is open from Wednesdays to Sundays), a host of special events are held here throughout the seasons.

HINTON PRIORY
7 miles N of Frome off the B3110

All that remains of the early Carthusian monastery founded here by Ela, Countess of Salisbury, are some wonderfully atmospheric ruins. As in other religious houses belonging to this order, the monks occupied their own small dwellings that were set around the main cloister, often with a small garden attached, and these communities were generally known for their reclusiveness. However, one outspoken monk from Hinton Priory, Nicholas Hopkins, achieved notoriety in Tudor times as the confessor and spiritual adviser to the 3rd Duke of Buckingham and his story is recounted by Shakespeare in *Henry VIII*. Several sections of the old priory remain, including the chapter house, parts of the guest quarters and the undercroft of the refectory.

WELLOW
7 miles N of Frome off the A367

On the southern edge of this attractive village, which has some fine old houses and a charming medieval circular dovecote, the road descends steeply to a ford on the **Wellow Brook** across which is a handsome medieval packhorse bridge. Close by can be found one of the finest examples of a Neolithic monument in the west of England, **Stoney Littleton Long Barrow**, which was built over 4,000 years ago. A striking multi-chambered tomb that has now been restored, the interior can be inspected by obtaining a key from nearby Stoney Littleton Farm.

BECKINGTON
3 miles NE of Frome off the A36

This former wool village lies on the opposite bank of the River Frome from Lullington and here,

amongst the fine stone houses, can be found the **Cedars** that was possibly once an ecclesiastical hospice for Augustinian canons. Here, too, is **Seymour Court** that takes its name from the St Maur family who became the lords of the manor of Beckington by marriage. First mentioned in the *Domesday Book*, Beckington has played host to various monarchs over the centuries and Charles II visited the village twice, once on his way to Longleat House and then again after his defeat at the battle of Worcester in 1663. George III and Queen Charlotte also rested here whilst making the same journey to Longleat House.

NUNNEY
2½ miles SW of Frome off the A361

This picturesque old market town is dominated by its dramatic moated **Castle** that was begun in 1373 by Sir John de la Mare on his return from the Hundred Years War with France. Thought to have been modelled on the Bastille, the fortress consists of four solidly built towers that stand on an island formed by a stream on one side and a broad water-filled moat on the other. The castle came under attack from Parliamentarian forces during the English Civil War and, despite having a garrison of only one officer, eight men and

Nunney Castle

a handful of civilian refugees, the castle held out for two days. However, the bombardment damaged the building beyond repair and it had to be abandoned thus leaving the romantic ruins that can still be seen today. One of the 30 pound cannonballs that were used by Cromwell's forces can be seen in the village's 13th century church.

MELLS
3 miles W of Frome off the A362

Once on the easternmost limit of the lands belonging to Glastonbury Abbey, in the 15th century Abbot Selwood drew up plans to rebuild the village in the shape of a St Anthony's cross (with four arms of equal length). However, only one street was ever completed – New Street – and this architectural gem can still be seen to the south of St Andrew's parish church. Whilst the exterior of the church is certainly imposing the main interest lies inside as, here, there is a remarkable collection of monuments that have all been designed by some of the 20th century's most acclaimed artists – Lutyens, Gill, Munnings and Burne-Jones. One of the memorials is to Raymond Asquith, the eldest son of the Liberal Prime Minister, Herbert Asquith, who was killed in World War I whilst another, to the pacifist and poet Siegfried Sassoon, can be found in the churchyard.

According to legend, the Abbot of Glastonbury, in an attempt to stave off Henry VIII's Dissolution of the Monasteries, dispatched his steward, John Horner, to London with a gift for the king consisting of a pie into which was baked the title deeds of 12 ecclesiastical manor houses. However, rather than attempting to persuade the king, Horner returned to Somerset the rightful owner of three of the manors himself – Mells, Nunnery and Leigh-upon-Mendip – for which he paid a total of £2,000. This blatant act of disloyalty is, supposedly, the inspiration for the famous nursery rhyme *Little Jack Horner* that describes how Jack "put in his thumb and pulled out a plum." The manor house at Mells, which is not open to the public, remained in the hands of the Horner family until the early 20th century when it passed to the Asquith family by marriage.

HOLCOMBE
6½ miles W of Frome off the A367

Mentioned in the *Domesday Book*, all that remains on the site today is the ancient, and now redundant, St Andrew's Church, which has one of the finest Norman arches in Somerset. Inside, the Jacobean pulpit and Georgian pews can still be seen and there is also no electric lighting so when the annual Christmas service is held here (the only service of the year) the building is illuminated by the gentle light of candles. The parents of Scott of the Antarctic lived at Holcombe Manor and they lie at rest in the well tended

THE KINGS HEAD
Lower Coleford, Nr Radstock, Somerset BA3 5LU
Tel: 01373 812346

The Kings Head is a long, two-storey 18th century inn tucked away down country lanes south of Radstock. New tenants Craig Jamieson and Helen Sheppard are working hard on renovations and refurbishment, including a coat of white paint for the frontage. A new kitchen is also in their plans, but meanwhile it's rolls and sandwiches only, with tea, coffee and a good range of real ales to wash them down. Darts, pool and skittles are the Kings Head's games, and there's occasional live music and a quiz every Sunday evening. The pub is open all day, every day.

RING O' ROSES INN

Stratton Road, Holcombe, near Bath, Somerset BA3 5EB
Tel: 01741 232478 e-mail: ringorosesholcombe@tesco.net
Fax: 01741 233737 website: ringoroses.co.uk

Found tucked away in the Mendip Hills, the **Ring o' Roses Inn** dates back to the 16th century and its name is a reminder of the plague that devastated this hidden village. Today's visitors will experience none of the horrors of those years as the inn is now a charming and delightful traditional country house hotel that offers superb hospitality in wonderfully peaceful and relaxing surroundings. Along with the cosy bar, customers can enjoy a quiet drink and conversation in the oak panelled lounge, indulge themselves at dinner from the imaginatively conceived menu and then retire to one of the luxurious and elegant en suite guest rooms for a restful night's sleep.

SEVEN STARS

North Road, Timsbury, Bath, Somerset BA2 0JJ
Tel: 01761 470398 Fax: 01761 470398

An attractive stone built rural pub that dates back to the 17th century, the **Seven Stars** is as charming inside as its superbly maintained exterior would suggest. Full of character with low exposed beams, the thick piled carpets and intimate lighting add an air of luxury and cosiness to this friendly, family run establishment. Very much a village local, with a fine selection of real ales, a glorious beer garden and play area for the children, Stephen and Diane Franks have also gained a fine reputation for the high standard of the food served here. Freshly prepared by chef Stephen, the ever-changing menu includes such delights as sword fish with lemon and thyme, and is a treat not to be missed.

LAMB INN

Fosse Way, Clandown, near Radstock, Somerset BA3 3BL
Tel: 01761 435777 e-mail: arkwright@sgrubb2.freeserve.co.uk

Situated in the village of Clandown, in the hills overlooking Radstock, the **Lamb Inn** is a large and spacious 19th century hostelry that provides a cosy and comfortable environment in which customers can enjoy the excellent hospitality offered by owners Jenny and Stephen. Along with a fine range of drinks, including real ales, at the bar, this young but experienced couple also provide a menu of simple yet superbly prepared traditional pub food at lunchtime that is proving to be exceedingly popular with a growing number of regulars. This is also a place where visitors do not remain strangers for long and everyone is encouraged to join in the Saturday evening live entertainment or try their hand at skittles or pool.

FRANKLYNS FARM

Chewton Mendip, Nr Bath, Somerset BA3 4NB
Tel/Fax: 01761 241372

A working farm of 500 acres provides an excellent base for a Bed & Breakfast stay in some of Somerset's loveliest rolling countryside. The Clothier family's cosy modern farmhouse has two bright, spacious and very comfortable bedrooms, both en suite, with tv, hospitality trays and great views over open countryside. Delicious breakfasts with free-range eggs set guests up for a day in the open-air or touring nearby attractions at Bath, Wells and Cheddar. The farm lies off the A39, on the B3114 road towards Emborough.

churchyard where, too, can be found a simple memorial to their famous son on their headstone. Not far from the church are Luccombe Ponds that were built by the monks of Keynsham Abbey in the Middle Ages for keeping their fish fresh.

STRATTON-ON-THE-FOSSE
7½ miles W of Frome on the A367

This former coal mining village is home to the famous Roman Catholic boys' public school, **Downside Abbey**, which occupies the site of a monastery that was founded in 1814 by a group of English Benedictines. The steady expansion of the school during the 20th century encouraged the monks to move to a new site on higher ground near the existing abbey church, an impressive building that took over 70 years to complete and numbered among its architects Sir Giles Gilbert Scott.

RADSTOCK
7 miles NW of Frome on the A362

This little coal mining town is unusual for the Somerset countryside in that it has a particularly industrial feel. At the interesting **Radstock Museum**, housed in a converted 18th century barn, more information can be found on the Somerset coalfield as the museum is devoted, in part, to the people of the local coal mines. However, there are also displays and exhibits featuring the local railways, the Somerset Coal Canal and reconstructions of a school room and a Co-op Shop. The museum is open Tuesday to Friday, Sunday and Bank Holiday Monday afternoons and all day Saturday. It is closed throughout December and January.

MIDSOMER NORTON
8 miles NW of Frome on the B3355

Although the history of the area around this town is one of mining, with coal being hewn from nearby Norton Hill until as recently as the 1970s, the surrounding countryside is beautiful and the sights and sounds of collieries have long since been replaced with that of open farmland being worked. Whilst Midsomer Norton itself is a pleasant mix of old and new – there are excellent shopping facilities along with attractive Georgian buildings and a late medieval tithe barn – in the churchyard of the town's parish church is a memorial to the 12 miners who were killed in an accident at Wellsway coal works in 1839.

CAMELEY
12 miles NW of Frome off the A37

This attractive village is home to a church that was referred to by John Betjeman as "Rip Van Winkle's Church" because of the remarkable series of medieval wall paintings that were discovered here, under layers of whitewash probably applied during the time of Cromwell, in the 1960s. The murals are believed to have been painted between the 11th and the 17th centuries and feature such diverse images as the foot of a giant St Christopher stepping through a fish and crab infested river, a charming 14th century jester complete with harlequin costume and a rare coat of arms of Charles I.

WELLS

This ancient ecclesiastical centre, which is also the smallest city in England, derives its name from a line of springs that rise up from the base of the Mendips. The first church here is believed to have been founded by King Ine in around AD700 and, after a diocesan tussle with Bath, the present **Cathedral of St Andrew**, first completely English Gothic cathedral, was begun in the 12th century. Taking over three centuries to complete this magnificent cathedral demonstrates the three main styles of Gothic architecture

THE SUN INN

Union Street, Wells, Somerset BA5 2PU
Tel: 01749 672854

The smiling face of the sun beams down from the sign outside this splendid old coaching inn just off the main street, and the greeting from Ron Baggs and his staff is equally welcoming. Behind the stone frontage, which in season is adorned by window boxes and hanging baskets, the **Sun Inn** has a pleasantly traditional look, and the home cooking brings a lunchtime clientele that includes all ages, from young families to senior citizens, who all appreciate the straightforward, wholesome fare and the kind prices. At the back of the inn is a covered courtyard where customers can drink and eat. Open hours are 11-11 Tuesday to Sunday, 12-2.30 & 7-11 Monday.

CARRINGTONS

12 Sadler Street, Wells, Somerset BA5 2SE
Tel: 01749 676435

In the centre of the city, just off the High Street, **is Carringtons** - a fully licensed restaurant and tea room in traditional style. Behind the large Victorian double frontage windows, among some interesting little shops, all is spick and span. The loyal clientele know that they will be well looked after by owner Anthony Brown and his excellent and courteous staff. The menu offers a selection of tasty, well prepared home cooked dishes, most of which are English classics such as Cottage Pie served with a selection of vegetables. This delightful establishment is open every day from 10am until 5pm.

MANOR FARM DULCOTE

Dulcote, Wells, Somerset BA5 3PZ
Tel/Fax: 01749 672125 e-mail: rosalind.bufton@ntlworld.com
website: www.wells-accommodation.co.uk

The house at **Manor Farm** is a superb 17th century stone farmhouse with climbing roses and clematis climbing over the front and a delightful garden with lawns,paved patio and flower beds. In this charming setting a mile away from Wells, Rosalind Bufton offers outstanding Bed & Breakfast accommodation in five beautifully furnished bedrooms, three en suite, the others with shared facilities.The Garden Suite has been adapted for wheelchair users . This is also a small working farm, with sheep, geese, ducks, hens,a goat and friendly cats. The hens provide eggs for a wonderful farmhouse breakfast. You can take a pleasant stroll across the fields to Wells Cathedral to hear Evensong.

RIVERSIDE RESTAURANT

Wells Road, Coxley, Nr Wells, Somerset BA5 1QT
Tel: 01749 672100 Fax: 01749 673891

Good home-cooked food is served in a friendly atmosphere at the **Riverside Restaurant**. In an L-shaped modern restaurant by a sleepy river, with lawns and a gazebo for outside dining at the front, Mike and Stella Griffiths are an excellent team with long experience in the licensed trade, Mike in the kitchen and Stella providing service with a personal touch. Superbly presented dishes include unmissable fish specials, steaks with all the trimmings and a super steak & kidney pudding, as well as a great choice for vegetarians. Traditional roasts are served all day on Sunday. Closed on Mondays.

and its 13th century west front, with over 100 statues of saints, angels and prophets gazing down on the cathedral close, is generally acknowledged to be its crowning glory – although this was defaced during the English Civil War. Inside, there are many superb features, including the beautiful scissor arches and the great 14th century stained glass window over the high altar. However, the cathedral's most impressive sight is its 14th century **Astronomical Clock**, one of the oldest working timepieces in the world, that shows the minutes, hours and phases of the moon on separate inner and outer dials and marks the quarter hours with a lively mechanised knights' tournament. The cathedral is also home to a 15th century library.

The large cathedral close is a tranquil and peaceful area right in the heart of the city and for centuries the ecclesiastical and civic functions of Wells have remained separate. The west front of the cathedral has an internal passage with pierced apertures and there is a theory that choirboys might have sung through these openings to give the illusion to those gathered on the cathedral green that the then lifelike painted statues were singing. Meanwhile, the cathedral green is surrounded by a high wall that is breached at only three castellated entrance points and one of these, the gateway into the Market Place, is known as **Penniless Porch**. It was here that the bishop allowed the city's poor to beg for money from those entering the cathedral close.

To the south of the cathedral's cloisters is the **Bishop's Palace**, a remarkable fortified medieval building that is surrounded by a moat fed by the springs, and here, too, is a 14th century **Gatehouse** that not only has its portcullis intact but also a chute down which boiling oil and molten lead were poured on to would-be invaders. Enclosed by a high wall, in order

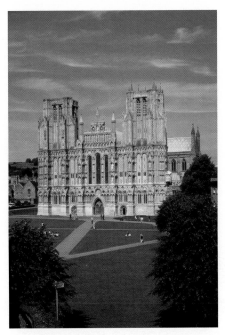

Wells Cathedral

to gain access to the palace from the Market Place, visitors must pass under a 13th century stone arch known as the **Bishop's Eye** and then cross a drawbridge that was last raised for defensive purposes in 1831. Although still an official residence of the Bishop of Bath and Wells, visitors can tour the palace's chapel and its Jocelin's hall. The **Palace Grounds and Gardens** are open on certain days during the summer whilst the Palace moat is home to a wealth of ducks and waterfowl that can be fed by the public, although the swans are not to be fed as it discourages them from the tradition of ringing a bell for food. Meanwhile, on the northern side of the cathedral green is the **Vicar's Close** and this 14th century cobbled thoroughfare is one of the oldest planned streets in Europe.

There is, of course, much more to Wells than just its ecclesiastical buildings and heritage and a visit to the **Wells Museum**, found near the west front of the cathedral, explains much of the history of the city and surrounding area through a collection of interesting locally found artefacts. Along with a new exhibition showing the techniques the medieval builders employed in constructing the great cathedral, there is a Jurassic ichthyosaur, needlework samplers and even a miniature antique shop. The museum is open daily from Easter to the end of October and from Wednesday to Sunday for the rest of the year.

The city also remains a lively market centre, with a street market held every Wednesday and Saturday, and, for those wanting to view Wells from a distance, there is an attractive footpath that starts from the Moat Walk and leads up to the summit of Tor Hill.

AROUND WELLS

SHEPTON MALLET
4½ miles E of Wells on the A371

Situated on the banks of the River Sheppey and just to the west of Fosse Way, this old market town has been a busy trading centre for 3,000 years and, along with the discovery of Bronze Age homesteads and pottery in 1995, there is **Maesbury Ring**,

an Iron Age town 950 feet up in the Mendips to the north of the town. The settlement's name is Saxon and it means, quite simply, 'sheep town' and this reveals its main commercial activity from the time before the Norman Conquest and through the Middle Ages when Shepton Mallet was a centre of first woollen production and then a weaving town. The industry reached its peak in the 15th century and it was around this time that the town's most striking building, its magnificent parish **Church of St Peter and St Paul**, was constructed. The church's imposing tower has a distinctive cap that was the base for a spire that was never added whilst, inside, there is one of the most impressive 'waggon' ceilings in the country that has 350 individual panels. Other reminders of Shepton Mallet's past can be seen around its market place where there is a 50 foot high **Market Cross**, which dates from around 1500 and was restored in Victorian times, whilst there is also **The Shambles**, a 15th century wooden shed where meat was traded. After the Duke of Monmouth's ill-fated Pitchfork Rebellion, several of his followers were executed at the Market Cross in 1685 on the orders of the infamous Judge Jeffreys. The town is also home to the oldest operational prison in the country and it was here, during World War II, that the *Magna Carta* and the *Domesday Book* were stored for safe

The Charlton Inn

Charlton Road, Shepton Mallet, Somerset BA4 5PH
Tel: 01749 342759
e-mail: richard@charltoninn.fsnet.co.uk

The Charlton Inn stands big and square on a corner site not far from the centre of town. Inside, it's spacious and comfortable, with open fires and high ceilings, while outside there's a beer garden and plenty of car parking space. Landlord Richard Pfyl, who spent some time training in Switzerland and at London's Savoy Hotel, engenders a pleasantly relaxed atmosphere at the inn, which serves straightforward, good-value food from 12 to 2.30 and from 6 to 9 every day. The inn is open for drinks all day. Tuesday is quiz night, and there are occasional live music nights. The lawned garden has picnic benches and a variety of swings, slides and climbing frames to keep the children amused.

keeping. Shepton Mallet has one other claim to fame as, reputedly, it was here that lager was first brewed in England by the Anglo-Bavarian Brewery, which was built here in the 1860s at a time when brewing was an important industry in the town.

Today, Shepton Mallet is a prosperous light industrial town that has a good selection of shopping and leisure activities and, for those wishing to find out more about its past, there is the interesting district **Museum** to visit. Meanwhile, each year the town plays host to two agricultural shows: the **Mid-Somerset Show** in August and, in May, the **Royal Bath and Wells Show** that has a permanent showground to the southeast of the town.

The limestone hills north of the town are littered with caves and caverns and the walls of one such cave are said to bear the marks of a terrible visitation by the Devil. Centuries ago, the cave was the home of a poor lady, Nancy Camel, and, on seeing her poverty, the Devil offered her both riches and an easy life in exchange for her soul. Nancy yielded to temptation and, although she continued to live in her cave, she never worked again and had all that

EAST SOMERSET RAILWAY

Cranmore railway Station,
Shepton Mallet, Somerset BA4 4QP
Tel: 01749 880417
Fax: 01749 880764
East Somerset Railway is run by a charitable trust and is based just outside Shepton Mallet at Cranmore railway station. The engine shed and workshops are open to the public, where you can see how to prepare and maintain the steam engines and rolling stock. The workshops contain engines and stock in process of restoration.

A Picnic Area and Children's playground are next to the station, and there is ample parking for cars and coaches. Disabled facilities include station access, disabled toilets and ramps onto trains. The Whistlestop Restaurant offers a range of snacks, meals and drinks for all the family, and is open every day trains are running.

she needed. As she grew older the time came for her to keep her part of the bargain with the Devil and, one stormy night, he brought a horse and cart to the cave ready to carry her to Hell. Piercing screams were heard from the cave along with the cracking of a whip and the creaking of wheels and, next morning, there was no sign of Nancy but the cave walls were stamped with the impressions of horse's hooves and cartwheel tracks.

To the southwest of the town lies a former residence of the abbots of Glastonbury, **Pilton Manor**, whose grounds have been planted with vines,

THE KINGS ARMS HOTEL

Leg Square, Garston Street, Shepton Mallet, Somerset
Tel: 01749 343781
website: www.dusthole.co.uk
The Kings Arms Hotel is a 17th century Somerset stone building with a tiled roof, ornate windows and a very distinctive interior that combines the charm of old England with French-style furniture. Tony Cockayne runs this convivial establishment with his two sons, and visitors can arrive throughout the day and evening to enjoy good hospitality, good beer and excellent home cooking that centres round a popular carvery. Barbecues take place in the beer garden, and there's occasional live music for entertainment; more regular entertainment is provided by the family of badgers who turn up at the front of the pub at about 8 o'clock every evening. The Hotel's accommodation comprises seven rooms, three with en suite facilities.

mostly of the German Riesling variety, and visitors are encouraged to stroll around the estate and also take the opportunity of sampling the vineyard's end product. Another legacy of Glastonbury Abbey can be found at **Pilton** village where there is a great cruciform tithe barn that stands on a hill surrounded by beech and chestnut trees although, unfortunately, the barn lost its arch-braced roof when it was struck by lightning in 1963.

DOULTING

6½ miles E of Wells on the A361

This ancient village dates back to the 8th century when King Ine gave the local estate to Glastonbury Abbey after his nephew, St Aldhelm, died here in AD709. The saint's body was taken back to Malmesbury – where he was abbot – via a circuitous route that is marked by a series of tall stone crosses. Meanwhile, in the garden of the village's former vicarage is a

THE HORSE & JOCKEY

Binegar Lane, Binegar, Somerset BA3 4UH
Tel: 01749 840537
e-mail: clivehowerd@btinternet.com

In a little village off the A37 Shepton Mallet-Midsomer Norton road, the **Horse & Jockey** is a very attractive and well-preserved old inn with young, go-ahead owners in Tonia Howerd and Ruth Williams. In the tiny little bars there's charm to spare, with part-wooden, part flagged floors, low ceilings and an open fire. Food is a major part of the business, and an extensive menu offers traditional home cooking with plenty of fresh local vegetables; booking is advised to be sure of a table in the lovely 35-cover restaurant. Any dish can be ordered to take away. Outside seating on the patio.

THE HORSESHOE INN

Bowlish, Shepton Mallet, Somerset BA4 5JG
Tel: 01749 342209

Landlord Alan Foot describes the **Horseshoe Inn** as a pub for all seasons - warm in winter and cool in summer. It's also a particularly friendly and sociable place, and Alan is on first name terms with most of his customers. Pool and bar billiards are played by the locals, and every other Saturday there's live music. Alan has many contacts in the music business, some of whose photographs are on the walls. Barbecues take place in the beer garden and there ia an excellent Sunday lunch with great-value roasts. To drink, there are three real ales and a good selection of draught lagers. Budget overnight accommodation is provided in four rooms that share a bathroom. The inn lies on the A371 Wells road half a mile out of Shepton Mallet.

THE STRODE ARMS

West Cranmore, Nr Shepton Mallet, Somerset BA4 4QJ
Tel: 01749 880450 Fax: 01749 880823

Dating back in part to the 14th century, the **Strode Arms** enjoys a splendid setting by the village pond in West Cranmore, 2 miles outside Shepton Mallet on the A361 Frome road. The landlords Helen and Ray McBain arrived here early in 2002 with many years of experience in the trade, and they look set to make their mark in this classic country pub, whose public rooms retain the period charm of stone-faced walls and low exposed beams. Freshness is the watchword in the kitchen, which produces excellent meals served every session by friendly, efficient staff. The inn has plenty of outside seating, either on the patio or in the rear beer garden, and there's ample off-road parking.

spring that, along with the church and a statue, is dedicated to St Aldhelm and the village's 15th century **Tithe Barn** is a reminder that the local tenant farmers paid a proportion of the crops each year to their ecclesiastical landlords.

Doulting is also home to one of the stations on the **East Somerset Railway** (see panel on page 135), that was founded by the wildlife artist David Shepherd in 1975, on the original broad gauge line that dates from the 1850s. Run by enthusiasts, the line stretches for three miles and it has an outstanding collection of steam locomotives that range in size from the tiny *Lord Fisher* to the mighty *Black Prince*.

BATCOMBE
10 miles SE of Wells off the A359

This secluded community, whose name comes from the Saxon for 'Bata's Valley', is surrounded by an Area of Outstanding Natural Beauty and it has one of the finest church towers in the whole of the county. The tower was built in the 16th century on the proceeds of the village's thriving wool industry and, at that time, there were nine cloth mills in the district that produced more woven fabric than those along the River Avon between Bath and Bristol.

CASTLE CARY
9½ miles SE of Wells on the B3152

This lovely little town's name is derived from 'Kari', a 7th century word that probably means pleasant stream, and both Iron Age and Bronze Age forts are thought to have been located nearby on Lodge Hill. The addition of the Castle came in the 12th century when Robert of Bampton constructed an impressive Norman fortification here of which nothing can be seen today. Thought to have been the fifth largest castle in Britain at that time, it featured heavily in the reign of King Stephen and was a central point of the

civil war between the king and his cousin the Empress Maud. The granting of a market charter by Edward IV in 1468 raised Castle Cary's status to a town and, whilst there was still a heavy reliance on agriculture and thatching, the wool trade was dominant. As the woollen industry in the southwest began to decline, horsehair weaving became a major employer in Castle Cary in the 19th century and, today, it is home to the only horsehair weaver in Britain and one of just two that survive in Europe – the other is in France.

Today, Castle Cary has an atmosphere of mature rural calm as well as some interesting old buildings. There is a handsome 18th century post office, a tiny lock-up gaol (one of only four left in the country) called the **Round House** that dates from the 1770s and a splendid Market House with a magnificent 17th century colonnade. Largely constructed in 1855, the Market House is now the home of the **Castle Cary District Museum**. However, perhaps the most interesting site here is the town's **War Memorial**, which stands in the middle of a pond that is said to be part of the old castle moat and where, in days gone by, scolds and witches received their punishment of a ducking.

BRUTON
11 miles SE of Wells on the A359

This remarkably well-preserved former clothing and ecclesiastical centre, beside the River Brue, is more like a small town than a village. The priory was first established here in the 11th century and although much of this has now gone the former priory church is now the parish church. With a rare second tower that was built over the north porch in the late 14th century, the interior of the **Church of St Mary** is well worth a visit as, not only is it light and spacious, but it contains a number of memorials to the Berkeley family, the local lords of the manor who also owned the land on which London's Berkeley Square now stands.

Across the river from the church is the **Patwell Pump**, a curious square structure that was the parish's communal water pump that remained in use until well into the 20th century and is a rare working example of a public pump. Meanwhile, further downstream a 15th century packhorse bridge can be seen near the site of the famous part 16th century King's School. However, **The Dovecote** is arguably Bruton's most distinctive building and it can be seen on the crest of a hill to the south of the bridge. Built in the 15th century, it is thought, due to its strategic position, to have doubled as a watchtower. For an insight into the history of this old fashioned town there is a good local **Museum** whilst, on the edge of Bruton, is a 1,000 year old working mill – **Gant's Mill**.

SPARKFORD
12½ miles SE of Wells on the A359

This village is home to the **Haynes Motor Museum** that is thought to hold the largest collection of veteran, vintage and classic cars and motorbikes in the United Kingdom. This unique collection has over 300 exhibits, including military vehicles, and each one is driven (or ridden) at least once every six months around a specially

constructed demonstration track. Open daily all year round, there is an adventure playground, restoration workshops to view, a restaurant and a souvenir and gift shop.

Just to the east of Sparkford lies **Cadbury Castle**, a massive Iron Age hill fort and a centre of craft, trade and religious worship that was developed from a modest Bronze Age settlement. First occupied over 5,000 years ago when it was probably the capital of the Durotriges, whose lands extended across central and southern Somerset and Dorset, the settlement was, at first, ignored by the Romans but they are then reputed to have carried out a massacre here in around AD 70 when they put down a revolt by the ancient Britons. A major excavation in the 1960s uncovered a wealth of Roman and pre-Roman remains on the site as well as confirming that there was certainly a 6th century fortification on the hilltop. This particular discovery certainly ties the castle in with King Arthur who, at around that time, was spearheading the Celtic British resistance against the advancing Saxons. Indeed, if Cadbury Castle had been Arthur's Camelot, it is likely that is would have been a timber fortification rather than the turreted stone structure described by the storybooks.

This easily defended hilltop was again fortified during the reign of Ethelred the

THE THREE OLD CASTLES INN

Castle Street, Keinton Mandeville, Somerton, Somerset TA11 6DX
Tel: 01458 223619 Fax: 01458 224092

The Three Old Castles is a long, two storey stone building in a village on the B3153, three miles east of Somerton. This is one of the most sociable pubs in the area, with a welcome for all the family from owner Lorraine Higgins and her cheerful staff. In the bar, a fine selection of beers, lagers, wines and spirits is served; food runs from a great selection of small plate dishes to curries and a hearty mixed grill, and the Sunday lunch is always very popular. In the Sports Bar major events are shown on big-screen tv, and the inn has a beer garden where barbecues take place, a play area for children and a skittle alley. Outside bar catering can be arranged.

Unready in the early 11th century and the poorly-advised king also established a mint here in around 1000 although most of the coinage minted at Cadbury was used to buy off the invading Danes in an act of appeasement that led to the term Danegeld. As a consequence, most of the surviving coins from the Cadbury mint are now to be found in the museums of Scandinavia.

The mile-long walk around Cadbury Castle's massive earthwork ramparts demonstrates the site's effectiveness as a defensive position but, although this allowed those at the castle to see enemy troop movements in days gone by, it now provides spectacular panoramic views for today's visitors.

WINCANTON
14 miles SE of Wells off the A303

This attractive old cloth-making town was also a bustling coaching town as it lies almost exactly half way between London and the long-established naval base at Plymouth. In the heyday of stagecoaches, up to 20 a day would stop here and, at that time, the inns could provide lodging for scores of travellers and stabling for over 250 horses. The oldest part of the town stands on a draughty hillside above the River Cale and a surprising number of fine Georgian buildings, some of which were constructed to replace earlier buildings

destroyed in a fire in 1747, can be found here.

Modern day Wincanton is a peaceful light industrial town whose best known attraction, **Wincanton National Hunt Racecourse**, harks back to the days when horses were the only form of transport. Horse racing began in the area in the 18th century and the racecourse moved to its present site to the north of the town centre in 1927. Regular meetings are held here between October and May and, recently, it is remembered as the course where Desert Orchid had his first race of each season during his dominance of steeple chasing in the 1980s. Meanwhile, for golf enthusiasts, the racecourse incorporates a challenging nine-hole pay and play course which is open throughout the year. Also worth visiting is the beautiful **Hadspen House Gardens** that are situated just to the northwest of the town.

TEMPLECOMBE
16 miles SE of Wells on the A357

To the east of the village is the unusual **Gartell Light Railway**, a rare 2-foot gauge line, that runs for around a mile through the beautiful countryside of Blackmore Vale on the trackbed of the Somerset and Dorset Railway that was closed over 30 years ago. The trains run every 15 minutes from Common Line Station, which also has a visitor centre, refreshment room and

shop. Meanwhile, the nearby **Templecombe Railway Museum** houses a fascinating collection of artefacts, photographs and models that tell the story of the nearby station that was once a busy junction where some 130 railwaymen worked.

BALTONSBOROUGH
6½ miles S of Wells off the A361

One of the 12 manors of Glastonbury Abbey, which lies just to the northwest, the lives of the people of the village were completely governed by the monks and the permission of the abbey had to be sought before a daughter could be married whilst on a man's death his chattels and beasts became the property of the abbey. It was also here, between AD909 and AD925, that St Dunstan is said to have been born and the ancient flour mill in the village is thought to have been owned by Dunstan's father. Before entering Glastonbury Abbey, Dunstan found favour at the court of King Athelstan but, once he had given up his worldly posessions, Dunstan restricted himself to a particularly austere regime. By setting himself apart from the abbey's other novices, Dunstan was soon to rise through the ranks of the religious house and he quickly became abbot whereupon he enforced the strict code of the Benedictines that had, before his appointment, been neglected by the monks. The wealth of Glastonbury grew under Dunstan and he also encouraged pilgrims to make their way here to see the holy relics. Along with being a great cleric and an entrepreneur, Dunstan was also an engineer and he was one of the first people to instigate the draining of the land in this area. From Glastonbury, Dunstan moved to Canterbury, where he was Archbishop up until his death.

PENNARD HILL FARM

East Pennard, Nr Shepton Mallet, Somerset BA4 6UG
Tel: 01749 890221 Fax: 01749 890665
e-mail: phebejudah@aol.com www.pennardhillfarm.co.uk

Phoebe Judah has meticulously renovated The **Pennard Hill Farm** Estate to suit her own high standards. The farm is on the summit of the southern most ridge of the Mendips, surrounded by pretty fields, far reaching views and tranquility. The accommodation offers luxury, privacy and a variety of styles and combinations, all with amazing decor and the house is a veritable Pandora's Box of objets d'art. Beds are antique with beautiful linen. Old fashioned good quality and service. Pheobe now presides over one of the most lavish and luxurious B&B's in the country.

Facing the house across the cobblestoned courtyard is a Victorian Barn, two thirds of which houses a superb heated pool. The remaining third forms an apartment for two with huge bedroom and bathroom upstairs and a fully equipped kitchen/living area downstairs. The main house offers the Master bedroom with its own staircase leading up from its private drawing room, or the Old Cellar suite with amazing Uzbek decor. There are also 3 single rooms.

In addition there are two cottages on the estate available on a nightly basis:The Golden Fleece offers a huge amount of living space: Drawing room with log fire, vast modern kitchen/dining room and sunroom. It has three double bedrooms and one single. Newly renovated, the cottage offers airy living space with great comfort in a contemporary style. It has its own garden and open views. The Lamb cottage is a retreat for two. Stylishly converted, it has a large double bedroom and bathroom upstairs and a kitchen/living room with log fire downstairs. Its all superb - and in its entirety can offer 16 beds.

THE ROSE & PORTCULLIS

Sub Road, Butleigh, Somerset BA6 8TQ
Tel: 01458 850287 Fax: 01458 850120

A delightful name for a delightful old inn. Tucked away down country lanes south of Glastonbury and Street, the **Rose & Portcullis** is a compact 17th century stone building in a peaceful rural hamlet. Neat and spotlessly kept by the proud owner, it has a cosy, inviting feel, and in the oak-furnished restaurant fresh, wholesome home-cooked dishes are served every lunchtime and evening. In fine weather the scene shifts to the garden, which has picnic benches, colourful tubs of flowers and a children's play area with swings and a slide. Back inside, it's skittles and darts at this super place.

STREET
7 miles SW of Wells on the A39

The oldest part of this now sprawling town lies around the 14th century parish Church of the Holy Trinity although most of the town itself dates from the 19th century when it began to expand from a small rural village into the light industrial town of today. Much of this growth was due to one family, the Clarks, when, in the 1820s, the Quaker brothers, Cyrus and James Clark began to produce sheepskin slippers from the hides of local animals. Many of the town's older buildings owe their existence to the family and, in particular, there is the **Friends' Meeting House** of 1850 and the building that housed the original **Millfield School**, still a thriving public school today with an international reputation particularly for sport. The oldest part of the Clark's factory has now been converted into a fascinating **Shoe Museum** and, although the company is one of the largest manufacturers of quality footwear in Europe, it continues to keep its headquarters in the town. Open daily, all year round, the museum explores the history of shoe-making from as far back as Roman times whilst **Clarks Village** is a large outlet shopping complex with restaurants and attractions for children.

GLASTONBURY
5½ miles SW of Wells on the A39

This ancient town of myths and legends, whose name is derived from the Saxon 'Glaestingaburgh' meaning hill fort of the Glaestings, is, today, an attractive market town that is still dominated by the ruins of its abbey that continue to bring visitors to the town. The dramatic remains of **Glastonbury Abbey** (see panel on page 142) lie in the heart of the old town and it is the site of the earliest Christian foundation in the British Isles. It is said that it was here that the followers of Jesus landed shortly after

Glastonbury Abbey

GLASTONBURY ABBEY

Glastonbury, Somerset BA6 9EL
Tel: 01458 832267 Fax: 01458 832267
e-mail: glastonbury.abbey@dial.pipex.com
website: www.glastonburyabbey.com

Set in the middle of the old market town, **Glastonbury Abbey** has been an influence on the lives of those who have lived in this part of the world for the past 1950 years and there are many people who believe that the 'Somerset Tradition' makes the association even longer than that. It is said that it was here that the followers of Jesus landed shortly after His death and set up the first Christian settlement with its own church in Britain. Some traditions go further and suggest that Christ

Himself came to Glastonbury as a boy on one of the boats of his great uncle, Joseph of Arimathea. The legends around Glastonbury suggest that it was Joseph of Arimathea, and not St Augustine centuries later, who started the Christian conversion of Great Britain in the 1st century.

What can be said with more certainty is that Glastonbury Abbey was a major Christian sanctuary during the 5th and 6th centuries. By the time of the Norman Conquest, it was considered to be the wealthiest and grandest abbey in the country. Such was its status within England during the Dark Ages that it would be logical that the great Celtic monarch, King Arthur, should be buried here after his long struggle against the Saxons.

Following the Dissolution in the 16th century, the abbey fell into ruins and King Arthur's tomb was destroyed. Nevertheless, a number of impressive remains have survived and these include **St Mary's Chapel**, the shell of the great church, and the 14th century **Abbot's Kitchen**. However, people coming here today come for three main reasons: to see where the first church might have existed, to see where King Arthur and Queen Guinevere might have been buried, and to enjoy the beautiful and peaceful parkland that surrounds the ruins.

The abbey is a private organisation run by trustees and, although a small concern, it remains open throughout the year. Along with the ruins and the parkland, there is an award winning museum and a small abbey shop. Visitors may also come across Brother Thomas Cleeve, the Guestmaster of 1538.

His death whilst some legends go further and suggest that Jesus Himself came to Glastonbury as a boy with his great uncle, Joseph of Arimathea and that it was Joseph, and not St Augustine centuries later, who started the Christian conversion of Great Britain in the 1ˢᵗ century. Certainly, by the 6ᵗʰ century, Glastonbury Abbey was a major Christian sanctuary and, at the time of the Norman Conquest, it was considered to be one of the wealthiest and grandest abbeys in the country.

However, it is the abbey's connection with King Arthur and his wife Queen Guinevere that draw most visitors to Glastonbury. During the 12ᵗʰ century the abbey was destroyed by a fire and when the foundations of the replacement great church were being excavated, a few years later, a wooden sarcophagus was discovered beneath the shafts of the abbey's two ancient crosses. Inside were found the bones of a large man and a slender woman and one story tells of how the woman's long golden hair seemed in perfect condition until a monk touched it and the tresses became dust. A lead cross was also found nearby and these finds convinced the abbot that he had discovered the remains of King Arthur and Queen Guinevere even though it was known that at least three kings from the later Saxon period were also buried here.

However, the abbot's findings were certainly timely as they helped to provide him with much needed funds to pay for the abbey's reconstruction. Glastonbury soon became an important place of pilgrimage and, when the main part of the new abbey had been completed in 1273, Edward I himself arrived to witness the re-interring of Arthur's bones in a magnificent tomb in the choir. The abbey continued to wield considerable power until the Dissolution forced its closure but, today, the picturesque ruins, with their associations with the legend of King Arthur, remain a great tourist attraction.

Along with the ruins of the abbey, the complex here also includes the **Abbot's Kitchen**, which dates from the 1340s and is the only complete building left of the abbey; **St Mary's Chapel**, the first building to be erected after the Great Fire and where, though now a shell, the elaborate carvings can still be seen; and an award winning **Museum** that describes the history and life of the abbey as well as displaying a model of the pre-Reformation abbey.

During the Middle Ages, Glastonbury Abbey was also an internationally renowned centre of learning and scholars, as well as pilgrims, from all over Christendom made their way here. Eventually the numbers of visitors became so great that a guest house was built outside the abbey walls. Originally constructed in 1475, the **George and**

Pilgrim Hotel is a striking building whose old timber beams are adorned with carved angels and whose interior is guarded by a series of curious monks' death masks. Close by is another 15th century building, the handsome **Tribunal** that is home to the town's Tourist Information Centre and the **Glastonbury Lake Village Museum**, which contains finds from one of Europe's most famous archaeological sites. Even the town's **Somerset Rural Life Museum**, which explores the life of farmers in this area during the 19th and early 20th centuries, cannot escape from the influence of the abbey as, although the museum is housed in a Victorian farmhouse and its associated buildings, there is also an impressive 14th century barn here that once belonged to Glastonbury Abbey. The museum is open all year round except non Bank Holiday Mondays and winter Sundays.

Glastonbury Tor

To the east of the town lies another site that is renowned for its ecclesiastical, secular and legendary connections. **Glastonbury Tor** is a dramatic hill that rises above the surrounding Somerset Levels that were drained in the 18th century. A dominant feature of the landscape, one of the earliest visitors to the tor was the early Christian trader, Joseph of Arimathea, who is said to have arrived here in around AD 60. Many legends abound but one tells that, whilst he was walking on the tor, Joseph drove his staff into the grown whereupon it took root and burst into leaf. Taking this as a sign that he should build a church, Joseph erected a simple church on the site that is now taken by the abbey, and his staff is reputed to have grown into the celebrated Christmas-flowering Glastonbury Hawthorn.

The 520 foot tor has been inhabited since prehistoric times and excavations on the site have revealed evidence of Celtic, Roman and pre-Saxon occupation. Because of its unusually regular conical shape the hill has long been associated with myth and legends and, in its time, it has been identified as the Land of the Dead, the Celtic Otherworld, a Druid's temple, a magic mountain, an Arthurian hill fort, a ley line intersection and a rendezvous point for passing UFOs. Along with its mystical energy, the tor also offers magnificent panoramic views across Somerset to Wells, the Mendips, the Quantocks and the Bristol Channel. The striking tower at the summit is all that remains of the 15th century **Church of St Michael**, an offshoot of Glastonbury Abbey. Meanwhile, between the tor and the town lies the wooded rise of **Chalice Hill**, where, it is said, Joseph buried the Holy Grail, the chalice used at the Last Supper, in a well.

To the northwest of the town is the site of a prehistoric **Lake Village** that was discovered in 1892 when Arthur Bulleid and his colleague, Harold St George Gray, noticed that the otherwise level fields was studded with irregular mounds. Thought to have been inhabited from 250 BC until 50 BC, the dwellings were built on a series of tall platforms that raised them above the surrounding marshland.

MEARE
6½ miles SW of Wells on the B3151

Just to the east of this attractive village is an unusual medieval building that is known as the **Abbot's Fish House**. Before around 1700, this isolated building stood on the edge of **Meare Pool**, once a substantial lake that provided nearby Glastonbury Abbey with a regular supply of freshwater fish and, before the lake was drained, this early 14th century building was used for storing fishing equipment and salting the catches.

Meanwhile, to the southwest of Meare, in terrain that is scarred by years of peat extraction, is the **Shapwick Heath Nature Reserve** that provides a safe haven for rare plants and wildlife. To the northwest, at **Westhay**, is the **Peat Moor Visitor Centre**, which offers visitors a fascinating insight into the history and ecology of the Somerset Levels and, through a series of imaginative displays, describes the development of commercial peat digging, the special trades that have grown up in this unique environment and the measures that have been taken to conserve the area's flora and fauna. The centre also has some interesting reconstructions including one of the Sweet Trace, the oldest known trackway in Britain that was discovered in the 1970s after having laid buried for around 5,000 years, and roundhouses from Glastonbury Lake Village. Open daily from April to the end of October, the centre has many other interesting Iron Age attractions and a small herd of Soay sheep that are similar to the breeds that were kept in ancient times.

WOOKEY HOLE
1½ miles NW of Wells off the A371

The village, in the rolling uplands of the Mendip Hills, is a popular place with

Wookey Hole

THE PHEASANT INN
Worth Wookey, Nr Wells, Somerset BA5 1LQ
Tel: 01749 672355

David Blomeley and his daughter Charlotte are maintaining a long tradition of hospitality at the **Pheasant Inn**, which stands on the B3139 a couple of miles west of Wells. Behind the fine old stone frontage the inn offers a pleasing mix of old-fashioned country charm (log fires, flag floors) and modern comfort that appeals to locals and tourists alike. Cooking is a blend of the best of English and Italian cuisine, and the steaks - large, tender and cooked to a T - are among the most popular orders. Lighter snacks are also available, and the inn has an off-road car park, a family garden and a skittle alley that doubles as a function room. Open 11-3 and 6-11.

THE SLAB HOUSE INN

West Horrington, Nr Wells, Somerset BA5 3EQ
Tel: 01749 840310 Fax: 01749 840358
website: www.slabhouseinn.co.uk

The **Slab House Inn** dates back to the 15th century and quality is the keynote throughout. Alan and Margaret Gripton's grand inn has a handsome stone frontage with a full-length veranda and a beautifully appointed interior with flag floors and exposed beams. In the restaurant, immaculate pink linen, sparkling crystal and gleaming cutlery create the setting for enjoying an excellent meal featuring top-quality ingredients on a menu offering traditional and modern dishes. Roast duckling served with an orange or black cherry & Dubonnet sauce is a speciality, and other favourites include poached salmon hollandaise and steaks. There's a good choice for vegetarians, and scrumptious desserts round off a fine meal.

walkers, cavers and motorised sightseers who are drawn to Wookey Hole not only by the tearooms but also by the natural formations found here. Throughout the centuries, the carboniferous limestone core of the hills has been gradually dissolved away by the small amount of carbonic acid in rainwater and this erosion has created over 25 caverns around Wookey Hole of which only the largest half dozen or so are open to the public. The **Great Cave** contains a rock formation known as the Witch of Wookey who is said to have been turned to stone for her evil ways. Legend tells how the witch, who lived in the cave, had been crossed in love and, out of vindictiveness, she cast spells on the local people who, frightened by her deeds, appealed to the Abbot of Glastonbury to remove the harridan. A monk was sent to the cave and, as she tried to flee as her spells were useless against good, the monk sprinkled her with holy water and she turned to stone. In 1912, excavations in the cave uncovered the skeleton of a Romano-British woman together with a comb, a dagger and a round stalagmite that looks like a witch's crystal ball. During prehistoric times, lions, bears and woolly mammoths lived in the area and, in a recess known as the **Hyena's Den**, a large cache of bones have been found and many of them show other animal's tooth marks.

The river emerging from Wookey Hole, the River Axe, has been harnessed to provide power since the 15th century and the present building here was originally constructed in the early 17th century as a paper mill.

Just to the northwest lies the dramatic **Ebbor Gorge** that is now a National Nature Reserve managed by English Nature. There are two walks here: the shorter one that is suitable for wheelchairs accompanied by a strong pusher and a longer walk that involves a certain amount of rock scrambling. However, the hard work is rewarded as there is a wealth of wildlife here, including badger and sparrow hawk in the woodland, lesser horseshoe bats in and around the caves and buzzard can often be seen flying overhead.

Wookey Hole

4 South and West Somerset (including Exmoor)

This region of Somerset is characterised by ancient Saxon towns and villages, willows growing on the old marshlands of the Somerset Levels and warm honey-coloured stone buildings. Despite having been founded by the Saxon King Ine in the 8th century, Taunton did not become the county town until the 1930s but this charming place, with many buildings of interest including the Somerset County Cricket Museum, is an excellent place from which to begin an exploration of the southern area of Somerset.

East Quantoxhead

To the north and east of Taunton lie the Somerset Levels, an area of marshland that, from medieval times onwards, have continued to be drained to provide rich and fertile farmland. Crossed by the Rivers Parrett, Isle and Cary, drainage ditches, locally known as rhines, have been constructed, and it is these, lined with rows of pollarded willows, that provide visitors with one of the regions most characteristic sights of the area. For centuries the willows, or withies, have been cut and woven into baskets and, today, the basket-weaving industry that has been so important to southern and central Somerset is once again enjoying a revival. Over the centuries, any land rising above the marshes has given rise to a host of legends and, in particular, there is Burrow Mump that is said to have been the site of a fortification belonging to King Alfred whilst it was nearby that he famously burnt the cakes.

The rich area of farmland is also littered with magnificent country and manor houses including Montacute House, which was built in the late 16th century for Elizabeth I's Master of the Rolls, the late medieval stone manor house of Lytes Cary and the Palladian Hatch Court. However, the fine houses are often over-shadowed by their gardens and there are some splendid examples here but, in particular, there are those that have been influenced by the early 20th century landscape gardener, Gertrude Jekyll such as Barrington Court, Hestercombe Gardens and Tintinhull House Gardens.

Once a major port to rival Bristol, Bridgwater's docks have not withstood the test of time as, gradually, the River Parrett silted up. Meanwhile, to the west of Bridgwater lie the Quantock Hills, an Area of Outstanding Natural Beauty that extend from just outside Taunton to the coast at Quantoxhead. Rich with Neolithic and Bronze Age remains as well as plant and wildlife, the southern area of hills provide some of the most fertile agricultural land in Somerset whilst the eastern slopes are famous as being the home of the village of Nether Stowey. In the late 18th century Samuel Taylor Coleridge moved to a cottage in the village and, during the short time that he and his family lived here, the poet composed most of his best known works whilst he also walked the surrounding countryside with his friend and fellow poet William Wordsworth.

Tarr Steps, Exmoor

Finally there is the high moorland plateau of Exmoor National Park, which straddles both Somerset and Devon, and borders the Bristol Channel. Famous for its wild Exmoor ponies, this area is rich in both flora and fauna and it is criss-crossed by a network of paths and bridleways that provide superb opportunities for discovering the hidden delights of this glorious landscape. Romantic Exmoor has become inextricably linked with RD Blackmore's novel *Lorna Doone*, published in 1869, which the novelist based in the area and wrote from childhood memories of the wild moorland whilst living in London.

PLACES TO STAY, EAT, DRINK AND SHOP

128	Fleet Air Museum, RNAS Yeovilton	Museum	page 151
129	The King's Arms Inn & Restaurant, Bishopton	Pub, Restaurant & Accommodation	page 151
130	Montacute TV And Radio Museum, Montacute	Museum	page 153
131	Halfway House, Chilthorne Domer, nr Yeovil	Pub, Restaurant & Accommodation	page 153
132	The Rose & Crown, Bower Hinton, nr Martock	Pub and Restaurant	page 154
133	The Buttercross Tearooms, Somerton	Café and Tea Shop	page 156
134	The Globe Inn, Somerton	Pub with Food	page 156
135	The Castlebrook Inn, Compton Dundon	Pub with Food	page 156
136	The Happy Return, Chard	Restaurant	page 160
137	Chard and District Museum, Chard	Museum	page 160
138	The Duke Of York, Shepton Beauchamp	Pub and Restaurant	page 161
139	Poulett Arms, Lopen Head	Pub with Food	page 162
140	Forde Abbey, Chard	Abbey	page 164
141	Monkton Inn, West Monkton, nr Taunton	Pub and Restaurant	page 168
142	The Old Ship Inn, Combwich, nr Bridgewater	Pub with Food	page 169
143	King William, Catcott, nr Bridgewater	Pub with Food	page 169
144	Laburnum House Hotel, West Huntspill	Hotel and Restaurant	page 170
145	Puriton Inn, Puriton, nr Bridgewater	Pub with Food	page 170
146	The Knowle Inn, Knowle, nr Bridgewater	Pub, Food & Accommodation	page 170
147	Apple View, Chedzoy, nr Bridgewater	Bed and Breakfast	page 170

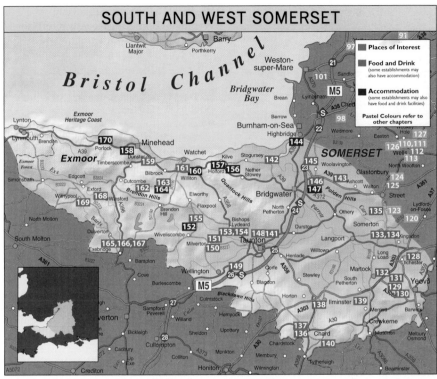

SOUTH AND WEST SOMERSET

Bristol Channel

Bristol Channel Bay

Places of Interest

Food and Drink
(some establishments may
also have accommodation)

Accommodation
(some establishments may also
have food and drink facilities)

**Pastel Colours refer to
other chapters**

SOMERSET

Exmoor

Exmoor Heritage Coast

© MAPS IN MINUTES ™ 2002   © Crown Copyright, Ordnance Survey 2002

148	Hestercombe Gardens, Cheddon Fitzpaine	Gardens	page 172
149	The Blackbird Inn, West Buckland	Pub, Food & Accommodation	page 173
150	The Globe, Milverton, nr Taunton	Pub, Food & Accommodation	page 175
151	New Inn, Halse, nr Taunton	Pub, Food & Accommodation	page 175
152	Langley House Hotel, Langley Marsh	Hotel and Restaurant	page 176
153	Bird in Hand, Bishops Lydeard, nr Taunton	Pub with Food	page 176
154	The Bell Inn, Bishops Lydeard, nr Taunton	Pub and Restaurant	page 176
155	Gaulden Manor Gardens and House, Exmoor	Gardens	page 177
156	Alfoxton Park, Holford, nr Bridgwater	Hotel	page 179
157	The Old Rectory, Kilve	Bed and Breakfast	page 179
158	Rose-Ash etc. Cottages, Tivington	Self Catering	page 180
159	Dunster Water Mill, Dunster	Water Mill	page 182
160	Daisy Cottage, Williton	Self Catering	page 185
161	Ceramics by Martin Pettinger, Williton	Pottery Gallery	page 185
162	The Royal Oak Inn, Luxborough	Pub, Restaurant & Accommodation	page 186
163	The Valiant Soldier, Roadwater, nr Watchet	Pub, Food & Accommodation	page 186
164	Wood Advent Farm, Roadwater	Hotel	page 186
165	Lion Hotel, Dulverton	Pub, Restaurant & Accommodation	page 188
166	Rock House Inn, Dulverton	Pub, Food & Accommodation	page 188
167	archiamma, Dulverton	Restaurant	page 188
168	The Royal Oak Inn, Winsford	Pub, Restaurant & Accommodation	page 188
169	The Royal Oak Inn, Withypool, nr Exmoor	Pub, Restaurant & Accommodation	page 189
170	Porlock Vale House, Porlock	Hotel and Restaurant	page 191

YEOVIL

Taking its name from the River Yeo (sometimes called the River Ivel) beside which it stands, the Romans were the first settlers here although the town really began to develop in the Middle Ages when a market was established that continues to be held here every Friday. Yeovil's parish **Church of St John the Baptist** is the only significant medieval structure to survive as most of its other early buildings were destroyed by a series of fires that struck the town in the 17th century. A substantial building, with a solid-looking tower, the church dates from the late 14th century and it has a surprisingly austere exterior given its exceptional number of windows. Indeed, it has so many windows that it is sometimes referred to as the 'Lantern of the West'.

During the 18th century, Yeovil developed into a flourishing coaching centre due to its strategic position at the junction of several main routes and industries such as glove-making, leather working, sailcloth making and cheese manufacture began to develop in the town. This rapid expansion was enhanced by the arrival of the railway in the mid 19th century and then, in the 1890s, James Petter, a local ironmonger and pioneer of the internal combustion engine, founded a business that went on to become one of the largest manufacturers of diesel engines in Britain. Although production was eventually transferred to the Midlands, a subsidiary set up to produce aircraft during World War I has since evolved into a helicopter plant.

Today, Yeovil retains its importance geographically and, along with being south Somerset's largest concentration of population, it is a thriving commercial, shopping, and market town that is, perhaps, best known as the home of

Westland Helicopters. Situated in Wyndham House, the recently refurbished **Museum of South Somerset** documents the social and industrial history of the town and surrounding area, from prehistoric times to the present. Through a series of imaginative displays and exhibits the fascinating atmosphere of times past, from the days of the Romans to the agricultural and industrial revolutions, are brought to life.

AROUND YEOVIL

YEOVILTON
4 miles N of Yeovil off the A37

This pleasant village, with its medieval church and some old stone cottages, is home to the **Fleet Air Arm Museum** (see panel opposite) one of the world's leading aviation museums that contains a unique collection of aircraft. Through the succession of superb exhibits, visitors can gain an excellent impression of the development of the country's flying Navy but there is much more to the museum than just a hangar full of old and not so old aircraft and the stories of the men and women of naval aviation are told here. The museum also has a children's adventure playground, a souvenir shop and airfield viewing galleries.

BARWICK
1½ miles S of Yeovil off the A37

Pronounced 'barrik', this village is home to **Barwick Park**, an estate that is littered with bizarre follies. Arranged at the four points of the compass, the eastern folly, known as **Jack the Treacle Eater**, is composed of a rickety stone arch topped by a curious turreted room. According to local stories, the folly is named after a foot messenger who ran back and forth between the estate and London on a diet

FLEET AIR ARM MUSEUM

RNAS Yeovilton, Ilchester, Somerset BA22 8HT
Tel: 01935 840565 Fax: 01935 842630
website: www.fleetairarm.com

The Fleet Air Arm Museum is one of the world's largest aviation museums, extending over 6.5 acres. Come and experience the exciting development of Britains Flying Navy, in a succession of superb exhibits. The museum is much more than a hanger full of vintage aircraft, it is a highly imaginative collection, telling the stories of men and women of naval aviation.

"Leading Edge" is a new exhibition providing an exciting new environment for visitors, with touch screen interactives, dramatic lighting, which when combined with the roar of Concorde's engines, creates a vivid and atmospheric interpretation. Visitors learn more about the history and background of the exhibits through video information stations.

The museum's ability to cater for all ages and interests come rain or shine is enhanced by excellent facilities, including car and coach park, disabled facilities, adventure playground, picnic area, viewing galleries, shop and restaurant.

of nothing more than bread and treacle. The estate also possesses a curious grotto and a handsome church with a Norman font and an unusual 17th century transeptal tower.

WEST COKER
3 miles SW of Yeovil on the A30

Found in the lanes just to the east of this village is the magnificent **Brympton d'Evercy Manor House** that originally dates from Norman times but that was significantly added to in the 16th and 17th centuries. In particular, there is the superb golden Hamstone south wing that was built in Jacobean times to a design by Inigo Jones. Among the many fine internal features the manor house is home to the longest straight single span staircase in Britain and an unusual modern tapestry that depicts an imaginary bird's eye view of the property during the 18th century. When viewed from a distance, the mansion house, the little estate church and the nearby dower house make a delightful lakeside grouping.

MONTACUTE
3½ miles W of Yeovil off the A3088

This charming village of golden Hamstone houses and cottages is also home to the magnificent Elizabethan mansion, **Montacute House** (National Trust) that was built in the 1590s for Edward Phelips, Elizabeth I's Master of the Rolls by, probably, William Arnold, the architect of Wadham College, Oxford. There have been, over the centuries, some alterations made to the house and the most notable of these was in the late 18th century when the west front was remodelled by another Edward Phelips. In

THE KING'S ARMS INN & RESTAURANT

Bishopton, Montacute, Somerset TA15 6UU
Tel: 01935 822513 Fax: 01935 826549 e-mail: dearsley@supernet.com

The King's Arms is a distinguished former cider and alehouse with a golden hamstone facade, small-paned windows and heavy oak doors. It nestles at the bottom of a steep hill in a picturesque village, offering relaxation, comfort, good food and first-class accommodation all overseen by owners Elizabeth and Richard Dearsley. Head chef Mark Lane and his team prepare an impressive range of menus running from bar snacks and lunchtime specials to an evening à la carte and daily table d'hote. In the Abbey Lounge, guests can relax in deep settees round a fire with the papers, or taking morning coffee, afternoon tea or coffee and liqueurs after dinner. The 15 en suite bedrooms include doubles, twins, a four-poster rooms and a family room for up to four guests.

the 19th century the fortunes of the Phelips family began to decline and, in the 1920s, following a succession of tenants, the house was put up for sale and, eventually, a gift from Ernest Cook (the grandson of the travel agent Thomas Cook) enabled the Trust to purchase this wonderful Elizabethan residence. The long gallery, one of the grandest of its kind in Britain, houses a fine collection of Tudor and

Montacute House

Jacobean portraits that are on permanent loan from London's National Portrait Gallery. Meanwhile, other noteworthy features include the stone and stained glass screen in the great hall and Lord Curzon's bath, an Edwardian addition that is concealed in a bedroom cupboard. An established story tells how Curzon, a senior Tory politician, waited at Montacute in 1923 for news that he was to be called to form a new government but the call never came. The house stands within a magnificent landscaped park that incorporates a walled formal garden, a fig walk, an orangery and a cedar lawn that is formally known as 'Pig's Wheaties's Orchard'. The house is open daily (except for Tuesdays) between April and the end of October.

Further back in time, some 500 years before Montacute House was built, a controversial castle was erected on the nearby hill by Robert, Count of Mortain. However, the count's choice of site angered the local Saxons as they believed the hill to be sacred as it is thought that King Alfred had buried a fragment of Christ's cross there. In 1068, they rose up and attacked the castle in one of the many unsuccessful revolts against the Norman occupation. Ironically, a subsequent Count of Mortain was found guilty of treason and forced

into founding and donating all his lands in the area to a Cluniac priory on the site that is now occupied by Montacute village. The castle has long since disappeared, as has the monastery, with the exception of its fine 16th century gatehouse (that is now a private home) and a stone dovecote.

Montacute village is also the home of the **TV and Radio Memorabilia Museum** (see panel opposite) where a vast collection of vintage radios, wireless receivers and television sets, from the 1920s through to the present day, are on display. Here, too, is a wealth of memorabilia on a wide range of classic television and radio programmes, from *The Archers* and *Coronation Street* to *Startrek* and *Thunderbirds*. The collection housed here today was started by Dennis Greenham who, in the 1930s, set up his own business charging accumulators before expanding it into an electrical business that still thrives today. The museum, which has itself featured in several television programmes, is open daily between Easter and October but is closed on Sunday mornings and some Tuesdays in the early and late season.

TINTINHULL
4 miles NW of Yeovil off the A303

This sprawling village is home to a number

MONTACUTE TV AND RADIO MUSEUM

1 South Street, Montacute, Somerset TA15 6XD
Tel: 01935 823024
website: www.montacutemuseum.co.uk

The Montacute TV and Radio Museum in the picturesque village of Montacute has been used in the filming of Jane Austen's *Sense and Sensibility* and featured on television, including Channel 4's *Collectors Lot* and the BBC's *Antiques Inspectors*. The museum has also made contributions to the BBC's *I Love the 70s* and *80s* series. The vast collection of fascinating memorabilia, including toys, books and games, is guaranteed to bring back memories of classic TV and radio programmes. The collection also includes the automated puppets from the favourite 1970s children's cartoon *Top Cat*.

The television themes covered at the museum include other children's favourites such as *Sooty*, *The Magic Roundabout* and *Twizzle*, westerns such as *Wagon Train* and *Gun Law*, science fiction featuring *Dr Who*, *Star Trek* and Gerry Anderson's *Thunderbirds*, quiz shows such as *Double Your Money*, comedy with *Sergeant Bilko* and everyone's favourite soap *Coronation Street*. There are over 500 radio exhibits ranging from vintage wirelesses of the 1920s to the colourful novelty transistors of today. There is *The Archers* and even the ventriloquist's doll from an early Archie Andrews show.

In addition to the vast collection of television and radio memorabilia, there is an extraordinary Alice in Wonderland collection, whilst the museum shop sells a vast range of television and radio related books and games. Visitors can enjoy a tasty meal or light snack along with homemade cakes and real West Country cream teas at the museum's tearooms and gardens. Bed and breakfast accommodation is also available and there are a number of village and woodland walks in the surrounding area.

of interesting buildings that include a remodelled, part-medieval rectory, Tintinhull Court; the 17th century Dower House; and St Margaret's parish church that is a rarity in Somerset as it is a rectangular single-cell church. Meanwhile, the village green is overlooked by another attractive building, Tintinhull House, an early 17th century manor farm (not open to the public) whose grounds, despite the age of the house, was laid out in the early 20th century. A series of distinctive areas, divided by walls and hedges, each with their own planting theme, **Tintinhull House Garden** (National Trust) also has a delightful pool garden with a lily and iris filled pond, a kitchen garden and a sunken garden that is cleverly designed to give the impression it has many different levels.

ILCHESTER

4½ miles NW of Yeovil on the A37

In Roman times, the settlement here stood at the point where the north-south route between Dorchester and the Bristol Channel crossed the Fosse Way. However, it was during the 13th

HALFWAY HOUSE AND COUNTRY LODGE

Chilthorne Domer, near Yeovil, Somerset BA22 8RE
Tel: 01935 840350

A substantial old inn that makes an ideal base from which to explore southwest Somerset, **Halfway House and Country Lodge** offers its customers the very best in country hospitality. A charming family run establishment, owner Paul Rowsell not only keeps an excellent cellar at his inn but there is also a delightful dining area where customers can enjoy a range of tempting dishes from the imaginative varied menu. However, the most outstanding feature of this inn is its superb, newly completed accommodation of eleven purpose-built en suite guest rooms that have all been decorated and furnished to the very highest standards. Finally, along with the friendly hospitality, Halfway House and Country Lodge has a fine beer garden, a children's play area and also a site for up to 20 caravans.

century that Ilchester reached its peak as a centre of administration, agriculture and learning and, like its near neighbour Somerton, this too was, for a time, the county town of Somerset and three substantial gaols were built here – one of which remained in use until the 1840s. Another indication of this town's former status is the 13th century **Ilchester Mace** that is England's oldest staff of office. Up until recently, the mace resided in the town hall but today a replica can be seen here whilst the original mace is now on display in the County Museum at Taunton.

The tiny **Ilchester Museum** can be found in the centre of the town, by the Market Cross, and here the story of the town from pre-Roman times to the 20th century is told through a series of exhibits that include a Roman coffin and skeleton. Ilchester was also the birthplace, in around 1214, of the celebrated scholar, monk and scientist, Roger Bacon, who went on to predict the invention of the aeroplane, telescope and steam engine although he was eventually imprisoned for his outspoken ideas.

STOKE SUB HAMDON
5 miles NW of Yeovil off the A303

Whilst the eastern part of this attractive village is home to a fine Norman church, in the western area of the village can be found the remains of a late medieval priory. **Stoke sub Hamdon Priory** (National Trust) was built in the 14th and 15th centuries for the priests of the now demolished chantry chapel of St Nicholas and the remains here include an impressive great hall.

Meanwhile, to the south of the village lies the 400 foot **Ham Hill** (or Hamdon Hill) that is the source of the beautiful honey coloured stone that has been used in so many of the surrounding towns and villages. This solitary limestone outcrop rises abruptly from the Somerset plain and from here there are breathtaking views of the surrounding countryside. A substantial hill fort was built here during the Iron Age that was, subsequently, overrun by the invading Romans. The new occupants built their own fortification on the site to guard their major route, the Fosse Way, and its important intersection with the road between Dorchester and the Bristol Channel at nearby Ilchester.

It was the Romans who discovered that the hill's soft, even grained limestone made a flexible and highly attractive building material and they used it in the construction of their villas and temples. Later, the Saxons and then the Normans came to share this high opinion of Hamstone and, by the time quarrying reached its height in the 17th century, a sizable settlement had grown up within the confines of the Iron Age fort though,

THE ROSE & CROWN
Bower Hinton, Nr Martock, Somerset TA12 6JY
Tel: 01935 822393
e-mail: elliegpbrooks@aol.com

A row of three cottages dating from the early 19th century make up this lovely little stone pub in a hamlet on the edge of Martock, a short drive north of the A303. Ellie and Roy Brooks (she cooks and he runs the bar) have kept as many original features as possible at the **Rose & Crown**, and the bar-lounge and restaurant are very quaint and charming, with old oak and pine featuring strongly. Ellie's fresh, wholesome dishes are served every session except Wednesday lunchtime, and the Sunday roast lunch is always a popular occasion. Skittle alley, Saturday quiz once a month, occasional live music.

today, only a solitary inn remains. A war memorial to 44 local men who died during World War I stands on the summit of Ham Hill, now designated a country park, and the combination of the views, the old earthwork ramparts and the maze of overgrown quarry workings make this an attractive place for recreation and picnics.

MARTOCK
6 miles NW of Yeovil on the B3165

This attractive, small town is surrounded by rich arable land and the area has long been renowned for its prosperous land-owning farmers and Martock's long established affluence is reflected in its impressive part 13th century parish church. A former abbey church that once belonged to the monks of Mont St Michel in Normandy, the church boasts one of the finest tie-beam roofs in Somerset and almost every part of it is covered in beautiful carvings.

The old part of Martock is blessed with an unusually large number of fine buildings and amongst these can be found the **Treasurer's House** (National Trust), a small medieval house of two stories that was built in the late 13th century. Visitors here can see the Great Hall that was completed in 1293, an interesting wall painting that is even older and the kitchen that was added to the building in the 15th century. Close by is the **Old Court House,** a parish building that served as the local grammar school for 200 years. Meanwhile, to the west is Martock's 17th century Manor House that was the home of Edward Parker, the man who exposed the Gunpowder Plot after Guy Fawkes had warned him against attending Parliament on that fateful night.

EAST LAMBROOK
7½ miles NW of Yeovil off the B3165

Close to this charming little hamlet is another beautiful garden, **Lambrook**

Manor Garden, which was laid out by the writer and horticulturalist, Margery Fish, who lived at the medieval Hamstone manor house from 1937 until her death in 1969. Her exuberant planting and deliberate lack of formality have created an atmosphere of romantic tranquillity that is maintained to this day. Now Grade I listed, the garden is also the home of the National Collection of cranesbill species geraniums.

The low-lying land to the north of East Lambrook is criss-crossed by a network of drainage ditches or rhines (pronounced reens) that eventually flow into the rivers Parrett, Isle and Yeo. Originally cut in the early 19th century, the ditches are often lined with double rows of pollarded willows, a sight that has come to characterise this part of Somerset. Despite having to be cleared every few years, the rhines provide a valuable natural habitat for a wide variety of bird, animal and plant life.

SOMERTON
8½ miles NW of Yeovil on the B3151

Although the town's claim that it was once a capital of Wessex under the Saxons is in dispute, it is certain that Somerton, which gave its name to the county, is an ancient place that grew up around an important crossroads. However, expansion towards the end of the late 13th century has altered

Somerton Market Cross

the town's original layout although it did create the present open market place that has become home to the distinctive **Market Cross** and town hall. Between 1278 and 1371, Somerton was the location of the county gaol and the meeting place of the shire courts although it continued to develop as a market town – a role that is reflected in the delightfully down-to-earth names of some of its streets such as Cow Square and Pig Street (now Broad Street).

Today, Somerton is a place of handsome old shops, inns and houses and its general atmosphere of mature prosperity is enhanced by the presence of a number of striking ancient buildings. Cow Square is home to Old Hall, an elegant town house that was built on the site of Edward I's late 13th century court of Assize and, close by, is **St Michael's Church**. Along with its fine Jacobean holy table that acts as the altar, the church is noted for its stunning 16th

THE BUTTERCROSS TEAROOMS

Market Place, Somerton, Somerset TA11 7NB
Tel: 01458 273168 e-mail: clive@thebuttercross.fsnet.co.uk

Nestling on the market square between shops and the parish church, the **Buttercross Tearooms** are the perfect place to pause on the tourist trail walk around Somerton. The business is owned and run by Clive and Carol Jones, Clive in the kitchen and Carol front of house. Open from 10 to 6 Monday to Saturday (10 to 5 in winter), the tearoom offers a well-balanced selection of home-made cakes and scones, morning coffee, light lunches and cream teas. A range of goodies is on sale at this delightful, traditional place, including own label jams and marmalades, fudge and toffee, Belgian chocolates, Moore's biscuits and Childhay Manor ice cream.

THE GLOBE INN

Market Place, Somerton, Somerset TA11 7LX
Tel: 01458 272474

Jenny Royle and her enthusiastic staff offer a warm and genuine welcome to the **Globe Inn**, a 17th century coaching inn that retains many original features, both inside and out, in its prime market-place setting . Handsome dark oak tables and chairs furnish the bar, which also has a carved oak counter and an open fire. The food is a major attraction here, from bar snacks to daily chalkboard specials and a tempting evening menu. A large upstairs room is a popular venue for private functions and parties. The Globe is open lunchtime and evening Monday to Saturday and all day Sunday.

THE CASTLEBROOK INN

Compton Dundon, Somerton, Somerset TA11 6PR
Tel: 01458 443632

Just over two miles north of Somerton on the B3151 road towards Street, the **Castlebrook Inn** is a charming 16th century building of whitewashed rough stone. Parasols are set over tables in the little front beer garden, and inside the picture is traditional on a small scale, with low beamed ceilings, flagged floors and a feature fireplace. The inn was taken over early in 2002 by Steven Doman, who pulls the pints, and Frances Brown, who runs the kitchen. Her good-value dishes include something for most tastes, with pies and steaks among the favourite orders. The inn is open Monday evening, Tuesday to Friday lunchtime and evening and all day Saturday and Sunday. No food Monday or Sunday evening.

century roof that was probably carved and decorated by the monks of Muchelney Abbey.

A couple of miles southeast of the town lies the charming manor, **Lytes Cary Manor** (National Trust), a late medieval stone house that was built by succeeding generations of the Lyte family. The best known member of the family was Henry Lyte, the Elizabethan herbalist who dedicated his 1578 translation of Dodoen's *Cruydeboeck* to Queen Elizabeth "from my poore house at Lytescarie." After the family left the house in the 18th century it fell into disrepair but, in 1907, it was purchased by Sir Walter Jenner, son of the famous Victorian physician, who restored the property. The present garden is an enchanting combination of formality and eccentricity – there is an open lawn lined with magnificent yew topiary, an orchard filled with quince, pear and apple trees, and a network of enclosed paths that every now and then reveal a view of the house, a lily pond or a classical statue.

Priest's House

MUCHELNEY
9 miles NW of Yeovil off the A372

This village's name means 'the Great Island' and it dates from the time when this settlement rose up above the surrounding marshland that has long since been drained to provide excellent arable farmland. Muchelney is also the location of an impressive part-ruined Benedictine monastery that is thought to have been founded by King Ine of Wessex in the 8th century – a claim that has, in part, been confirmed when, in the 1950s, an archaeological dig unearthed an 8th century crypt. During medieval times **Muchelney Abbey** (English Heritage) grew to emulate its great rival at Glastonbury and it was, at one time, the second largest abbey in Somerset. However, after the

Dissolution in 1539, the buildings, most of which date from the 15th and 16th centuries, gradually fell into disrepair and much of its stone was removed to provide building material for the surrounding village. In spite of this, a substantial part of the original structure, including the south cloister and 16th century abbot's lodge with its carved stone doorways, can still be seen today.

Meanwhile, opposite the parish church, which is noted for its remarkable early 17th century illuminations, stands the **Priest's House** (National Trust), a late medieval hall house that was built by the abbey, in 1308, for the parish priest. Little changed since the 17th century, when the building was divided, the interesting features to see here are the Gothic doorway, the beautiful tracery windows and a massive 15th century stone fireplace. The house is still a dwelling today and it is opened on a limited basis.

HUISH EPISCOPI
10 miles NW of Yeovil on the A372

This village's unusual name means 'belonging to a bishop' and, fittingly, it is home to one of the finest examples of a late medieval Somerset tower in the county that can be found at the village church. At its most impressive in high summer when it can be viewed through the surrounding greenery, this ornate structure is adorned with striking tracery, pinnacles and carvings. The church also has an elaborate Norman doorway, which still shows signs of the fire that destroyed much of the earlier building in the 13th century, and a window in the south chapel that was designed by Edward Burne-Jones, the 19th century Pre-Raphaelite.

DRAYTON
10½ miles NW of Yeovil off the A378

Close to the village lies the privately-owned **Midelney Manor** that was originally an island manor belonging to Muchelney Abbey. A handsome manor house that shows architectural features from the 16th, 17th and 18th centuries, this has been in the hands of the Trevilian family since the early 1500s and the estate incorporates a heronry, a series of delightful gardens, a unique 17th century falcon's mews and woodland walks.

LANGPORT
10½ miles NW of Yeovil on the A378

The old part of this former market town stands on a rise above an ancient ford across the River Parrett and, just a short distance downstream from this point, the river is joined by the Rivers Isle and Yeo. Defended by an earthwork rampart during Saxon times, by AD930 Langport was an important commercial centre that minted its own coins. The only surviving part of the town's defences is the east gate that incorporates a curious 'hanging' chapel that sits above the arch on an upper level whilst the tower of that church at nearby Huish Episcopi can be seen through its barrel vaulted gateway.

During the 18th and 19th centuries, Langport flourished as a banking centre and the local independent bank, Stuckey's, became known for its impressive branches,

many of which can still be seen in the surrounding towns and villages even though the bank has long since been taken over by NatWest. At the time of this amalgamation in 1909, Stuckey's had more notes in circulation than any other bank in the country except for the Bank of England.

Throughout history, the **Langport Gap** has been the site of a number of important military encounters. Two of the most significant occurred over 1,000 years apart: in the 6th century Geraint, King of the Dumnonii, was involved in a battle here whilst, in July 1645, the Parliamentarian victory at the Battle of Langport gave Cromwell's forces almost total control of the West Country during the English Civil War. More about life on the Somerset Levels and the Moors can be learnt at the **Langport and River Parrett Visitor Centre** through its series of hands-on exhibits and displays.

ALLER
12½ miles NW of Yeovil on the A372

It was at the church here that, in 878, King Alfred converted Guthrum the Dane and his followers to Christianity following a battle on Salisbury Plain. The low wooded rise to the east of Aller is criss-crossed by a network of ancient country lanes and these pass through some pleasant hamlets and villages including **High Ham**, the home of the last thatched windmill in England. Dating from 1822, **Stembridge Tower Mill** (National Trust) continued to operate until 1910.

STOKE ST GREGORY
14½ miles NW of Yeovil off the A378

This elongated village boasts at least eight farmhouses that date from the 16th and 17th centuries along with a 14th century church with an unusual font of the same age. Renowned for its willow industry, the moors around Stoke St Gregory contain withy beds where the raw materials are grown and appropriately enough the village is home to the **Willows and Wetlands Centre**. Open from Monday to Saturday, the centre is an ideal place to gain an understanding of the processes involved in growing the withies and all manner of willow basket, furniture and sculpture making. A wide range of willow items, handcrafted at the centre, are also for sale here.

BURROW BRIDGE
15 miles NW of Yeovil on the A361

This village, on the River Parrett, is home to one of several pumping stations that were built in Victorian times to drain the Somerset Levels and the **Pumping Station** is open to the public occasionally throughout the year.

Just to the northeast is the conspicuous conical hill, **Burrow Mump**, which rises dramatically from the surrounding wetlands. Situated at a fording point on the River Parrett, this knoll has at its summit the picturesque remains of an unfinished chapel dedicated to St Michael that was begun in 1793 but for which funds ran out before its completion. This isolated hill is reputed to be the site of an ancient fortification belonging to King Alfred, and it was to here that he is said to have retreated to escape from invading Vikings. It was during his time here that he is rumoured to have sought shelter in a hut in the nearby village of **Athelney** and whilst he was sitting at the peasant's hearth, absorbed in his own thought, he burnt the cakes that the housewife had been baking. Not recognising the king, the peasant boxed his ears for ruining all her hard work and, during the 19th century, a stone was placed on the site that recalls that, in gratitude for his hospitality, King Alfred founded a monastery on the Isle of Athelney.

Burrow Mump is situated in the heart of the low lying area known as **King's Sedge Moor**, an attractive part of the Somerset Levels that is drained by the Rivers Cary (although here it is called the King's Sedgemoor Drain) and Parrett. A rich area of wetland, the moor is known for its characteristic pollarded willows whose straight shoots, or withies, have been cultivated on a substantial scale ever since the taste for wicker developed during the 19th century. The traditional craft of basket-weaving is one of Somerset's oldest commercial activities and it once employed thousands of people. Although the industry has been scaled down over the last 150 years, it is still alive and, today, enjoying something of a revival.

Just to the west of Burrow Bridge, the **Bridgwater and Taunton Canal** winds its way through some of the most attractive countryside in the Somerset Levels and the restored locks, swing bridges, engine houses and rare paddle gearing equipment add further interest to this already picturesque walk. The canal also offers a variety of recreational facilities including boating, fishing and canoeing whilst the canal banks are alive with both bird and animal life.

CHARD

First established in 1235, during the Middle Ages Chard was a prosperous wool centre with its own mayor, or portreeve, and burgesses. However, few buildings date from before 1577 as, that year, there was a devastating fire that raged through the town and left most of it razed to the ground but one building that did survive the destruction was the fine Perpendicular parish church. The town was rebuilt and, today, many of these 16th and 17th century buildings remain, including the courthouse and the old grammar school,

THE HAPPY RETURN

East Street, Chard, Somerset TA20 1EP
Tel: 01460 63152

Found at one end of Chard's busy main street, **The Happy Return** is, despite the seemingly austere exterior, a surprisingly cosy yet stylish restaurant that is owned and run by Peter and Lynne Lee and Geoff and Doris Sibthorpe. Although the two couples have only been here a short while they have already put The Happy Return on the culinary map of the area and this charming restaurant is fast gaining an enviable reputation for the excellence of Lynne's cuisine. All the carefully chosen dishes here are made freshly to order and, along with the house speciality of Lasagne, the ever changing menu presents a wealth of both imaginative and more traditional dishes. Open every day, at both lunchtime and in the evening, dining at this intimate restaurant is a real treat.

whilst Chard is also home to some striking Georgian and Victorian buildings of which the most notable is the neoclassical town hall, built in 1835, which has an impressive two-tier portico. Meanwhile, the unusual round toll house, with its conical thatched roof, on the outskirts of the town, is a reminder of the days of stagecoaches and turnpike roads.

Although Chard has expanded rapidly since World War II – its population has more than doubled in the last 55 years – the centre of this light industrial town still retains a pleasant village-like atmosphere that is most apparent in its broad main shopping street. At the western end of the town's High Street, and housed in the attractive thatched Godworth House, is the award winning **Chard Museum** (see panel) that is an ideal place for visitors to find out more about this town's eventful past. Though many visitors may not have been here before the town may

seem familiar as it was used as a location for the television situation comedy *To the Manor Born* that was filmed, chiefly, in and around Cricket House.

To the northwest of the town is a 200 year old corn mill, **Hornsbury Mill**, set in landscaped water gardens, whose impressive water wheel is still in working order and where there is also a collection of agricultural and milling artefacts along with a restaurant from where there is an excellent view of the water wheel. Meanwhile, to the northeast lies **Chard Reservoir Nature Reserve**, a conservation area that is an important habitat for wildlife and one where kingfisher, great crested grebe and other rare species of birds have made their home in and around the

CHARD AND DISTRICT MUSEUM

Godworthy House, High Street, Chard, Somerset, TA20 1Q
Tel: 01460 65091

Chard Museum, on the A30 a few hundred yards west of the town centre, is housed in buildings dating from the 16th to the 20th century. It has displays illustrating the history of Chard and its surrounding area, including exhibitions devoted to the work of two notable Victorians, John Stringfellow, who flew a steam powered flying machine in 1848, and James Gillingham, a pioneer in the development of artificial limbs. Other displays show rural crafts (blacksmith, wheelwright, carpenter, cooper), local industries (lace making, agricultural machinery) and aspects of social life (domestic, religion, education, costumes). Most of the Museum is accessible to disabled visitors.

lake. The nature reserve also has a two-mile circular footpath that takes in rustling reed beds, broadleaved woodland and open hay meadows.

AROUND CHARD

HATCH BEAUCHAMP
7½ miles N of Chard off the A358

This pleasant rural village's name originates from 'Hache', a Saxon word meaning gateway, and this refers to the ancient forest of Neroche whose boundary was just to the north and west. Meanwhile, the suffix comes from the Norman family who owned the local manor and their house stood on the land that is now taken up with one of the finest country houses in the area, **Hatch Court**. Built of attractive honey coloured limestone it was a rich local clothier, John Collins, who commissioned the Axbridge architect, Thomas Prowse, to design the house and the resulting magnificent Palladian mansion was completed in 1755. Among its finest features are the hall with its cantilevered stone staircase, the curved orangery with its arched floor-to-ceiling windows and the semicircular china room with its elegant display of rare porcelain and glass. There is also a fine collection of 17th and 18th century English and French

furniture, 19th and 20th century paintings and a small **Military Museum** commemorating Britain's last privately raised regiment, the Princess Patricia's Canadian Light Infantry. The extensively restored grounds incorporate a walled kitchen garden, rose garden, arboretum and deer park. Behind this spectacular mansion is the Church of St John the Baptist that is the final resting place of Colonel John Chard, a hero of the late 19th century battle of Rorke's Drift during the Zulu War and who was played by Stanley Baker in the film *Zulu*.

DOWLISH WAKE
4 miles NE of Chard off the A358

In the village church is the tomb of John Hanning Speke, the intrepid Victorian explorer who journeyed for over 2,500 miles through Africa to confirm that Lake Victoria was, indeed, the source of the River Nile. After his epic journey, Speke returned to England a hero but, tragically, on the very morning that he was due to report his findings to the British Geographical Association he accidentally shot himself whilst out partridge shooting.

ILMINSTER
4½ miles NE of Chard on the B3168

This ancient ecclesiastical and agricultural centre, whose name means 'minster on the

---

THE DUKE OF YORK

North Street, Shepton Beauchamp, Ilminster, Somerset TA19 0LW
Tel: 01460 240314

The Duke of York is a grand old pub standing proudly on the main street of Shepton Beauchamp. The facade is stone and inside, the look is pleasantly traditional, with several cosy corners in the public bar and a feature wood-burning fire. At the back is a lounge/dining area where tasty, wholesome food is served. Cod & chips and big juicy steaks are among the favourites, and the regular curry nights are always popular. The food is prepared by enthusiastic landlord Paul Rowlands with assistance from his wife Hayley, who also runs the bar. The pub has a beer garden and a skittle alley, and entertainment includes a live band monthly on a Saturday and a quiz night monthly on a Sunday.

River Isle', takes its name from the church that was founded here by the Saxon King Ine in the 8th century. By the time of the *Domesday Book*, in 1089, the borough had grown and it was recorded as having a market and three mills whilst, during the Middle Ages, it expanded into a thriving wool and lace-making town. This period of prosperity is reflected in the town's unusually large parish church whose massive multi-pinnacled tower is modelled on that of Wells cathedral. Any walk around the old part of Ilminster will reveal a number of delightful old buildings, many constructed in golden Hamstone, and they include the chantry house, the old grammar school and a colonnaded market house.

On the outskirts of Ilminster is another lovely old building, the handsome part Tudor mansion, **Dillington House**, which is the former home of the Speke family. In the time of James II, John Speke was an officer in the Duke of Monmouth's ill-fated rebel army that landed at Lyme Regis in 1685. However, following the rebellion's disastrous defeat at the Battle of Sedgemoor, Speke was forced to flee abroad, leaving his brother, George (who had done no more than shake the duke's hand), to face the wrath of Judge Jeffreys. The infamous 'hanging' judge sentenced George to death, justifying his decision with the words, "His family owes a life and he shall die for his brother."

HINTON ST GEORGE
6½ miles NE of Chard off the A356

This pretty and unspoilt former estate village was, for centuries, owned by the Poulett family and it is thanks to them that Hinton St George has been left virtually untouched over the years. The Pouletts came here in the 15th century and the house that they rebuilt then, Hinton House, now forms the main structure of the present day mansion. Although this has now been converted into apartments, the building is still said to be haunted by the ghost of a young Poulett woman who died of a broken heart after her father shot dead the man with whom she was planning to elope.

Several ostentatious monuments to members of the Poulett family can be seen in the village's 15th century Church of St George whilst another noteworthy building here is the so called Priory, a 16th century residence with a 14th century window at its eastern end that is thought to have once belonged to Monkton Farleigh Priory in Wiltshire.

On the last Thursday in October, 'Punkie Night', it is traditional for Hinton children to beg for candles to put inside their intricately fashioned turnip and pumpkin lanterns. It is considered very unlucky to refuse to give a child a candle as each lantern is thought to represent the spirit of a dead person who, unless illuminated, will rise up at Hallowe'en.

BARRINGTON
7½ miles NE of Chard off the B3168

To the east of this pretty estate village is the beautiful **Barrington Court** (National Trust) that is famous for its enchanting garden that was influenced by the great 20th century garden architect Gertrude Jekyll. This estate originally belonged to the Daubeney family but it passed through several hands before becoming the property of William Clifton, a wealthy London merchant, who was responsible for building the house in the mid 16th century. In 1907, the now dilapidated Barrington Court became the first country house to be purchased by the Trust and it was restored in the 1920s by Col AA Lyle to whom the Trust had let the property. The garden, too, was laid out during this time in a series of themed areas that include an iris garden, a lily garden, a white garden and a fragrant rose garden. Gertrude Jekyll was brought in to advise on the initial planting and layout and the garden remains the finest example of her work in the Trust's care. There is also an exceptionally attractive kitchen garden with apple, pear and plum trees trained along the walls that, in season, produces fruit and vegetables for the licensed restaurant that can be found here.

Meanwhile, to the north of Barrington is the tranquil community of **Westport**, a peaceful village that is a former inland port that was built at the height of the canal era by the Parrett Navigation Company. From here wool and stone were exported whilst coal and building materials were taken inland.

CREWKERNE
7 miles E of Chard on the A30

A thriving agricultural centre during Saxon times, Crewkerne even had its own mint in the decades that led up to the Norman invasion whilst evidence of this ancient former market town's importance and prosperity can still be seen in the magnificence of its parish church that was built using money generated by the late medieval boom in the local wool industry. A building of minster-like proportions, **St Bartholomew's Church** is one of the grandest of the many fine Perpendicular churches to be found in south Somerset. The interior has a wonderful airy feel with a soaring nave decorated with angels and it is said that, in the early 16th century, Odolina, the first in a series of female hermits, occupied a cell at the church.

Unlike many other towns in Wessex whose textile industries suffered an almost total decline in later years, Crewkerne was rejuvenated in the 18th century when the availability of locally grown flax led to an expansion in the manufacture of sailcloth and canvas webbing. Among the many thousands of sails to be made here were those for HMS *Victory*, Admiral Nelson's flagship at the Battle of Trafalgar. This resurgence was also boosted by the development of the London to Exeter stage coach route and this led to the rebuilding of Crewkerne with elegant Georgian buildings. Many of the fine houses and inns can still be seen from that era and the main areas, around Church and Abbey Streets, have now been designated an Area of Outstanding Architectural Interest. The town's local **Museum**, found in a beautifully restored 18th century house, illustrates the history of Crewkerne and the surrounding area and also has a special area dedicated to Lord Nelson's captain, Sir Thomas Hardy, who was educated at Crewkerne grammar school.

To the west of Crewkerne lies the aptly named **Windwhistle Hill**, a high chalk topped ridge from the summit of which there are dramatic views southwards to Lyme Bay and northwards across the Somerset Levels to, on a clear day, the mountains of South Wales. Meanwhile, the town also lies close to the source of the River Parrett and from here the 50 mile long **River Parrett Trail** follows the river through some of the country's most ecologically sensitive and fragile areas, the Somerset Levels and Moors. Old mills, splendid churches, attractive villages and ancient monuments as well as orchards, peaceful pastureland and traditional industries such as cider-making and basket-weaving can all be found along the route.

HASELBURY PLUCKNETT
9½ miles E of Chard on the A3066

This delightfully named and particularly pretty village has a large part-Norman church whose churchyard contains a series of unusual 'squeeze stones' whilst, in the 12th century, there was a cell on the village outskirts that was the home of Wulfric. A gentle saint who is best remembered for his love of animals, it is said that, when a wren nested above his bed he moved to a draughty corner so that he did not disturb the fledglings. Just to the west of the village the lovely **Haslebury Bridge**, a medieval packhorse bridge, crosses the River Parrett.

CLAPTON
6 miles SE of Chard on the B3165

This village is home to the varied and interesting **Clapton Court Gardens** that feature, among their 10 acres, formal terraces, a rose garden, a rockery and a water garden. The grounds also incorporate a large wooded area that contains a massive ash tree that, at over 230 years old and 28 feet in girth, is believed to be the oldest and the largest in

Forde Abbey

Chard, Somerset TA20 4LU
Tel: 01460 220231 Fax: 01460 220296

Originally founded by Cistercian monks in the 12th century, **Forde Abbey** lay empty for over 100 years after the Dissolution of the Monasteries before its was sold to Edmund Prideaux, Oliver Cromwell's Attorney General in 1649.

The remains of the abbey were incorporated into the grand private house of the Prideaux family. The old chapter house became the family chapel. Later additions include the magnificent 17th century plaster ceilings and the renowned Mortlake Tapestries brought over from Brussels by Charles I. Today, Forde Abbey is the home of the Roper family and it stands at the heart of this family run estate.

Along with the collection of tapestries, period furniture and paintings to see in the house, there is the refectory and dormitory that still survive from the time of the medieval monastery and the abbey is also home to the famous Eeles Pottery exhibition.

The house is surrounded by wonderful gardens described by Alan Titchmarsh as "one of the greatest gardens in the West Country." There are sloping lawns, herbaceous borders, a bog garden, lakes and a working kitchen garden that supplies the abbey's restaurant with produce whilst rare and unusual plants are for sale at the Plant Centre. The estate is also known for its pedigree herd of cattle. The house, with its restaurant and tearoom, can be visited between April and October whilst the gardens and grounds are open all year round.

mainland Britain. There is also a fine metasequoia that is already over 80 feet tall although it was only planted in 1950 from a seed brought back from China.

TATWORTH
2 miles S of Chard on the A358

Forde Abbey

To the northeast of this village, which was established as late as the 19th century, lies a meadow that is the last remaining sign of 'common' land that was enclosed in 1819. Changes in the ownership of the land during the 1820s allowed too many farmers with grazing rights on the land and the meadow suffered from being over stocked. Therefore, in 1832, the holders of those rights met and, calling their meeting the Stowell Court, they auctioned off the meadow for one year and shared the proceeds. So an annual tradition was born and the Stowell Court still meets on the first Tuesday after April 6th every year. Although many more customs have been added over the years, the auction proceedings are unique and they begin when a tallow candle of precisely one inch in length is lit and they end with the last bid before the candle goes out. Today, Stowell Mead is now managed as a Site of Special Scientific Interest and, as the land is not treated with fertilisers, pesticides or herbicides, it is home to many plants that are generally quiet rare elsewhere. There is no right of way across the land but it can be seen from the road.

A short distance to the southeast of Tatworth lies **Forde Abbey**, which was founded in the 12th century by Cistercian monks after they had made an unsuccessful attempt to found an abbey in neighbouring Devon. Over the years it became one of the richest and most learned monasteries in the country but it had already declined greatly by the time of the Dissolution in 1536 and it remained empty until 1649 when it was bought by Edward Prideaux, Attorney General to Oliver Cromwell. What remained of the abbey was incorporated into the Prideaux family's grand mansion, the old chapter house became the family chapel, and later additions include the magnificent 17th century plaster ceilings and the renowned Mortlake Tapestries that were brought over from Brussels by Charles I. Now the home of the Roper family, this charming country house holds collections of tapestries, period furniture, paintings and the famous Eeles Pottery exhibition. Meanwhile, the gardens are equally magnificent, with sloping lawns, herbaceous borders, lakes and a working kitchen garden, whilst the estate is well known for its pedigree herd of cattle. The house, with its restaurant and tearoom, is open between April and October while the gardens and grounds remain open all year round.

WAMBROOK
2 miles SW of Chard off the A30

Situated close to the county border with Dorset visitors interested in animal welfare will be keen to take in the **Ferne Animal**

Sanctuary which lies just outside the village. Originally founded in 1939 by the Duchess of Hamilton and Brandon while she was living at Berwick St John near Shaftesbury, the sanctuary moved to its present position in the valley of the River Yarty in 1975 and this pleasant 51 acre site incorporates a nature trail, conservation area, dragonfly pools and picnic areas.

Taunton High Street

BUCKLAND ST MARY
4½ miles NW of Chard off the A303

This village is thought to be the place where red-clothed fairies were last seen in Somerset and, it is claimed, that they were defeated in a battle with the pixies and, afterwards, all the land west of the River Parrett became Pixyland. The fairies were then believed to have fled to Ireland though, some say, a few settled in Devon and Dorset.

STABLE FITZPAINE
7 miles NW of Chard off the B3170

Close to the remains of the ancient Forest of Neroche, it was near this village that Robert, Count of Mortain, a half-brother to William the Conqueror, converted an old Saxon fortress into a residential castle. However, by the late 13th century the castle was already in a very run down state and all that can be seen today of the old fortress is an immense ditch that is overshadowed by trees.

TAUNTON

Despite a settlement being founded here by the Saxon King Ine in the 8th century, Taunton, the county town of Somerset, has only been its sole centre of administration

since 1935 and, up until that date, both Ilchester and Somerton had been the county town. By Norman times the Saxon settlement had grown to have its own Augustinian monastery, a minster and a **Castle** – an extensive structure whose purpose had always been more as an administrative centre than as a military post. However, this did not prevent the castle from being the focus of two important sieges during the English Civil War and, a few years later, it was here that the infamous Judge Jeffreys sentenced over 150 followers of the Duke of Monmouth to death during the Bloody Autumn Assizes. Even today, the judge's ghost is said to haunt the castle grounds on September nights.

The town's historic castle is now the home of the **Somerset County Museum**, a highly informative museum that contains a large collection of exhibits on the archaeology and the natural and human history of the county. Along with wooden trackways from the Somerset Levels and the Low Ham Roman mosaic, there are fossils, glassware, costumes, ceramics and silver. Meanwhile, the local industrial history is explored in a series of exhibits that trace the development of steam, oil and electric engines. Also at the castle site is the **Somerset Military Museum** and there are some medieval almshouses in the courtyard. The museums are open from Tuesday to Saturday all year round.

Another of the town's old building's is still making itself useful today, as Somerset's famous County Cricket Ground occupies part of the priory grounds that once extended down to the river and a section of the old monastic gatehouse, known as the Priory Barn, can still be seen beside the cricket ground. Dating from the late 15th or early 16th century, the barn has been restored and this wonderful old building houses the fascinating **Somerset County Cricket Museum**, with its collection of cricket memorabilia, photographs, autographed bats and equipment and its extensive reference library. The museum is open from Monday to Friday between April and October.

Like many other Somerset towns and villages, Taunton was a thriving wool, and later silk, cloth-making centre during the Middle Ages and the profits earned by the medieval clothiers went into buildings and here, in particular, their wealth was used in the construction of two huge churches: St James' and St Mary's. The town is also home to **Mary Street Unitarian Chapel**, one of the few unspoilt early 18th century chapels in the southwest, whose interior still contains the original wood panelling, square pillars, pulpit and galleries fashioned from Flemish oak. In 1798, Samuel Taylor Coleridge walked here from his home at Nether Stowey to preach in place of the minister, Dr Joshua Toulmin, whose daughter had drowned herself. Meanwhile, the rest of the town centre is scattered with fine buildings including the timber-framed Tudor House in Fore Street. Taunton is still a thriving place today with an important commercial centre, a weekly market and a busy light industrial sector that benefits from some excellent transport

River Tone, Taunton

links with the rest of the country.

Today, the **Bridgwater and Taunton Canal** towpath has been reopened following an extensive restoration programme and it provides pleasant waterside walks along its 14 miles. A relative latecomer, the canal first opened in 1827 and it was designed to be part of an ambitious scheme to create a freight route between Exeter and Bristol that would avoid the treacherous sea journey around the Cornwall peninsula. For many years, the canal was the principal means of importing coal and iron from South Wales to the inland towns of Somerset and of exporting their wool and agricultural produce to the rest of Britain.

Taunton's attractive **National Hunt Racecourse** lies on the opposite side of the motorway from the town and the combination of good facilities, excellent

MONKTON INN

West Monkton, near Taunton, Somerset TA2 8NP
Tel: 01823 412414 e-mail: themonktoninn@btopen.com
Fax: 01823 413310 website: www.homestyleinn.co.uk

Anyone passing **The Monkton Inn** should disregard the pub's sign – "The famous Monkton Inn, Bad Food, Bad Management, we recommend you don't come in" – as this is certainly misleading! A former 18th century manor house with stone floors and a large interior that incorporates a small public bar, spacious lounge bar and a stylish restaurant, this inn has been run by Marcus and Diane Williams, on behalf of Mr & Mrs Banwell, for just over a year. A head chef by profession, Marcus's Italian heritage plays a great part in the preparation of the excellent dishes that appear on the superb menu here whilst the couple's natural flair for entertaining ensures that this is a place with a friendly and relaxed atmosphere.

racing and glorious location make it one of the best country racecourses in Britain.

AROUND TAUNTON

ENMORE
6 miles N of Taunton off the A39

To the north of the village is the small redbrick country mansion of **Barford Park**, a delightfully proportioned Queen Anne house that is set in extensive grounds that incorporate a walled flower garden, a water garden and a large area of broadleaf woodland. Meanwhile, the house, which contains some exceptionally fine examples of Queen Anne furniture, is still in daily family use and is only open by prior appointment.

Meanwhile, to the west of Enmore the ground rises up into the **Quantock Hills**, an Area of Outstanding Natural Beauty that runs from near Taunton to the Bristol Channel at Quantoxhead. Rising to a high point of 1,260 feet at **Wills Neck**, this delightful area of open heath and scattered woodland supports one of the country's last remaining herds of wild red deer. The exposed hilltops are littered with Neolithic and Bronze Age remains, including around 100 burial mounds, many of which now resemble nothing more than a pile of

stones. The richer soil in the south sustains arable farms and pockets of dense woodland and this varied landscape offers some magnificent walking with splendid views over the Bristol Channel, the Vale of Taunton Deane, the Brendon Hills and Exmoor. It was this glorious classical English landscape that the poets Wordsworth and Coleridge so admired whilst they were living in the area.

Situated in one of the loveliest areas of the southern Quantocks, to the southwest of Enmore, is **Fyne Court** (National Trust) that is home to the headquarters of the Somerset Wildlife Trust and a visitor centre for the Quantocks. The main house was built in the 17th century by the Crosse family but it was largely destroyed by fire in the 1890s and the only surviving parts are the library and music room that have been converted into the visitor centre. Meanwhile, the house's grounds, which incorporate a walled garden, two ponds, an arboretum and a lake, have been designated a nature reserve. The most renowned occupant of the house was Andrew Crosse, an early 19th century scientist who was a pioneer in the field of electrical energy. Known locally as the 'thunder and lightning man', one of Crosse's lightning conductors can still be seen on an oak tree in the grounds and local stories tell how, during one of his electrical experiments, Crosse created tiny live insects. It was this claim that helped to inspire Mary Shelley to write her Gothic horror story, *Frankenstein*, in 1818.

HINKLEY POINT
13 miles N of Taunton off the A39

Hinkley Point is perhaps best known for its great power station and, at the **Hinkley Point Visitor Centre**, visitors can find out just how the adjacent power station releases the energy in the uranium and converts it into electricity. Meanwhile, there are other exciting exhibitions and displays that outline the natural history of the Earth but the environment around the power station also teems with wildlife and should not be forgotten. The **Hinkley Point Nature Trail** leads walkers through a wide diversity of habitats and, along with the many species of birds and wild flowers found here, some visitors may be lucky enough to see glow worms on the guided night-time walks.

The trail also includes an early Bronze Age mound, known locally as **Pixie's Mound**, which dates back to 1500 BC and was excavated in 1906.

Just inland lies the ancient village of **Stogursey** that was, in the 13th century, the lair of the renegade lord Fulke de Breaute, who terrorised the surrounding population with a band of ruthless followers until he was hunted down and brought to justice. The remains of his castle can still be seen near the village.

BRIDGWATER
10 miles N of Taunton on the A38

Situated at the lowest bridging point of the River Parrett in medieval times, Bridgwater is, today, an ancient inland port and industrial town. Yet, despite having been fortified from before the Norman Conquest, the settlement that grew up around the castle remained little more than a village until the international trade

THE OLD SHIP INN

Ship Lane, Combwich, near Bridgewater,
Somerset TA5 2QT
Tel: 01278 652348

A small and quaint 18th century country pub, **The Old Ship Inn** has a wonderfully traditional interior with low beamed ceilings, a stone fireplace and alcove windows that all adds to the appeal of this warm and friendly inn. A well known place locally for the high standard of both beer and food served here, including superb seafood, landlady Diana Harris ensures that there are always new and interesting dishes appearing on the menu. This is a charming, hidden away inn that is well worth taking the time to discover.

KING WILLIAM

Lippets Way, Catcott, near Bridgwater, Somerset TA7 9HU
Tel/Fax: 01278 722374

Originally a small 17th century stone cottage, the **King William** has been enlarged over the years without loosing any of its appeal or its inside well and, today, it is an attractive and atmospheric country inn that prides itself on offering excellent hospitality. Along with a fine selection of real ales at the bar, landlords, Malcolm and Linda Bullimore, have gained an enviable reputation for the high standard of cuisine served here. The extensive menu includes many favourites as well as the house speciality, King William pie, with its secret ingredients!

LABURNUM HOUSE LODGE HOTEL

Sloway Lane, West Huntspill, Highbridge,
Somerset TA9 3RJ
Tel: 01278 781830 Fax: 01278 781612
e-mail: laburnumhh@aol.com
website: www.laburnumhh.co.uk

Less than a mile from the coast and on the edge of a nature
reserve **Laburnum House Lodge Hotel** offers its visitors
the opportunity to relax in a comfortable and attractive hotel and enjoy a get away from it all holiday.
Along with excellent accommodation, a modern leisure complex, a superb restaurant and an informal
pub, there are numerous sports facilities at the hotel, including tennis, horse riding, golf, water sports
and sailing, and with the Huntspill River at the back of the hotel's grounds there is also angling.

PURITON INN

Puriton, near Bridgewater, Somerset TA7 8AF
Tel: 01278 683464 Fax: 01278 683516

Situated on the edge of this small village, the **Puriton
Inn** is a charming early 19th century inn. Summertime
it has a colourful display of flowers with front and
back beer gardens. This is a cosy inn with subtle
lighting creating a warm and intimate atmosphere,
where customers are treated to not only an excellent
range of real ales but also a varied and delicious menu
of freshly cooked dishes which include vegetarian and
many house specialities.

THE KNOWLE INN

Bawdrip, Knowle, near Bridgewater, Somerset TA7 8TL
Tel: 01278 683330 Fax: 01278 685646

A wonderful former coaching inn that dates from the 16th
century, **The Knowle Inn** has a lovely, atmospheric interior
that is enhanced by the stone floors, ancient beams and
splendid log burning stove in the main bar. A family run inn
that attracts customers from far and wide, landlady Carol
Singleton and her husband not only offer an excellent range
of real ales but there is also a superb menu of new English
style cuisine, which specialises in fresh fish and seafood. The
Knowle Inn, too, has two charming en suite guest rooms.

APPLE VIEW

Temple Farm, Chedzoy Lane, Chedzoy, near Bridgwater, Somerset TA7 8QR
Tel/Fax: 01278 423201
e-mail: temple-farm@hotmail.com

Situated on the edge of the Somerset Levels and, as its name suggests, with
orchard views, **Apple View** is a superb family run bed and breakfast establishment
based around a charming 200-year-old farmhouse. Along with comfortable en
suite accommodation, which includes many little extras, guests can wander
around the working farm, feed the chickens and meet the cheeky resident pony
and friendly collie. An ideal place for children, Apple View also has a room that
is particularly suited to less able guests. Evening meal available with 24 hours
notice. ETC grading 4 Diamonds and Silver Award NAS Category 2.

in wool, wheat and other agricultural products began to develop in the late Middle Ages. Bridgwater grew and, at one time, it was the most important town between Bristol and Barnstaple and it was the fifth busiest port in the country though this is hard to believe now. The largely 14th century parish church, with its disproportionately large spire, is the only building to remain from those prosperous medieval times as the castle was dismantled after the English Civil War and both the town's 13th century Franciscan friary and St John's hospital disappeared long ago. However, whilst the buildings in the town are mainly Georgian – and amongst them are some of the best examples of domestic architecture of that period in the county – Bridgwater has maintained its original medieval layout.

Before the construction of a canal dock in the early 19th century, the ships arriving at Bridgwater used to tie up on both sides of the river below the town's medieval bridge and here, too, can be seen the last remnant of the castle, **The Water Gate**, on West Quay. After a long period of decline in the textile industry and as the river was beginning to silt up, Bridgwater underwent something of an industrial renaissance as new industries were established here during the early 19th century. The manufacture of Bridgwater glass, which had begun the previous century, continued to expand, and a canal terminus, complete with dock and warehouses, was built. The river mud that caused the decline of the town's port also proved to have hidden benefits as, when it was baked in oblong blocks it was found to be an excellent scourer and, as Bath Brick, it was used for nearly a century to clean grates and stone steps. The canal terminus, where the brickworks also stood, was finally closed in 1970 but, today, the site has been restored and it is now a fascinating area of industrial archaeology.

Bridgwater Parish Church

Bridgwater's most famous son is the celebrated military leader, Robert Blake, who was born here in 1598 and went on to become an important officer in Cromwell's army, twice defending Taunton against overwhelming Royalist odds. Just a decade later, he was given command of the British navy and he went on to win a number of important battles against the Dutch and the Spanish and, in so doing, he restored the nation's naval supremacy in Europe. The house in which he was born is now home to the **Admiral Blake Museum** that contains a three-dimensional model of the Battle of Santa Cruz, one of Blake's most famous victories, along with a collection of his personal effects. However, Blake is not the only military leader to have stayed in Bridgwater as, during the late 17th century, the Duke of Monmouth stayed here before his disastrous defeat at the nearby Battle of Sedgemoor and the museum suitably illustrates this decisive battle in the duke's quest for the English throne. This is also a museum of local history and there is a large collection of locally discovered artefacts on display that date from Neolithic times right up to the days of World War II.

CHEDDON FITZPAINE
2 miles NE of Taunton off the A361

Just to the north of this village and situated on the south-facing foothills of the Quantocks are the beautiful **Hestercombe Gardens** (see panel below), an outstanding example of the professional collaboration of architect Sir Edwin Lutyens and landscape designer Gertrude Jekyll. The estate here goes back to Saxon times but, from the 14th to the late 19th century, the Hestercombe estate was owned by one family and it was Coplestone Warre Bampfylde who first

Hestercombe House

designed and laid out the magnificent landscape gardens here in the mid 18th century. In the 1870s the estate was acquired by Viscount Portman and, in 1904, his grandson, Edward Portman, commissioned Lutyens and Gertrude Jekyll to created a new and wonderful formal garden that has now been restored to its

HESTERCOMBE GARDENS

Cheddon Fitzpaine, near Taunton, Somerset TA2 8LG
Tel: 01823 413923 Fax: 01823 413747
e-mail: info@hestercombegardens.com
website: www.hestercombegardens.com

On the southern slopes of the Quantocks, **Hestercombe Gardens** lie on an estate that goes back to Saxon times but from the 14th to the late 19th century it was owned by one family. Coplestone

Warre Bampfylde designed and laid out the magnificent landscape garden in the mid 18th century. In 1872, the estate was acquired by the 1st Viscount Portman. His grandson, Hon Edward Portman, in 1904, commissioned Sir Edwin Lutyens to create a new formal garden that was planted by Gertrude Jekyll. Follies abound in this wonderful place and any walk around this 40-acre garden will include lakes, temples and magnificent views.

original glory. The church at nearby Kingston St Mary is the final resting place of the landscape garden's creator, Coplestone Bampfylde.

LYNG
7 miles NE of Taunton on the A361

Found on a low rise above the surrounding wetlands, this pretty village was once, like many other villages in this region of Somerset, a centre of withy growing and basket-weaving. The original village church of St Bartholomew was the chapelry of the monastery that King Alfred founded at Athelney and, whilst Alfred was sheltering nearby, his biographer described the village as being surrounded "by water and vast impassable peat bog."

WESTONZOYLAND
10 miles NE of Taunton on the A372

To the northwest of the village, on the southern bank of what is now the **King's Sedgemoor Drain**, is the site of the last battle to be fought on English soil. In July 1685, the well-equipped forces of James II heavily defeated the followers of the Duke of Monmouth in the bloody **Battle of Sedgemoor** that was to bring an end to the ill-fated Pitchfork Rebellion that aimed to replace the catholic King James with the protestant Duke of Monmouth, the illegitimate son of Charles II. Around 700 of Monmouth's followers were killed on the battlefield whilst several hundred

survivors were rounded up and taken to Westonzoyland churchyard where many of them were then hanged. The duke himself was taken to London where, ten days after the battle, he was executed on Tower Hill. However, it was during the infamous Judge Jeffrey's Bloody Assizes that the greatest terror was inflicted on the surviving followers of the duke when over 300 men were condemned to death and a further 600 were transported to the colonies. Today, a stark memorial marks the site of the lonely battlefield.

The village lies in the Somerset Levels and, in the 19th century, a steam-powered **Pumping Station** was built here to drain the water from the levels into the River Parrett. The oldest pumping station of its kind in the area, the current engine here was in operation from 1861 until 1952 and, now fully restored, it can be seen in steam at various times throughout the year. The station itself is a grade II listed building and also on the site is a small forge, a tramway and a number of other exhibits from the steam age. The Pumping Station is open on the first Sunday of the month and on both Sunday and Monday of Bank Holiday weekends in the afternoons only.

WEST BUCKLAND
4½ miles SW of Taunton off the A38

To the northeast of this village lies **Sheppy's Cider Farm Centre**, a traditional

THE BLACKBIRD INN
West Buckland, near Wellington, Somerset TA21 9HS
Tel: 01823 461273

First opened as an inn in 1773, **The Blackbird Inn**, which was originally two buildings, is a well-known landmark on this busy road between Taunton and Wellington and it is well worth taking the time to stop off here. Retaining its olde worlde character throughout, this inn not only has a fine reputation for its welcoming bar but also it has a superb and extensive menu of traditional, rural cuisine and has gained fame throughout the area and beyond. Along with the wonderful range of succulent steaks there is a large choice that is supplemented daily by the specials selection. Comfortable bed and breakfast accommodation is available too in a choice of three en suite guest rooms.

cider farm that is owned by the Sheppy family who have been producing cider in the West Country for over 200 years. Renowned for their quality ciders, visitors to the farm can see the cellars here along with the modern Press Room where the apple crop is processed each autumn. There are also guided tours of the cider orchards, where traditional apples such as Kingston Black and Dabinett grow, as well as a **Rural Life Museum** where a collection of vintage agricultural and cider equipment, along with cooper's tools, are displayed. The farm centre and its shop are open from Monday to Saturday all year round and, between Easter and Christmas, on Sunday early afternoons.

WELLINGTON
6 miles SW of Taunton on the B3187

Once an important producer of woven cloth and serge, this pleasant old market town owes much of its prosperity to Quaker entrepreneurs and, later, the Fox banking family. Fox, Fowler and Co were the last private bank in England to issue notes and they only ceased in 1921 when they were taken over by Lloyds. One of the last private bank notes to be issued can be seen at the **Wellington Museum**, a local history museum that, among its other mementoes of the town, has a display devoted to the Duke of Wellington and a working model of Wellesley cinema. The museum is open from Monday to Saturday between Easter and the end of September and, for the rest of the year, on Saturday mornings only. The broad streets around the town centre are peppered with fine Georgian buildings, including the neoclassical **Town Hall**, and, at the eastern end of the town, there is the much altered church that contains the ostentatious tomb of Sir John Popham, the judge who presided at the trial of Guy Fawkes.

To the south of the town stands the **Wellington Monument** (National Trust), a 175 foot high obelisk that was erected not long after the duke's great victory at Waterloo. The foundation stone was laid in 1817 by Lord Somerville but the monument was only completed in 1854. The duke himself visited the site and the town, from which he took his title, only once, in 1819. There are some 235 steps inside the monument and the climb is worth the exertion as, from the top, there are superb views of the Blackdown Hills and, on a clear day, Wales can be seen some 70 miles away.

THORNE ST MARGARET
8½ miles SW of Taunton off the A38

The broad valley between the southern Quantocks and the Devon border is known as the **Vale of Taunton Deane** and it contains some of the most fertile farmland in Somerset. Due to its prolonged agricultural prosperity, the area is dotted with some fine country houses and three can be found in the lanes around this village. **Cothay Manor Gardens** has been described as "one of the most perfect smaller English manor houses of the late 15th century" and its gardens, beside the River Tone, are worth seeing. The gardens are open on certain days between May and September. **Greenham Barton** is slightly older and it retains its early 15th century two-storey porch and open hall while **Wellisford Manor** was built of brick in around 1700 in a style that reflects the contemporary architecture of nearby Devon.

NORTON FITZWARREN
2 miles W of Taunton on the B3227

Large finds of Roman pottery have been excavated in and around this village and they have helped to confirm that Norton Fitzwarren was the Roman settlement of Theodunum. However, the village's name is derived from the Saxon 'north tun' (meaning north farm) and the Norman

THE GLOBE

Fore Street, Milverton, near Taunton, Somerset
Tel: 01823 400534 Fax: 01823 401201
e-mail: stuart@nettcomuk.co.uk

Despite its red brick Georgian façade parts of **The Globe**, found in
a prominent position in the centre of this small town, date back
over 500 years and the antiquity of the building is reflected in the
simply decorated and furnished interior. However, the unassuming
character of this friendly inn is complemented by the exceptional
food that is served here. In the three years that landlord, Stuart Mudge, has been at The Globe, it has
gained an enviable reputation for its interesting and imaginative cuisine that draws people here from all
over this part of Somerset. Those travelling from further afield will be interested to know that The Globe
also has three comfortable en suite guest rooms.

NEW INN

Halse, near Taunton, Somerset TA4 3AF
Tel: 01823 432352 Fax: 01823 432363

Found in this tucked away village, **New Inn** is a charming 17th
century former coaching inn that has been tastefully extended over
the years. A quaint, old place that is a quintessential English country
inn, not only is the New Inn well known for its fine ales – it has
been recognised by CAMRA – but landlords Mark Leadeham and
Maggie Harris have also gained an excellent reputation for their
delicious, traditional country pub food. From succulent steaks to freshly prepared sandwiches and
children's meals, the menu here is extensive and visitors to the area will be pleased to hear that the inn
also offers equally superb accommodation in a choice of five en suite guest rooms.

family who were given the manor here
after the Conquest. Norton Fitzwarren's
antiquity and former importance gave rise
to the old rhyme "When Taunton was a
furzy down, Norton was a market town."
Today, although the village has all but
been consumed by its now much larger
neighbour it has still managed to retain
some of its individuality.

The land around Norton Fitzwarren is
damp and fertile and, for hundreds of
years, cider apples have been grown here.
Today, this suburb is a great centre of cider
making and the drink is now transported
all over the world but until the early 19th
century cider was a beverage very much
confined to Somerset and the West
Country. It was the Rev Thomas Cornish,
a local clergyman, who first brought cider
to the attention of the rest of the nation
when he produced a drink so appetizing
that it found great favour with Queen

Victoria. Close to one of the largest cider
breweries in the area are the remains of an
early Bronze Age bank and ditch enclosure
and artefacts excavated from here can be
seen in the county museum in Taunton.

WIVELISCOMBE
9 miles W of Taunton on the B3227

This ancient and isolated village was home
to a Roman fort and a quantity of 3rd and
4th century coins have been found here
whilst, later, in medieval times, the local
manor house was used as a summer
residence of the bishops of Bath and Wells.
The remains of the house, which include a
striking 14th century archway, can still be
seen and they have now been incorporated
into a group of cottages. During World
War II, the church's crypt was used to store
priceless historic documents and
ecclesiastical treasures that were brought
here from other parts of Somerset that

LANGLEY HOUSE HOTEL AND RESTAURANT

Langley Marsh, Wiveliscombe, Somerset TA4 2UF
Tel: 01984 623318 Fax: 01984 624573
e-mail: langley.house@virgin.net

Tucked away in the gentle folds of the Brendon Hill, **Langley House Hotel and Restaurant** is an exceptional country house hotel that offers its customers the chance to enjoy top class hospitality in splendidly elegant Georgian surroundings. Owners, Stuart and Sue Warnock, have won awards for the interior design of the hotel and attention to the smallest detail of anyone's stay here is extended to eight individually designed guest rooms. Naturally, the cuisine here matches the same high standards and diners can look forward to a superb dinner of imaginative, freshly prepared dishes that are created by the hotel's classically trained chef.

were considerably more at risk from aerial attack.

WATERROW
11 miles W of Taunton on the B3227

The original name for this delightful hamlet on the banks of the River Tone is derived from the Old Norse word 'Skir' meaning clear, bright and pure (a reference to the stream) and the Saxon word 'Dael' meaning a valley. Indeed, the fields on the hills surrounding Waterrow suggest a Saxon layout and traces of both Iron Age and Celtic occupation have been found in the area.

BISHOP'S LYDEARD
4½ miles NW of Taunton off the A358

This large village is the southern terminus of the **West Somerset Railway**, the privately operated steam railway that runs to Minehead further down the Bristol

BIRD IN HAND

Bishops Lydeard, near Taunton, Somerset TA4 3LH
Tel: 01823 432090

An early 19th century pub found in the heart of this village, the **Bird in Hand** not only has a traditional English country pub interior with oak beams and wood burning stove in the fireplace, but it is also well known for its simple menu of excellent pub food. An ideal place for lunch whilst walking or cycling in the area, landlords Louise and Richard Cadwallader have made this a very popular local and, along with occasional live music evenings, they also hold a quiz night to which all are welcome.

THE BELL INN

Bishops Lydeard, near Taunton, Somerset TA4 3AU
Tel: 01823 432968

Found next to the village's ancient church is **The Bell Inn**, a wonderful and quaint 15th century pub that, with its large walled beer garden to the front, has the cosy feel of a large cottage rather than an inn. Despite alterations over the years, including the addition of a conservatory style restaurant, there are many original features still to be seen such as the superb open fireplace and the exposed stone walls. Well known for

its delicious cuisine and good choice of real ales, this warm and friendly inn has, under landlord David Jones and his family, become very much part of village life.

Channel coast. At nearly 20 miles it is the longest line of its kind in the country and it was formed when British Rail's branch line between Taunton and Minehead closed in 1971. Running a summer service between Easter and the end of October, there are ten stations along the route and its special attractions include the first class Pullman dining car and the *Flockton Flyer*, a steam locomotive that some passengers may recognise as it has made numerous television and film appearances.

GAULDEN MANOR GARDENS AND HOUSE

Tel: 01984 667213
Set in a beautiful valley between the Brendon and the Quantock hills is the historic **Gaulden Manor**, a medieval house surrounded by a series of gardens that include the rose garden, a well-stocked herb garden, a bog garden and a butterfly garden. Tucked away lies the Secret Garden planted with white shrubs and roses whilst beyond is the Monk's Fish Pond and island. A grassy walk with old shrub roses and geraniums leads back to the house. Not an overly neat garden, this is a place to explore with something new and different around each corner. Plants propagated from the garden are for sale.

WEST BAGBOROUGH
6 miles NW of Taunton off the A358

Set in the heart of the Quantocks, from this attractive village there are wonderful views down over to Taunton and, from the village church, the late Georgian house where Wordsworth stayed briefly in 1841 can be seen. The village is also home to the Quantock Pottery whose decorative stoneware depicts the stunning views and varied wildlife of the area.

TOLLAND
8½ miles NW of Taunton off the B3138

Close to this village is the delightful **Gaulden Manor** (see panel above), an estate that dates from the 12th century although the present house is largely 17th century. The manor's intriguing gardens, which are open from the beginning of June to the end of August, include a rose garden, a herb garden and a Secret Garden that is planted with white shrubs and roses. Gaulden Manor once belonged to

the Turberville family whose name was borrowed by Thomas Hardy for use in his novel, *Tess of the D'Urbervilles*.

CROWCOMBE
9 miles NW of Taunton off the A358

Situated in the western foothills of the Quantocks, Crowcombe is one of the area's most attractive villages and was once an important stopping place on the road to the Bristol Channel. The impressive village church not only contains a striking 17th century family pew of the Carews and an 18th century screen, pulpit and altar designed by Thomas Parker but also a wonderful collection of bench ends and, in particular, there is one dated 1534 that depicts a green man, a mermaid and a pair of naked men trying to spear a dragon – all of which have pagan significance. Thomas Parker was also the architect of **Crowcombe Court**, the somewhat dilapidated looking brick mansion that dominates the village. However, Parker was not able to see his commission through to completion as he was dismissed in 1734 due to the spiralling costs of the building work. The village is also home to a rare part-Tudor **Church House** that served as the parish hall and a Jacobean brewery with mullioned windows that was later converted into almshouses with a school on the upper floor.

NETHER STOWEY
9 miles NW of Taunton off the A39

An attractive village of 17th and 18th century stone cottages and houses, Nether Stowey is best known for its late 18th century literary connections but it has a much longer history and, at one time, it was a small market town. A castle was built here in Norman times and the earthwork remains can still be seen to the west of the village centre whilst its substantial manor house, **Stowey Court**, stands on the eastern side of the village. The construction of the manor house was begun by Lord Audley in 1497 shortly before he joined a protest against Henry VII's taxation policy although, sadly, he was not able to see the finished house as he was executed soon afterwards. The clock tower in the centre of the village dates from 1897 and it replaced the village's market cross.

In 1797, a local tanner, Tom Poole, lent a dilapidated cottage at the end of his garden to his friend, Samuel Taylor Coleridge, who stayed here for three years with his wife and child and so began Nether Stowey's association with poets and writers. It was whilst here that Coleridge wrote most of his famous works, including *The Rime of the Ancient Mariner* and *Kubla Khan*, and, when not writing, he would go on long walks with his friend and near neighbour William Wordsworth who had moved close to Nether Stowey from a house in Dorset at around the same time. Other visitors to the cottage included

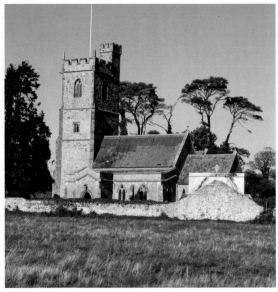

Nether Stowey Parish Church

Charles Lamb but it was not long before Coleridge's opium addition and his rocky marriage began to take their toll on his work. These, however, were not the only problems for the poet as local suspicion was growing that he and Wordsworth were French spies and, after William Wordsworth and his sister Dorothy left for a visit to Germany, Coleridge and his family also moved away. The home in which the Coleridges lived for three years is now **Coleridge Cottage** (National Trust) and it contains mementoes of the poet.

A lane leads southwest from the village to the nearby village of **Over Stowey** and the starting point of the Forestry Commission's **Quantock Forest Trail**, a three mile walk that is lined with specially planted native and imported trees. Meanwhile, to the northwest of Nether Stowey lies the small privately owned manor house, **Dodington Hall**, which is occasionally open to visitors. A fine example of Tudor architecture, the great hall features a splendid oak room and a carved stone fireplace, whilst outside there are attractive semi-formal gardens.

HOLFORD
11 miles NW of Taunton on the A39

A track from this village, on the edge of the Quantocks, leads up to the large Iron Age hill fortification **Dowsborough Fort** whilst, close by, there are the dramatic viewpoints of **Beacon Hill** and **Bicknoller Hill**, where there is another Iron Age relic – a livestock enclosure known as **Tendle Ring**.

KILVE
12 miles NW of Taunton on the A39

Lying at the foot of the Quantocks, this village is home to the ruins of a medieval chantry, or college of priests, and from here a track can be taken from the churchyard that leads down to a boulder-strewn beach that is reputed to be a favourite haunt of glats – conger eels. Once known as St Keyne's serpents, local people used to search for the eels, which hide among the rocks near the shore, using trained fish dogs.

EAST QUANTOXHEAD
12½ miles NW of Taunton off the A39

A picturesque village of thatched cottages with a mill and its millpond, East Quantoxhead is also home to a handsome old manor house, **Court House**, which stands on a rise overlooking the sea. The original owner's family bloodline can be traced back to the 11th century and the *Domesday Book* but, in the 13th century, the manor passed by marriage to the Luttrell family, who were also to become the owners of Dunster Castle. The manor house seen today dates from the 16th and 17th centuries and was constructed by successive generations of the same family.

ALFOXTON PARK

Holford, near Bridgwater, Somerset TA5 1SG
Tel: 01278 741211 e-mail: alfoxton.park@tinyworld.co.uk
website: www.alfoxtonpark.co.uk

Nestling in the gentle folds of the Quantock Hills, **Alfoxton Park** is a glorious Queen Anne period house that was once the home of poet William Wordsworth and his sister Dorothy. Surrounded by 50 peaceful acres and with fabulous, unspoilt views across the Bristol Channel, the grounds include a traditional walled kitchen garden where the vegetables and fruit used in the cooking are grown. Homemade bread, soups, pates, puddings, jam and marmalade all add to the enjoyment of meals in the gracious dining room. The house has retained its classical elegance and along with the carefully chosen furnishings, this delightful hotel, which also has a self catering cottage in the grounds, has a charm all of its own.

THE OLD RECTORY

Kilve, Somerset TA5 1DZ
Tel/Fax: 01278 741520
e-mail: oldrectorykilve@yahoo.co.uk
website: www.oldrectorykilve.btinternet.co.uk

The Old Rectory is a charming 17th century stone house from which Jan and Chris Alder offer superb bed and breakfast accommodation in a choice of three tastefully furnished and decorated en suite guest rooms. A friendly and welcoming establishment, this is an ideal base for exploring north Somerset and the Quantock Hills. Anyone looking for more privacy but the same high standard of accommodation should take advantage of The Old Rectory's three self-catering cottages.

MINEHEAD

Despite sounding like a product of the industrial age, Minehead is a popular seaside town, which lies at the foot of the wooded promontory known as **North Hill**, as well as being one of the oldest settlements in Somerset. A busy Bristol Channel port since the time of the Celts, the old harbour is sheltered by North Hill, which makes it one of the safest landing places in the West Country. At one time, ships arrived here with their cargoes of wool and livestock from Ireland, crops from the plantations of Virginia, coal of the South Wales' valleys and day trippers from Cardiff and Bristol. However, today the merchants and paddle steamers have gone and the harbour is the peaceful haunt of sailing dinghies and pleasure craft.

There is a good view of the old port from the **North Hill Nature Reserve** and a three mile walk that starts near the lifeboat station on the harbour side is an excellent way to explore this particular area of Minehead and its surroundings. Minehead's parish Church of St Michael stands in a prominent position below North Hill and, for centuries, a light was kept burning in the tower of this 14th century church to help guide ships into the harbour. Meanwhile, inside, the church contains a number of unusual features, including a rare medieval prayer book, or missal, which once belonged to Richard Fitzjames, a local vicar who went on to become Bishop of London in 1506.

Minehead's decline as a port was offset by its gradual expansion as a seaside resort and the town went to great lengths to attract a suitably respectable clientele. So much so, in fact, that there was a local bylaw in force until 1890 that forbad anyone over 10 years of age from swimming in the sea "except from a bathing machine, tent or other effective screen." The arrival of the railway in 1874 failed to trigger the rapid expansion experienced by some other seaside resorts and, during World War I, Minehead was able to provide an escape from the ravages of war at timeless establishments such as the Strand Hotel where guests were entertained by such stars as Anna Pavolva and Gladys Cooper.

Improvements to Minehead over the years have been gradual but the most momentous change came in 1962 when Billy Butlin opened a holiday camp at the eastern end of the esplanade. Now updated and renamed **Somerwest World** this popular attraction has done much to transform present day Minehead into an all round family resort.

The town is also the terminus of the **West Somerset Railway**, the privately owned steam railway that runs for 20 miles between the resort and Bishop's Lydeard, just northwest of Taunton.

ROSE-ASH, WILLOW AND LITTLE THATCH COTTAGES

Troytes Farmstead, Tivington, near Minehead, Somerset
Tel: 01643 704531

Found in Minehead, at the foot of the historic Church Steps, these three charming and attractive thatched cottages are part of the group that date back to the 15th and 16th centuries. Each has been sympathetically and carefully restored to provide the very best in self-catering holiday accommodation whilst not losing any of the buildings' original features such as the exposed beams and inglenook fireplaces. Each makes an ideal holiday base in north Somerset and, whilst the interiors are just the place so spend a relaxing evening, each also has an enclosed garden and dogs are welcome at each of the cottages.

Despite its seemingly modern day seaside attractions, Minehead does continue one particularly ancient ceremony when, on May Day eve, the town's Hobby Horse makes its first appearance and then, for the next three days, can be seen dancing at unexpected times around the town accompanied by a drum and an accordion. Hobby Horse ceremonies in the southwest of England are not unusual and are thought to have been based on ancient spring fertility rites; however, Minehead's custom, so local legend suggests, has a different derivation. During the 9th century, the town was under constant attack by the Vikings but the raiders are said to have fled when a Minehead crew disguised its ship as a sea serpent and it is this victory that the ceremony celebrates. In confirmation, it is also pointed out that Minehead's Hobby Horse does bear some resemblance to a longship.

AROUND MINEHEAD

DUNSTER
2 miles SE of Minehead on the A396

Although Dunster is one of the most popular of Exmoor's villages, this ancient settlement is one of the least typical as it lies in the fertile valley of the River Avill and no visitor will be surprised to learn that it was this glorious landscape that inspired Mrs Alexander to compose the hymn *All Things Bright and Beautiful*. The village is dominated by **Dunster Castle** that stands on the top of the wooded Conygar Hill and was founded by William de Mohun on this natural promontory above the River

Avill just a few years before the *Domesday Book* was compiled. The castle passed into the hands of the Luttrell family in 1379 and remained in that family until it was given to the National Trust in 1976 by Lt Col GWF Luttrell. The medieval castle was remodelled in 1617 by William Arnold and, during the English Civil War, Dunster Castle was one of the last Royalist strongholds in the West Country to fall and here the garrison only surrendered after a siege lasting 160 days. Whilst several Jacobean interiors have survived, the castle underwent some major alterations during the latter part of the 17th century and some of the finest features here date from that period – in particular, there is the superb plasterwork in the dining room and the magnificent balustraded main staircase with its delicately carved flora and fauna. However, the overall medieval character of the exterior of the present day castle is due to restoration work undertaken by Anthony Salvin in the 1860s when the castle was transformed into a comfortable and opulent country mansion. The steeply terraced gardens, with their striking collection of rare shrubs and subtropical plants, were also laid out around this time and the castle and gardens are surrounded by a 28 acre deer park through which there

Dunster

are several footpaths. The castle is open on selected days between April and the end of October whilst the gardens and grounds are open daily all year round.

The parkland of Dunster Castle is also home to **Dunster Working Watermill** (see panel - also National Trust) that was built on the site of a pre Norman mill in the 18th century. Now restored to working order, the mill, which is run as a private business, has a shop selling mill flour, museli and mill souvenirs and there is also a tearoom by the riverside.

Remnants of the ancient feudal settlement that grew up in the shelter of the castle can still be seen in the village today, particularly in the wide main street at the north end of which lies the former **Yarn Market**. This small octagonal building was erected by the Luttrells in the early 17th century when the village was an important cloth trading centre and, in fact, such was Dunster's influence in this trade that a type of woollen cloth, renowned for its quality and strength, bears the village's name. Meanwhile, the nearby **Luttrell Arms** is over a century older and it was converted from a private residence into an inn in the mid 17th century. Distinguished by its fine 15th century porch, the inn is one of the few places in the country where the once common custom of burning the ashen faggot is still observed. On Christmas Eve, the faggot, a bundle of 12 ash branches bound with green ash bands, is burnt in the inn's great fireplace and, as each band burns through, another round of hot punch is ordered from the bar. Whilst the ash is burning the audience also sing the ancient Dunster Carol and, when the faggot is finally consumed, a charred

DUNSTER WATER MILL

Mill Lane, Dunster, Somerset TA24 6SW
Tel: 01643 821759

Built in 1680, the mill is set in magnificent surroundings alongside the River Avill overlooking Exmoor National Park, only minutes from Dunster Castle and High Street. You can see how flour is produced as the wheat grain is fed down to the grinding stones before being bagged up for the local bakeries and observe the fascinating collection of ancient agricultural machinery in the integral museum.

The *Domesday Book* recorded two mills on the Mohun Estate at Dunster in 1086, but the upper one has long disappeared. Although there are records of the Lower Mill from medieval times, it began to assume its present appearance in 1779-82 when it was almost completely rebuilt. The Mill survived various periods of disuse between the wars and, continued to produce flour and grind feed for the home farm until 1962. In 1979 the Mill was again repaired and put into working order. The bridge adjacent to the Mill was built in  the eighteenth century by Henry Fownes Luttrell to replace the medieval Mill-bridge. The romantic charm of the Mill made it a favourite haunt of artists in the nineteenth century when its rough rendered walls were covered in ivy. In June 1990, renovation of the Old Mill Stables was completed to provide an attractive tea room and riverside garden.

You can visit the Mill Shop, where the stoneground wholemeal flour, home made muesh and other products are available or morning coffee, home made cakes and scones, cream teas, light lunches may be enjoyed in our delightful tea room or riverside garden.

remain is taken from the embers ready to light the following year's fire.

This ancient inn once belonged to Cleeve Abbey whilst the village's principal religious house, **Dunster Priory**, was an outpost of Bath Abbey. Now largely demolished the only parts of the priory to survive are its splendid priory church and an unusual 12th century dovecote that can be seen in a nearby garden: it still contains the revolving ladder that was used to reach the roosting birds. Meanwhile, the priory church is now one of the most impressive of Somerset's parish churches and it was rebuilt as early as 1100 by monks in a rose pink sandstone. The church tower was added in the 15th century but its most outstanding feature is undoubtedly the fan vaulted rood screen that extends across the nave and aisles.

Along with its buildings of great antiquity, the village is also home to the **Dunster Dolls Museum** that was established in the early 1970s and is based on a unique doll collection that was started by Mollie Harwick some 20 years earlier. Of particular interest here are the ethnic dolls which illustrate the great many lands and cultures of the world whilst there are also character dolls, advertising figures and dolls made from many unusual materials. The museum can be found in the Memorial Hall.

CARHAMPTON
3½ miles SE of Minehead on the A39

A small inland village that was the site of a Viking victory in the 9th century, Carhampton's original village church was named after St Carantoc, an early Celtic missionary from across the Bristol Channel who is reputed to have chosen this site for his ministry by throwing his stone altar overboard and following it to the shore. The present church building, though much restored, contains a remarkable 15th century painted screen that extends across

the entire church whilst the old inn, near the churchyard lych gate, has, in its cobbled floor, the date 1638 picked out in sheep's knuckle bones.

Each January, the residents of Carhampton re-enact the ancient custom of wassailing the apple trees. A toast is made to the most productive apple tree in the district and cider is poured on to its trunk in a charming ceremony that probably has pagan origins. Meanwhile, local folklore tells of a mysterious woman from the village, Madam Carne, who died in 1612 after having done away with three husbands. According to legend, her ghost returned home after her funeral to prepare breakfast for the mourners.

WASHFORD
6 miles SE of Minehead on the A39

This village, which is spread out across Vallis Florida, the flowery valley that is dedicated to 'Our Blessed Lady of the Cliff', is home to **Cleeve Abbey** (English Heritage), the only monastery in Somerset that belonged to the austere Cistercian order. Founded in 1198 by the Earl of Lincoln, the abbey is fortunate in that it was not allowed to fall into disrepair after the Dissolution of the Monasteries, like many great monastic houses, but the cloister buildings at Cleeve were put to domestic use and they are now among the most complete in the country. Although the cruciform abbey church has been reduced to its foundations, the refectory, chapter house, monks' common room, dormitory and cloisters all remain. Most impressive of all is the great hall – a magnificent building with tall windows, a wagon roof that is decorated with busts of crowned angels and medieval murals, and a unique set of floor tiles with heraldic symbols. Meanwhile, the curved dormitory staircase has particularly fine archways and mullioned windows whilst the combined gatehouse and almonry, the last building to be constructed before the Dissolution, makes an imposing entrance to the abbey precinct. The abbey is open daily all year round and a programme of special events are staged here.

Whilst the abbey has dominated Washford for centuries, just to the east of the village lies a more recent attraction **Tropiquaria**, a wildlife park that particularly features, as its name suggests, tropical animals. There is also an aquarium here along with an aviary and visitors are offered the chance to stroke snakes, handle tarantulas and in many other ways get in touch with their wilder side.

WATCHET
6½ miles SE of Minehead on the B3191

Established as a port long before the Norman Conquest, it was at Watchet that, in the 6th century, St Decuman is said to have landed from Wales with his cow that he brought with him to provide sustenance. The town's name is derived from the Welsh for 'under the hill' but more recently it has lent itself to a fashionable colour – Charles I was once described as wearing a waistcoat of Watchet blue – that is possibly taken from the very distinctive colour of the cliffs here that were worked for their alabaster. By the 10th century the Saxon port and settlement here was important enough to have been sacked by the Vikings on at least three separate occasions and Watchet, today, is the only port of any significance in this part of the county. During the mid 19th century thousands of tons of iron ore from the Brendon Hills were being exported through the docks each year and, unlike many similar sized ports that fell into disuse following the arrival of the railway, Watchet docks continue to export goods principally bound for the Iberian Peninsula. It was from Watchet that

Watchet Lighthouse

Coleridge's imaginary crew set sail in *The Rime of the Ancient Mariner*, the epic poem that was written whilst the poet was living at nearby Nether Stowey. **Watchet Harbour** is now a focal point for various activities and, along with being a venue for concerts, boat trips can also be taken from here. Meanwhile, the first part of the **Old Mineral Line**, the local railway line that brought goods to and from the harbour, is now a pleasant footpath that runs between Watchet and Washford. Found beside the station and housed in an old Victorian goods shed, is the **Watchet Flatner Boat Museum** that houses the largest collection of these local boats in the world. Used for carrying peat and other materials on the rivers and moors of Somerset, these flat bottomed boats were once a common sight in the town and the museum is open most afternoons from Easter to October.

The scale of Watchet's parish church reflects the town's long standing importance and prosperity: it is set well back from the town centre and contains several fine tombs belonging to the Wyndham family, the local lords of the manor who did much to develop the potential of the port. There is a local story that suggests that one 16th century member of the family, Florence Wyndham, had to be buried twice. The day after her first funeral the church sexton went down into church vaults to secretly remove a ring from her finger and, on opening the coffin, the old woman suddenly awoke! In recent years, the town has become something of a coastal resort and one of its attractions is the small **Market House Museum** that has a host of displays of artefacts that illustrate Watchet's colourful past from Viking invasions to the story of the Mineral Line Railway. The museum is open throughout the summer and other holidays.

WILLITON
7½ miles SE of Minehead on the A39

This large village was once a Saxon royal estate and, during the 12th century, the manor was the home of Sir Reginald FitzUrse, one of the knights who murdered Thomas à Becket, and to atone for his terrible crime, Sir Reginald gave half the manor to the Knights Templar. The other half of the manor remained in the FitzUrse

family until the death of Sir Ralph, in 1350, where upon it was divided between his daughters. The village today is the home of the diesel locomotive workshops of the West Somerset Railway and the **Bakelite Museum**, a fascinating place that provides a nostalgic look at the 'pioneer of plastics'. The only museum in Britain to be devoted to Bakelite, which was invented in 1907, and other vintage plastics, there are thousands of objects for visitors to see that touch on all aspects of 20th century life. This fascinating place, where the astonishing range of colours and textures of the plastics is sure to amaze, is open from Easter to the end of September from Thursdays to Saturdays during term time and daily in the main school holidays.

SAMPFORD BRETT
8½ miles SE of Minehead on the A358

Recorded in the *Domesday Book*, this historic village's name is derived from both

DAISY COTTAGE

Bridge Street, Williton, Somerset TA4 4NR
Contact Mrs A. Bishop, 6 North Street, Williton, Taunton, Somerset TA4 4SL Tel/Fax: 01984 632657

Found in the oldest part of this village, near the church, stream and old mill (now the Bakelite Museum), **Daisy Cottage** is a delightful thatched cottage providing attractive self-catering accommodation for up to four in two bedrooms. The cottage has been recently refurbished with all the latest conveniences, while retaining charm and character with beamed ceilings and inglenook fireplace complete with cast iron gas fired stove. Outside the cottage has a pretty and secluded garden. Within easy walking distance of the shops and pubs, the cottage is an ideal base for exploring the Exmoor National Park, the Quantock Hills and the coast.Parking for 3 cars. ETB 4 Keys (and Silver Award)

CERAMICS BY MARTIN PETTINGER

Williton Pottery, Half Acre, Williton, near Taunton, Somerset TA4 4NZ
Tel: 01984 632150
e-mail: martinpettinger@hotmail.com

Established in 1982, **Williton Pottery** now has a refitted showroom where the extensive range of pots created by this established potter can be viewed in an attractive contemporary setting. Developed over the last 25 years, the range of ceramics here not only reflects the making of pots in the West Country for the last four centuries but also modern day needs and, in all cases, they are decorated with the attractive slip ware technique. The distinctive designs of his pots make Martin Pettinger's ceramics particularly sought after and along with those on sale in the gallery he also undertakes commission work.

the sandy ford that crossed the Doniford stream close by and the local de Brett family. It was Sir Adam de Brett who obtained the village's first charter to hold a market (in 1306) and, today, Sampford Brett remains a lovely and unspoilt place.

MONKSILVER
8½ miles SE of Minehead on the B3188

This pretty village of charming old houses and thatched cottages has, in its

churchyard, the graves of Elizabeth Conibeer and her two middle aged daughters, Anne and Sarah, who were murdered in June 1775 in the nearby hamlet of **Woodford**. Their tombstone bears a message to the unidentified murderer:

"Inhuman wretch, whoe'er thou art
That didst commit this horrid crime,
Repent before thou dost depart

THE ROYAL OAK INN
Luxborough, Somerset TA23 0SH
Tel: 01984 640319 Fax: 01984 641561
e-mail: royalaokof.luxborough@virgin.net

Surrounded by the glorious wilderness of Exmoor, **The Royal Oak** Inn is a charming traditional country inn that is formed by a collection of attractive 14th century cottages and outbuildings. A rambling and interesting place, the inn offers both the full pub atmosphere in the bustling bar area whilst there are several smaller rooms that provide a cosy and intimate environment for eating and drinking. A place that offers superb food, accommodation and hospitality, however, what makes the Royal Oak particularly special is what it does not offer – there are no juke boxes or piped music, no fruit machines, no reproduction furniture and no mobile phone reception.

THE VALIANT SOLDIER
Roadwater, near Watchet, Somerset TA23 0QZ
Tel: 01984 640223 Fax: 01984 641244

A typical rural inn found just on the fringes of Exmoor, **The Valiant Soldier** dates from the 18th century and its traditional interior and roaring log fires draw both locals and visitors alike. Cosy, warm and friendly, this charming inn not only has a fine selection of real ales and ciders but also an interesting menu of food that combines the best of English cuisine with more adventurous dishes from around the world. Landlords, Tracey and Michael Twine, also offer accommodation in a choice of five comfortable en suite guest rooms and, for the children, there is a special kiddies play garden.

WOOD ADVENT FARM
Roadwater, Somerset TA23 0RR
Tel/Fax: 01984 640920 e-mail: info@woodadventfarm.co.uk
website: www.woodadventfarm.co.uk

Built in the early 19th century, **Wood Advent Farm** has been in the Brewer family since the 1700's and today, whilst John Brewer manages the farm, his wife Diana looks after their guests who are fortunate enough to have discovered this glorious haven amidst Exmoor National Park. Along with the charming en suite guest rooms, John and Diana provide a wealth of local information and maps in the Chintzed Room while the elegant Drawing Room is just the place to relax quietly with a book. Meanwhile, in the stylish Dining Room guests are treated to wonderful home-cooked dishes that can be complemented by either wine or the farm's own spring water.

To meet thy awful Judge Divine."

Just to the south of the village is a particularly handsome manor house, **Combe Sydenham Hall** that was built in the middle of the reign of Elizabeth I by George Sydenham on the site of a monastic settlement and, above the entrance, there is a Latin inscription that translates to: "This door of George's is always open except to ungrateful souls." This was also the home of Elizabeth Sydenham, George's daughter, who was to become the second wife of Sir Francis Drake but, after becoming engaged, Sir Francis left his fiancée to go off looting for Spanish gold. Elizabeth grew so weary waiting for her betrothed to return that she resolved to marry another gentleman and while on her way to the church, according to local stories, a meteorite flew out of the sky and smashed into the ground in front of her. Taking this as a sign that she should wait for Sir Francis she called off the wedding and, eventually, the couple were reunited. The meteorite, now known as 'Drake's Cannonball', is on display in the great hall and it is said to bring good luck to those who touch it. Meanwhile, the 500 acre grounds around the hall have been designated a **Country Park** and they contain a working corn mill complete with waterwheel, a herb garden, a peacock house and a herd of fallow deer. The estate also incorporates a modern trout farm that stands on the site of a fully restored Tudor trout hatchery that dates from the end of the 16th century.

A mile or so to the west lies another ancient manor, **Nettlecombe Court** that was once the home of the Raleigh family, relations of another great Elizabethan seafarer Sir Walter Raleigh. Later, the manor passed, by marriage, to the Cornish Trevelyan family and it is now a field studies centre that is only open by appointment.

Exmoor River

To the southwest of the village are the **Brendon Hills**, the upland area within the Exmoor National Park from where, in the mid 19th century, iron ore was extracted in significant quantities and then carried down a steep mineral railway to the coast for shipment to the furnaces of South Wales. At one time the Ebbw Vale Company employed almost a thousand miners here and this strictly Nonconformist concern imposed a rigorous teetotal regime on its workers. (Those wanting a drink had to walk across the moor all the way to Raleigh's Cross.) The company also founded a miners' settlement with a temperance hotel and three chapels that became renowned for the achievements of its choir and fife and drum band. Meanwhile, those walking the slopes of the hills can still see sections of the old Mineral Railway and there is a two mile stretch leading down to the coast at Watchet that is now a pleasant footpath.

DULVERTON
12 miles S of Minehead on the B3222

Dulverton's name is derived from a Saxon name meaning 'the secret place' and it lies, rather aptly, in the wooded Barle Valley on the edge of Exmoor. A pretty little town, it is home to the headquarters of the Exmoor National Park Authority that can be found in an old converted workhouse.

LION HOTEL

Bank Square, Dulverton, Somerset TA22 9BU
Tel: 01398 323444 Fax: 01398 323980

Found in the heart of this pretty Exmoor village, the early 19th century **Lion Hotel** offers customers a real taste of traditional English hospitality as well as being an ideal location from which to explore the delights of the surrounding countryside. Along with the two comfortable bars, guests can also enjoy a delicious home-cooked meal from the traditional menu of homemade pies, pates and local specialities in the bar or the more formal surroundings of the dining room. Finally, staying here in one of the charming en suite guest rooms provides the ideal opportunity for visitors to fully appreciate the relaxed and friendly atmosphere of this delightful inn.

ROCK HOUSE INN

1 Jury Road, Dulverton, Somerset TA22 9DU
Tel: 01398 323131
website: www.rockhouseinn.co.uk

Overlooking Dulverton from its elevated position the **Rock House Inn** is, for many visitors, one of the first places they see. A charming old inn dating back to the mid 19th century, this is very much a village pub and the cosy and inviting interior creates just the right atmosphere for both locals and visitors alike to mingle and enjoy the excellent hospitality on offer here. Along with the bar, landlords Tony and Lindsay Wright provide a traditional menu of good pub food that is particularly noted for its freshness and they also offer comfortable bed and breakfast accommodation at the inn.

ARCHIAMMA

26 High Street, Dulverton, Exmoor National Park, Somerset TA22 9DJ
Tel: 01398 323397 Fax: 01398 323918 website: www.archiamma.co.uk

Found in the heart of Dulverton, down one of its many narrow streets that are crammed with antique and crafts shops, is **archiamma** restaurant. Within this beautiful 19th century building, lies a stylish, unique restaurant serving contemporary food. Owner, Nelisha, is passionate about food and works closely with local suppliers and the Head Chef to create menus influenced by regional and European styles. All produce is bought daily from local farms and fisheries and food is prepared to order. As well as a changing menu, the wine list is regularly revised and all wines on this inspiring list are offered by the glass. Booking is advisable.

THE ROYAL OAK INN

Winsford, Exmoor National Park, Somerset TA24 7JE
Tel: 01643 851455 e-mail: enquiries@royaloak-somerset.co.uk
Fax: 01643 851009 website: www.royaloak-somerset.co.uk

Dating back to the 12th century, **The Royal Oak Inn** has a fairytale appearance from the outside whilst the inside is charming, with lots of character, and retaining many of its original features such as the inglenook fireplaces and oak beams. Decorated and furnished to create a cosy and relaxing as well as stylish environment, this inn offers customers the very best in country house hospitality. The bar is an ideal place to begin an evening before moving through to enjoy a superb dinner prepared by the inn's excellent head chef. Following a nightcap by the fire in one of the elegant lounges, guests can then retire to one of the 14 exquisite and individually designed en suite rooms. AA 3 star, RAC 3 star and ETC 3 star ratings.

Meanwhile, at the **Guildhall Heritage and Arts Centre** there are a series of displays on the history of Dulverton over the last 100 years along with the Exmoor Photographic Archive whilst the gallery hosts an exhibition of arts and crafts by local artists. The centre is open from the end of March to the beginning of November.

This was also the town where, in RF Delderfield's novel *To Serve Them All My Days*, the main character David Powlett-Jones falls asleep at the station on his way to begin teaching at a public school in Exmoor. Delderfield had grown up on the edge of Exmoor and he used Somerset and neighbouring Devon as settings for this and his other novels.

Selworthy

CHALLACOMBE
17½ miles SW of Minehead on the B3358

Famous for its ancient inn, The Black Venus, Challacombe lies just inside Exmoor National Park whilst, the **Edgerley Stone** that marks the border between Somerset and Devon lies just a mile and a half away. There has been a settlement here for centuries and it was the ancient Britons who gave the village its name although experts cannot agree whether the name means 'cold valley' or 'calves' valley' but either interpretation would be valid as the wind is never still here and beef cattle are raised on the surrounding moorland.

SELWORTHY
3 miles W of Minehead off the A39

This picturesque and much photographed village is situated on the side of a wooded hill whilst just to the northwest lies **Selworthy Beacon**, one of the highest points on the vast **Holnicote Estate** (National Trust) that covers some 12,500 acres of Exmoor National Park and includes a four mile stretch of coastline between Minehead and Porlock Weir. There are few estates in the country that offer such a variety of landscape as this and, along with north facing cliffs along the coast, there are traditional villages and hamlets of cottages and farms and the **Horner and Dunkery National Nature Reserve** that is home to **Dunkery Beacon**, which is the highest point on Exmoor at 1,700 feet. Virtually the full length of the River Horner lies within the estate, from its source on the

THE ROYAL OAK INN

Withypool, Exmoor, Somerset TA24 7QP
Tel: 01643 831506 Fax: 01643 831659
e-mail: enquiries@royaloakwithypool.co.uk
website: www.royaloakwithypool.co.uk

Found right in the heart of Exmoor National Park, **The Royal Oak Inn** has been offering superb countryside hospitality for over 300 years and, among its many visitors, have been General Eisenhower and RD Blackmore whilst, in the 1930s, the inn was owned by Maxwell Knight, the spy-master who inspired Ian Fleming's character 'M'.However, it is now owned and personally run by Gail Sloggett. As well as its atmospheric bars the Inn has an elegant restaurant, renowned for the quality and presentation of its food, and individually styled guest rooms with the most comfortable beds you ever slept in. At the rear of the Inn are two beautiful self catering cottages.

high moorland to Bossington Beach – one of the best examples of a shingle storm beach in the country – were it flows into the sea. The whole area is noted for its diversity of wildlife and there are also many rare plant species to be found.

This estate has over 100 miles of footpaths through fields, moors and villages for walkers to enjoy whilst the **South West Coast Path** curves inland at Hurlstone Point to avoid the possibility of landslips in the soft Foreland sandstone. Among the settlements in the estate is this village of Selworthy that was created by Sir Thomas Dyke-Acland to house his estate workers.

ALLERFORD
4 miles W of Minehead on the A39

Another estate village, Allerford is home to an elegant twin arched **Packhorse Bridge** whilst its old school, which closed in 1981, is now a **Museum** that is dedicated to the rural life of west Somerset. Among its many imaginatively presented displays is a Victorian schoolroom with the original desks and forms, a kitchen and a laundry. Outside there is a riverside garden and a playground and the museum is open at Easter and then from May to October on weekdays and Sundays.

PORLOCK
5 miles W of Minehead off the A39

An ancient settlement that was once frequented by Saxon kings, in recent decades Porlock has become a popular riding and holiday centre. Of the village's many lovely old buildings, there is the 15th century **Dovery Manor**, with its striking traceried hall window, and the largely 13th century parish church that lost the top section of its spire during a thunderstorm in the 17th century. Porlock has long had the feel of a community at the end of the world as it lies at the foot of **Porlock Hill**, a notorious incline were the road rises 1,350 feet in less than three miles and, in places, has a gradient of 1 in 4.

PORLOCK WEIR
6½ miles W of Minehead off the A39

Today this hamlet's small tide-affected harbour is populated by pleasure craft but Porlock Weir was once an important seaport. The Danes sacked it on a number of occasions in the 10th century and, in 1052, Harold, the future king of England, landed here from Ireland to begin a short-lived career that ended at the Battle of Hastings in 1066. Now a pleasant and picturesque place, a short distance off shore a **Submerged Forest**, a relic of the Ice Age, can be seen at low tide.

From Porlock Weir a pretty mile-long walk leads up through woodland to **Culbone Church**, the smallest church in regular use in England. A true hidden treasure that measures only 33 feet by 14 feet, this superb part Norman building is set in a wooded combe that once supported a small charcoal burning community.

Allerford Packhorse Bridge

PORLOCK VALE HOUSE

Porlock Weir, Porlock, Somerset TA24 8NY
Tel: 01643 862338 Fax: 01643 863338
e-mail: info@porlockvale.co.uk
website: www.porlockvale.co.uk

Nestling on the sheltered slopes of Exmoor, with spectacular views and 25 acres of grounds running down to the sea, **Porlock Vale House** is a small, friendly hotel retaining much of the character and elegance from its hunting lodge origins. In summer guests can sit outside on the terrace and soak up the peace and tranquility or in winter, relax in front of a roaring fire. A drink can be enjoyed in the oak panelled bar and tasty traditional food can be savoured in the dining room with its excellent views. All the individually styled bedrooms are en-suite with every comfort and amazing outlooks. There are numerous and varied activities to partake of in the area including fishing, shooting, walking and horse riding (the Hotel has its own riding centre). An absolute must!

DOONE VALLEY
11 miles W of Minehead off the A39

This scenic valley, with its long enclosed sweep of green pasture and mature woodland, was immortalised by RD Blackmore in his classic romantic novel, *Lorna Doone* and the now demolished medieval farm known as Hoccombe Combe is thought to have been the home of a wild and unruly Exmoor family whose real-life exploits provided the inspiration for the story. Meanwhile, the beautiful little 15th century church to the east, at **Oare**, is thought to be the setting of the heroine's dramatic, interrupted wedding. Inside the church, where RD Blackmore's grandfather was once rector, there is a fine set of 19th century box pews and an unusual piscine that is shaped like a man's head.

To the north, on the coast and at the county border with Devon is **County Gate**, one of several dramatic viewpoints along this stretch of spectacular coastline. Here, the great whale-backed hills of Exmoor plunge down to the sea and there are breathtaking views across the Bristol Channel to South Wales. Meanwhile, this headland is also home to one of the few Roman remains on Exmoor, a lookout station for observing cross-channel raiding parties.

LYNMOUTH
15½ miles W of Minehead on the A39

For centuries this was a village scraping a living from the land and the sea and it was particularly noted for its catches of herring most of which were also cured here. Thankfully, just as the herring shoals were moving to new waters this part of the Exmoor coast began to benefit from two great enthusiasms: romantic scenery and sea bathing. Both Coleridge and Wordsworth came here on a walking tour in the 1790s, Shelley visited in 1812 but it was Robert Southey, later to become the Poet Laureate, who first used the phrase "English Switzerland" to describe the dramatic scenery here that Gainsborough considered the "most delightful" for a landscape painter. However, by the mid 19th century the steep cliff between Lynmouth and its neighbour along the coast, Lynton, was affecting the growing tourist trade and so Bob Janes, a local engineer designed the **Lynton-Lynmouth Cliff Railway.** Opened on Easter Monday 1890, this ingenious railway, which still runs today, rises some 450 feet in just 900 feet and it is powered by water, with each of the two carriages having a huge water tank beneath them. The tank is filled at the top of the cliff to carry that carriage down to the bottom (taking the other carriage to the top) and then the tank is emptied whilst the other carriage's tank is filled to bring them back to their original positions and so on. The trip takes just 90 seconds and so good were Janes's designs for the braking and hydraulic systems that they have not been changed since the railway was built.

Lynmouth lies at the confluence of the East and West Lyn Rivers and it has a tiny harbour surrounded by wooded hills, a curious tower on its pier and Mars Hill, an eye-catching row of thatched cottages. Although Lynmouth's setting beside its twin rivers is undeniably beautiful, it has also proved to be tragically vulnerable and, on the night of 16th August 1952, a cloudburst over Exmoor deposited nine inches of rain on to an already soaked moorland. In the darkness the normally placid East and West Lyn Rivers became raging torrents and, having burst their banks, they swept trees and boulders away in their wake. The debris-filled torrent smashed its way through the village and destroyed dozens of houses leaving 34 people dead and many injured. Following the devastation, the village was rebuilt, along with its harbour and the **Rhenish Tower**, the folly at the end of the pier.

However, this is not the first storm to hit Lynmouth and, in 1899, the Lynmouth lifeboat was involved in a tale of epic endurance during another exceptional storm. A full-rigged ship, the *Forest Hill*, was in difficulties off Porlock but the storm was so violent it was impossible to launch the lifeboat at Lynmouth. Instead the crewmen dragged their three and a half ton boat, the *Louisa*, 13 miles across the moor and, in the process, they had to negotiate Countisbury Hill, with its gradient of 1,000 feet over two miles.

Once at Porlock Weir the lifeboat was successfully launched and every crewmember of the stricken ship was saved.

To the east of the village, in a picturesque valley, lies **Watersmeet House**, an old fishing lodge that has been a tea garden since 1901 and from where several scenic walks begin. Along with offering refreshments, the house is also a National Trust shop and information point.

LYNTON
16 miles W of Minehead off the A39

Lymouth's twin, Lynton, has a very different character: the younger of the two settlements, it sits on top of the great cliff whilst Lynmouth lies far below. A bright and breezy village, of chiefly Victorian architecture, Lynton is home to the **Exmoor Museum** that is housed in a restored 16th century dwelling and here an intriguing collection of tools and the bygone products of local craftsmen can be seen along with other exhibits that recount the area's history. Meanwhile, to the west of Lynton is one of the most remarkable natural features in Devon, the **Valley of the Rocks**. When the poet Robert Southey visited here in 1800, he was most impressed by this natural gorge and he described it as "covered with huge stones" and with "rock reeling upon rock." In *Lorna Doone*, RD Blackmore transforms the site into the Devil's Cheesewring where Jan Ridd visits Mother Meldrun who is sheltering under a lichen-covered rock. Coleridge was equally inspired by the valley, which he walked in the company of Wordsworth and his sister Dorothy, and the result was his immortal poem *The Rime of the Ancient Mariner*.

List of
Tourist Information Centres

GLOUCESTERSHIRE

BOURTON-ON-THE-WATER
Victoria Street
Bourton-on-the-Water
Gloucestershire GL54 2BU
Tel: 01451 820211

CHELTENHAM
77 Promenade
Cheltenham
Gloucestershire GL50 1PP
Tel: 01242 522878
Fax: 01242 255848
e-mail: tic@cheltenham.gov.uk

CHIPPING CAMPDEN
Rosary Court
High Street
Chipping Campden
Gloucestershire GL55 6AL
Tel: 01386 841206

CIRENCESTER
Corn Hall
Market Place
Cirencester
Gloucestershire GL7 2NW
Tel: 01285 654180
Fax: 01285 641182

COLEFORD
High Street
Coleford
Gloucestershire GL16 8HG
Tel: 01594 812388
e-mail: tourism@fdean.gov.uk

GLOUCESTER DOCKS
National Waterways Museum
Llanthony Warehouse
Gloucester Docks
Gloucestershire

GLOUCESTER
28 Southgate Street
Gloucester
Gloucestershire GL1 1PD
Tel: 01452 421188
Fax: 01452 504273
e-mail:tourism@gloscity.gov.uk

or

7 Church Street
Newent
Gloucestershire GL18 1PU
Tel: 01531 822468

KEYNES COUNTRY PARK
Shorncote
Cirencester
Gloucestershire GL7 6DF
Tel: 01285 861459

MORETON-IN-MARSH
Cotswold District Council Offices
High Street
Moreton-in-Marsh
Gloucestershire
Tel: 01608 650881

NAILSWORTH
1 Fountain Street
Nailsworth
Stroud
Gloucestershire
Tel: 01453 832532

PAINSWICK
The Library
Stroud Road
Painswick
Gloucestershire
Tel: 01452 813552
(Seasonal)

STOW-ON-THE-WOLD

Hollis House
The Square
Stow-on-the-Wold
Gloucestershire GL54 1AF
Tel: 01451 831082

STROUD

1 John Street
Stroud
Gloucestershire GL5 1AE
Tel: 01453 765768

TETBURY

Shop 1
33 Church Street
Tetbury
Gloucestershire
GL8 8JG
Tel: 01666 503552
e-mail: tetburytourism@yahoo.co.uk

TEWKESBURY

The Museum
64 Barton Street
Tewkesbury
Gloucestershire GL20 5PX
Tel: 01684 295027

WINCHCOMBE

The Town Hall
High Street
Winchcombe
Gloucestershire GL54 5LJ
Tel: 01242 602925 *(seasonal)*

WOTTON-UNDER-EDGE

The Heritage Centre
The Chipping
Wotton-under-Edge
Gloucestershire
Tel: 01453 521541

SOMERSET

BATH

Abbey Chambers
Abbey Church Yard
Bath
BA1 1LY
Tel: 01225 477101
Fax: 01225 477787
e-mail: tourism@bathnes.gov.uk

BRIDGWATER

50 High Street
Bridgwater
Somerset TA6 3BL
Tel: 01278 427652
Fax: 01278 453489
e-mail: bridgwater.tic@sedgemoor.gov.uk

BRISTOL

The Annexe
Wildscreen Walk
Harbourside
Bristol BS1 5DB
Tel: 0117 926 0767
Fax: 0117 922 1557
e-mail: ticharbourside@bristol-city.gov.uk

BURNHAM-ON-SEA

South Esplanade
Burnham-on-Sea
Somerset TA8 1BU
Tel: 01278 787852
Fax: 01278 781282
e-mail: burnham.tic@sedgemoor.gov.uk

CHARD

The Guildhall
Fore Street
Chard
Somerset TA20 1PP
Tel: 01460 67463

CHEDDAR

The Gorge
Cheddar
Somerset BS27 3QE
Tel: 01934 744071
Fax: 01934 744614
e-mail: cheddar.tic@sedgemoor.gov.uk

FROME
The Round Tower
Justice Lane
Frome
Somerset BA11 1BB
Tel: 01373 467271
Fax: 01373 451733
e-mail: frome.tic@ukonline.co.uk

GLASTONBURY
The Tribunal
9 High Street
Glastonbury
Somerset BA6 9DP
Tel: 01458 832954
Fax: 01458 832949
e-mail: glastonbury.tic@ukonline.co.uk

MINEHEAD
17 Friday Street
Minehead
Somerset
TA24 5UB
Tel: 01643 702624
Fax: 01643 707166
e-mail: mineheadtic@visit.org.uk

PODIMORE
South Somerset Visitor Centre Services Area
(A303) Podimore
Nr Yeovil
Somerset BA22 8JG
Tel: 01935 841302
Fax: 01935 841294
e-mail: podimore.tic@ukonline.co.uk

SEDGEMOOR
Somerset Visitor Centre
Sedgemoor Services
M5 South
Axbridge
Somerset BS26 2UF
Tel: 01934 750833
Fax: 01934 750755
e-mail: sominfo@msn.com

SHEPTON MALLET
70 High Street
Shepton Mallet
Somerset BA4 5AS
Tel: 01749 345258
Fax: 01749 345258
e-mail: sheptonmallet.tic@ukonline.co.uk

STREET
Clark's Village
Farm Road
Street
Somerset BA16 0BB
Tel: 01458 447384
Fax: 01458 447393
e-mail: street.tic@ukonline.co.uk

TAUNTON
Paul Street
Taunton
Somerset TA1 3XZ
Tel: 01823 336344
Fax: 01823 340308
e-mail: tautic@somerset.gov.uk

WELLINGTON
30 Fore Street
Wellington
Somerset TA21 8AQ
Tel: 01823 663379
Fax: 01823 667279

WELLS
Town Hall
Market Place
Wells
Somerset BA5 2RB
Tel: 01749 672552
Fax: 01749 670869
e-mail: wellstic@ukonline.co.uk

WESTON-SUPER-MARE
Beach Lawns
Weston-super-Mare
Somerset BS23 1AT
Tel: 01934 888800
Fax: 01934 641741

YEOVIL
Petter's House
Petter's Way
Yeovil
Somerset BA20 1SH
Tel: 01935 471279
Fax: 01935 434065
e-mail: yeoviltic@southsomerset.gov.uk

WILTSHIRE

AMESBURY

Redworth House, Flower Lane
Amesbury
Wiltshire SP4 7HG
Tel: 01980 622833
Fax: 01980 625541
e-mail: amesburytic@salisbury.gov.uk

BRADFORD-ON-AVON

34 Silver Street
Bradford-on-Avon
Wiltshire BA15 1JX
Tel: 01225 865797 (01225 868722)
Fax: 01225 868722

CHIPPENHAM

The Citadel, Bath Road
Chippenham
Wiltshire SN15 2AA
Tel: 01249 706333
Fax: 01249 460776
e-mail: tourism@northwilts.gov.uk

CORSHAM

Arnold House, 31 High Street
Corsham
Wiltshire SN13 0EZ
Tel: 01249 714660
Fax: 01249 716164
e-mail: corshamheritage@northwilts.gov.uk

DEVIZES

Cromwell House, Market Place
Devizes
Wiltshire SN10 1JG
Tel: 01380 729408
Fax: 01380 730319

MALMESBURY

Town Hall, Market Lane
Malmesbury
Wiltshire SN16 9BZ
Tel: 01666 823748

MARLBOROUGH

George Lane Car Park
Marlborough
Wiltshire SN8 1EE
Tel: 01672 513989
Fax: 01672 513989

MELKSHAM

Church Street
Melksham
Wiltshire SN12 6LS
Tel: 01225 707424
Fax: 01225 707424
e-mail: visitmelksham@westwiltshire.gov.uk

MERE

The Square, Mere
Warminster
Wiltshire BA12 6JJ
Tel: 01747 861211
Fax: 01747 861127

SALISBURY

Fish Row
Salisbury
Wiltshire SP1 1EJ
Tel: 01722 334956
Fax: 01722 422059

SWINDON

37 Regent Street
Swindon
Wiltshire SN1 1JL
Tel: 01793 530328 (01793 466454)
Fax: 01793 434031
e-mail: infocentre@swindon.gov.uk

TROWBRIDGE

St Stephen's Place
Trowbridge
Wiltshire BA14 8AH
Tel: 01225 777054
Fax: 01225 777054
e-mail: visittrowbridge@westwiltshire.gov.uk

WARMINSTER

Central Car Park
Warminster
Wiltshire BA12 9BT
Tel: 01985 218548
Fax: 01985 846154

WESTBURY

The Library, Edward Street
Westbury
Wiltshire BA13 3BD
Tel: 01373 827158
Fax: 01373 827158

Index of Towns, Villages and Places of Interest

A

Aller 158
  High Ham 158
  Stembridge Tower Mill 158
Allerford 190
  Museum 190
  Packhorse Bridge 190
Avebury
  Avebury Stone Circles 73
Avening 38
  Avening Long Stone 39
Axbridge 119
  Gypsy Folklore Collection 120
  King John's Hunting Lodge 120
  Local History Museum 120
  Webbington Loxton 120
  Wheelwright's Working Museum 120

B

Badminton 41
  Badminton Park 41
Baltonsborough 140
Banwell 121
  Banwell Camp 121
  Banwell Castle 121
  Bone Caves 121
  Puxton 121
Barnsley 54
  Barnsley House Garden 54
Barrington 163
  Barrington Court 163
  Westport 163
Barrow Gurney 114
Barwick 150
  Barwick Park 150
  Jack the Treacle Eater 150
Batcombe 137
Bath 105
  Assembly Rooms 107
  Bath Abbey 106
  Bath Museum 107
  Bath Postal Museum 107
  Bath Racecourse 108
  Bath Skyline Walk 107
  Great Bath 105
  Holburne Museum 107
  Jane Austen Centre 107
  Museum of Costume 107
  Museum of East Asian Art 107
  Pulteney Bridge 106, 107
  Pump Room 107
  Roman Baths 105
  Royal Crescent 107
  Vaults Museum 106
Bathampton 108
  Bathampton Down 108
Bathford 108
  Brown's Folly 108
  Eagle House 108
Beckington 128
  Cedars 128
  Seymour Court 128
Berkeley 45
  Berkeley Castle 45
  Butterfly Farm 46
  Jenner Museum 46
  The Jenner Museum 46
  Vale of Berkeley 45
Bibury 53
  Arlington Mill 54
  Arlington Row 54
Bishop's Lydeard 176
  West Somerset Railway 176
Bisley 37
  Seven Wells of Bisley 37
Blagdon 118
  Blagdon Lake 118
  Chew Valley Lake 118
Bleadon 120
Blockley 12
  Batsford Arboretum 12
  Burton House Garden 12
  Mill Dene Garden 12
Bourton-on-the-Water 51
  Birdland 53
  Bourton Model Railway 52
  Cotswold Motor Museum and Toy
    Collection 52
  Cotswold Perfumery 52
  Dragonfly Maze 52
  Model Village 52
Brean 120
  Brean Down 120
  Steep Holm 120
Bridgwater 169
  Admiral Blake Museum 171
  The Water Gate 171

Bridgwater and Taunton Canal 159, 167
Bristol 110
  @ Bristol 111
  Avon Gorge Country Park 113
  Avonmouth 111
  Blaise Hamlet 114
  Bristol Cathedral 110
  Bristol Industrial Museum 111
  Bristol Old Vic 112
  Bristol Zoo Gardens 113
  British Empire and Commonwealth
    Museum 112
  Castle Park 110
  Church of St Mary Redcliffe 112
  City Museum and Art Gallery 112
  Clifton 113
  Clifton Suspension Bridge 112
  Clifton Suspension Bridge Visitor Centre 113
  Floating Harbour 111
  Georgian House 112
  Goldney Grotto 113
  Goldney House 113
  John Wesley's Chapel 112
  Llandoger Trow 112
  Maritime Heritage Centre 111
  Redcliffe Caves 112
  Severn Way 114
  St Augustine's Reach 111
  The Red Lodge 112
  Theatre Royal 112
  Westbury College Gatehouse 114
  Westbury on Trym 114
Bruton 137
  Church of St Mary 137
  Gant's Mill 138
  Museum 138
  Patwell Pump 138
  The Dovecote 138
Buckland St Mary 166
Burnham-on-Sea 119
  Brent Knoll 119
  Highbridge 119
  Low Lighthouse 119
Burrow Bridge 159
  Athelney 159
  Burrow Mump 159
  King's Sedge Moor 159
  Pumping Station 159

C

Cameley 131
Carhampton 183
Castle Cary 137
  Castle Cary District Museum 137
  Round House 137
  War Memorial 137

Challacombe 189
  Edgerley Stone 189
Chard 159
  Chard Museum 160
  Chard Reservoir Nature Reserve 160
  Hornsbury Mill 160
Charterhouse 117
  Black Down 118
  Burrington Combe 118
  Witham Priory 118
Cheddar 115
  Cheddar Gorge 115
  Cox's Cave 117
  Gough's Cave 117
  Jacob's Ladder 115
  Museum 117
  Pavey's Lookout Tower 117
Cheddon Fitzpaine 172
  Hestercombe Gardens 172
Cheltenham 4
  Cheltenham Art Gallery & Museum 5
  Cheltenham Ladies College 6
  Cheltenham Racecourse 6
  Elephant Murals 6
  Holst Birthplace Museum 5
  Imperial Gardens 5
  Montpellier Gardens 5
  Neptune's Fountain 5
  Pittville Park 5
  Pittville Pump Room Museum 5
  Promenade 4
  Wishing Fish Clock 6
Chew Magna 109
  Chew Court 109
  Church House 109
Chipping Campden 10
  Cotswold Olympics 11
  Dover's Hill 11
  Grevel's House 11
  Market Hall 11
  Old Campden House 11
  Woolstaplers Hall 11
Chipping Sodbury 42
  Dodington House 42
  Little Sodbury Manor 42
  Old Sodbury 42
Cinderford 22
  Cyril Hart Arboretum 23
  Forest of Dean 22
  Linear Park 22
Cirencester 47
  Church of St John the Baptist 47
  Corinium Museum 47
Clapton 164
  Clapton Court Gardens 164

Claverton 108
American Museum and Gardens 108
Claverton Manor 108
Clearwell 29
Clearwell Caves 29
St Peter's Church 29
Clevedon 123
Clevedon Court 124
Clevedon Pier 124
Manor House 124
Market Hall 124
Poet's Walk 124
Walton-in-Gordano 124
Clifton Suspension Bridge 112
Clifton Suspension Bridge Visitor Centre 113
Coleford 31
Clearwell Caves 29
Clock Tower 31
Great Western Railway Museum 31
Perrygrove Railway 31
Congresbury 117
Cranham 14
Prinknash Abbey Park 14
Prinknash Bird and Deer Park 14
Crewkerne 163
Museum 163
River Parrett Trail 164
St Bartholomew's Church 163
Windwhistle Hill 163
Crowcombe 177
Church House 177
Crowcombe Court 177

D

Deerhurst 18
Odda's Chapel 19
Doone Valley 191
County Gate 191
Oare 191
Doulting 136
East Somerset Railway 137
Tithe Barn 137
Dowlish Wake 161
Drayton 158
Midelney Manor 158
Dulverton 187
Guildhall Heritage and Arts Centre 189
Dunster 181
Dunster Castle 181
Dunster Dolls Museum 183
Dunster Priory 183
Dunster Working Watermill 182
Luttrell Arms 182
Yarn Market 182

Dymock 23
Church of St Mary 23
Dymock Poets 24
Dyrham 42
Dyrham Park 42

E

East Lambrook 155
Lambrook Manor Garden 155
East Quantoxhead 179
Court House 179
Enmore 168
Barford Park 168
Fyne Court 168
Quantock Hills 168
Wills Neck 168
Exmoor Museum 192

F

Fairford 54
St Mary's Church 55
Farleigh Hungerford 127
Chapel of St Leonard 127
Farleigh Hungerford Castle 127
Fleet Air Arm Museum 150
Fovant
Fovant Badges 85
Frampton-on-Severn 33
Arlingham 35
Arlingham Peninsula 35
Epney 35
Frampton Court 33
Frampton Manor 33
Saul 35
Severn Way 35
Sharpness Canal 33
Frome 124
Blue House 125
Bridge 125
Frome Cheese Show 125
Frome Museum 125

G

Glastonbury 141
Abbot's Kitchen 143
Chalice Hill 144
Church of St Michael 144
George and Pilgrim Hotel 143
Glastonbury Abbey 141
Glastonbury Lake Village Museum 144
Glastonbury Tor 144
Lake Village 144
Museum 143
Somerset Rural Life Museum 144
St Mary's Chapel 143

Gloucester 16
Birdlip Mirror 17
Gloucester Cathedral 16
Gloucester City Museum and Art Gallery 17
Gloucester Docks 17
Gloucester Folk Museum 17
Gloucester Transport Museum 17
House of the Tailor of Gloucester 17
Llanthony Abbey 18
Maverdine House 17
*Museum of Advertising and Packaging: The
Robert O 18*
National Waterways Museum 17
Soldiers of Gloucestershire Museum 17
St Ann's Well 18

H

Haselbury Plucknett 164
Haslebury Bridge 164
Hatch Beauchamp 161
Hatch Court 161
Military Museum 161
Henbury 114
Blaise Castle House Museum 114
Hidcote Bartrim 11
Hidcote Manor Garden 11
Kiftsgate Court Garden 12
Hinkley Point 169
Hinkley Point Nature Trail 169
Hinkley Point Visitor Centre 169
Pixie's Mound 169
Stogursey 169
Hinton Priory 128
Hinton St George 162
Holcombe 129
Holford 179
Beacon Hill 179
Bicknoller Hill 179
Dowsborough Fort 179
Tendle Ring 179
Holnicote Estate 189
Horner and Dunkery National Nature
Reserve 189
Dunkery Beacon 189
Horton 41
Norton Court 41
Huish Episcopi 157

I

Ilchester 153
Ilchester Mace 154
Ilchester Museum 154
Ilminster 161
Dillington House 162

K

Kempley 23
Church of St Mary 23
Keynsham 109
Museum 109
Kilve 179

L

Langport 158
Langport and River Parrett Visitor Centre 158
Langport Gap 158
Lechlade upon Thames 55
Cotswold Water Park 55
Father Thames 56
Ha'penny Bridge 55
Littledean 27
Littledean Hall 27
Lullington 125
Orchardleigh Park 125
Rode Bird Gardens 126
Lydney 27
Dean Forest Railway 28
Lydney Park Spring Gardens and Museum 28
Norchard Railway Centre 28
Taurus Crafts 28
Lyng 173
Lynmouth 191
Lynton-Lynmouth Cliff Railway 191
Rhenish Tower 192
Watersmeet House 192
Lynton 192
Exmoor Museum 192
Valley of the Rocks 192
Lynton-Lynmouth Cliff Railway 191

M

Marshfield 43
Marshfield Mummers 43
St Catherine's 43
Tolzey Market Hall 43
Martock 155
Old Court House 155
Treasurer's House 155
Meare 145
Abbot's Fish House 145
Meare Pool 145
Peat Moor Visitor Centre 145
Shapwick Heath Nature Reserve 145
Westhay 145
Mells 129
Mendips 117
Midsomer Norton 131

Minehead 180
North Hill 180
North Hill Nature Reserve 180
Somerwest World 180
West Somerset Railway 180

Miserden 56
Miserden Park Gardens 56

Mitcheldean 23
St Anthony's Well 23
Wintle's Brewery 23

Monksilver 186
Brendon Hills 187
Combe Sydenham Hall 187
Country Park 187
Nettlecombe Court 187
Woodford 186

Montacute 151
Montacute House 151
TV and Radio Memorabilia Museum 152

Moreton-in-Marsh 13
Batsford Park 13
Cotswold Falconry Centre 14
Four Shires Stone 13
Moreton Show 13

Muchelney 157
Muchelney Abbey 157
Priest's House 157

N

Nailsworth 38
Ruskin Mill 38
Stokescroft 38

National Hunt Racecourse 167

Nether Stowey 178
Coleridge Cottage 178
Dodington Hall 178
Over Stowey 178
Quantock Forest Trail 178
Stowey Court 178

Newent 24
Crime Through Times, the Black Museum 24
Mary's Church 24
May Hill 25
National Bird of Prey Centre 25
Newent Heritage Centre 24
Onion Fayre 24
*The Shambles of Newent, a Museum of
    Victorian Life 24*
Three Choirs Vineyard 24
Vale of Leadon 24

Newland 31
Cathedral of the Forest 31

North Cerney 48
Cerney House Gardens 48

Northleach 48
Church of St Peter and St Paul 48
Cotswold Heritage Centre 49
*Keith Harding's World of Mechanical Music
    49*

Norton Fitzwarren 174

Norton St Philip 126
George Inn 126

Nunney 128
Castle 128

O

Oldbury-on-Severn 45
Oldbury Power Station 45

P

Painswick 14
Cotswold Way 16
King Charles' Stone 15
Painswick Beacon 16
Painswick House 15
Painswick Rococo Garden 15
Slad Valley 16
Spoonbed 15

Parkend 27
Nagshead Nature Reserve 27

Pauntley 18
Pauntley Court 18

Pilton 136
Pilton Manor 135

Porlock 190
Dovery Manor 190
Porlock Hill 190

Porlock Weir 190
Culbone Church 190
Submerged Forest 190

Portishead 115
Portishead Point 115

Priston 108
Priston Mill 108

Q

Quantock Forest Trail 178

R

Radstock 131
Radstock Museum 131

Rodmarton 39
Long Barrow 39
Rodmarton Manor 40
Windmill Tump 39

Roman Baths 105

Ruardean 32
St John's Church 32

S

Salisbury
Old Sarum 79
Sampford Brett 185
Selworthy 189
Holnicote Estate 189
Selworthy Beacon 189
Severn Way 114
Shepton Mallet 134
Church of St Peter and St Paul 134
Maesbury Ring 134
Market Cross 134
Mid-Somerset Show 135
Museum 135
Royal Bath and Wells Show 135
The Shambles 134
Sherborne 53
Ice House 53
Lodge Park 53
Pleasure Grounds 53
Sherborne Park Estate 53
Water Meadows 53
Slimbridge 33
Wildfowl and Wetlands Trust 33
Somerset County Cricket Museum 167
Somerset County Museum 166
Somerset Military Museum 167
Somerton 155
Lytes Cary Manor 157
Market Cross 155, 156
St Michael's Church 156
South West Coast Path 190
Sparkford 138
Cadbury Castle 138
Haynes Motor Museum 138
St Briavels 28
Bread and Cheese Ceremony 28
St Briavels Castle 29
St Mary's Church 28
Stable Fitzpaine 166
Stanton 9
Snowshill Manor 9
Stanton Court 9
Stanton Drew 108
Hauteville's Quoit 109
Standing Stones 109
The Cove 109
Wansdyke 109

Stanway 9
Baroque Water Garden 9
Hailes Abbey 9
Stanway House 9
Staunton 31
All Saints' Church 31
Buckstone 31
Suck Stone 32
Stoke St Gregory 158
Willows and Wetlands Centre 159
Stoke sub Hamdon 154
Ham Hill 154
Stoke sub Hamdon Priory 154
Stow-on-the-Wold 50
Crooked House 51
Sheep Street 50
Shepherd's Way 50
St Edward's Hall 51
Toy and Collectors Museum 51
Stratton-on-the-Fosse 131
Downside Abbey 131
Street 141
Clarks Village 141
Friends' Meeting House 141
Millfield School 141
Shoe Museum 141
Stroud 35
Old Town Hall 36
Sapperton Tunnel 36
Stratford Park 36
Stratford Park Museum 37
Stroudwater Navigation 35
Subscription Rooms 36
Thames and Severn Canal 35
Swindon
STEAM 61

T

Tatworth 165
Forde Abbey 165
Taunton 166
Castle 166
Mary Street Unitarian Chapel 167
National Hunt Racecourse 167
Somerset County Cricket Museum 167
Somerset County Museum 166
Somerset Military Museum 167
Templecombe 139
Gartell Light Railway 139
Templecombe Railway Museum 140
Tetbury 40
Chavenage House 40
Chipping Steps 40
Market House 40
Tetbury Police Museum 40

Tewkesbury 19
Abbey Mill 21
Battle of Tewkesbury 21
John Moore Countryside Museum 21
Little Museum 21
Tewkesbury Abbey 19
The Royal Hop Pole Hotel 21
Town Museum 19
Thornbury 43
Castle 44
Thorne St Margaret 174
Cothay Manor Gardens 174
Greenham Barton 174
Vale of Taunton Deane 174
Wellisford Manor 174
Tintinhull 152
Tintinhull House Garden 153
Tolland 177
Gaulden Manor 177
Tortworth 44
Tortworth Arboretum 44
Tortworth Chestnut 44

U

Uley 35
Coaley Peak 35
Hetty Pegler's Tump 35
Nympsfield Long Barrow 35
Owlpen Manor 35
Uley Bury 35
Upleadon 25
St Mary's Church 25
Upper and Lower Slaughter 49
Old Mill 50
Upper Soudley 27
Dean Heritage Centre 27
Soudley Ponds 27

W

Wallsworth 18
Nature in Art 18
Wallsworth Hall 18
Wambrook 165
Ferne Animal Sanctuary 165
Wardour
Old Wardour Castle 86
Washford 183
Cleeve Abbey 183
Tropiquaria 184
Watchet 184
Market House Museum 185
Old Mineral Line 184
Watchet Flatner Boat Museum 184
Watchet Harbour 184

Waterrow 176
Wedmore 119
Wellington 174
Town Hall 174
Wellington Monument 174
Wellington Museum 174
Wellow 128
Stoney Littleton Long Barrow 128
Wellow Brook 128
Wells 131
Astronomical Clock 133
Bishop's Eye 133
Bishop's Palace 133
Cathedral of St Andrew 131
Gatehouse 133
Palace Grounds and Gardens 133
Penniless Porch 133
Vicar's Close 133
Wells Museum 134
West Bagborough 177
West Buckland 173
Rural Life Museum 174
Sheppy's Cider Farm Centre 173
West Coker 151
Brympton d'Evercy Manor House 151
West Somerset Railway 176, 180
Westbury-on-Severn 25
Westbury Court Garden 25
Weston-super-Mare 122, 123
Grand Pier 123
Helicopter Museum 123
Mendip Way 122
Sand Point 123
Sea Life Aquarium 123
Time Machine Museum 123
Uphill 122
Weston Miniature Railway 123
Winter Gardens 123
Woodspring Museum 123
Woodspring Priory 123
Worlebury Camp 122
Westonbirt 41
Westonbirt Arboretum 41
Westonzoyland 173
Battle of Sedgemoor 173
King's Sedgemoor Drain 173
Pumping Station 173
Williton 185
Bakelite Museum 185
Willows and Wetlands Centre 159
Wincanton 139
Hadspen House Gardens 139
Wincanton National Hunt Racecourse 139

Winchcombe 7
Sudeley Castle 8
Winchcombe Folk and Police Museum 8
Winchcombe Railway Museum and Garden 8
Wiveliscombe 175
Wookey Hole 145
Ebbor Gorge 146
Great Cave 146
Hyena's Den 146
Wotton-under-Edge 32
Church of St Mary 32
Midger Wood Nature Reserve 33
Nan Tow's Tump 33
Newark Park 33
Wraxall 114
Noah's Ark Farm Centre 114

Y

Yanworth 48
Chedworth Roman Villa 48
Yeovil 150
Church of St John the Baptist 150
Museum of South Somerset 150
Yeovilton 150
Fleet Air Arm Museum 150

List of Advertisers

A

Alfoxton Park	Holford, nr Bridgwater, Somerset	179
Apple Tree Inn	Morgan Vale, nr Salisbury, Wiltshire	83
Apple View	Chedzoy, nr Bridgwater, Somerset	170
archiamma	Dulverton, nr Exmoor National Park, Somerset	188
Aubergine Caffe Bar	Tewkesbury, Gloucestershire	19
Avebury Stone Circles	Avebury, Wiltshire	73

B

The Barleycorn Inn	Collingbourne Kingston, nr Marlborough, Wiltshire	68
Bath Arms Hotel	Cheddar, Somerset	116
Bath Lodge Hotel	Norton St Philip, nr Bath, Somerset	126
Batsford Park: Arboretum	Batsford Park, nr Moreton-in-Marsh, Gloucestershire	13
The Bear Inn	Bisley, nr Stroud, Gloucestershire	37
Beckford Inn	Beckford, nr Tewkesbury, Gloucestershire	20
Beechworth Lawn Hotel	Cheltenham, Gloucestershire	4
The Bell & Castle	Horsley, nr Nailsworth, Gloucestershire	38
The Bell & Crown	Zeals, Wiltshire	86
The Bell @ Ramsbury	Ramsbury, nr Marlborough, Wiltshire	66
The Bell Inn	Bishops Lydeard, nr Taunton, Somerset	176
The Bell Inn	Moreton-in-Marsh, Gloucestershire	13
The Berkely Arms	Tewkesbury, Gloucestershire	21
Biddestone Arms	Biddestone, nr Chippenham, Wiltshire	100
Bird in Hand	Bishops Lydeard, nr Taunton, Somerset	176
The Blackbird Inn	West Buckland, nr Wellington, Somerset	173
The Bridge at Woodford	Upper Woodford, nr Salisbury, Wiltshire	80
The Buttercross Tearooms	Somerton, Somerset	156

C

Carmella's Restaurant	Nailsworth, Gloucestershire	38
The Carpenters Arms	Easton Town, nr Sherston, Wiltshire	94
Carringtons	Wells, Somerset	132
The Castlebrook Inn	Compton Dundon, nr Somerton, Somerset	156
The Catherine Wheel	Marshfield, Gloucestershire	43
Ceramics by Martin Pettinger	Williton, nr Taunton, Somerset	185
Chancellors Tea Rooms	Painswick, Gloucestershire	15
Chard and District Museum	Chard, Somerset	160
The Charlton Inn	Shepton Mallet, Somerset	134

Cheltenham Art Gallery/Museum Cheltenham, Gloucestershire   5
Clearwell Caves   Near Coleford, nr Royal Forest of Dean, Gloucestershire 29
Court Close House B&b   North Wraxall, nr Chippenham, Wiltshire   100
The Courtyard & Regency
  Maisonette   Cheltenham, Gloucestershire   6
The Cross Hands Inn   Salford Hill (A44), nr Moreton-in-Marsh, Gloucestershire 14
The Crown At Kemerton   Kemerton, nr Tewkesbury, Gloucestershire   20
The Crown Inn Hotel   Blockley, nr Moreton-in-Marsh, Gloucestershire   12
The Crown Inn   Minchinhampton, nr Stroud, Gloucestershire   39
The Cuckoo Inn   Hamptworth, nr Salisbury, Wiltshire   83

D

Daisy Cottage   Williton, Somerset   185
The Dandy Lion   Bradford-upon-Avon, Wiltshire   97
The Daneway Inn   Sapperton, Gloucestershire   55
The Drummer Boy   Market Lavington, Wiltshire   92
The Duke at Bratton   Bratton, nr Westbury, Wiltshire   91
The Duke Of Wellington Inn   Bourton-on-the-Water, Gloucestershire   52
The Duke Of York   Shepton Beauchamp, nr Ilminster, Somerset   161
Dunster Water Mill   Dunster, Somerset   182

E

East Somerset Railway   Cranmore, nr Shepton Mallet, Somerset   135
Eastcott Manor   Easterton, Wiltshire   93
The Eight Bells   Chipping Campden, Gloucestershire   10

F

The Fleece Hotel   Cirencester, Gloucestershire   47
The Fleece Inn   Lightpill, nr Stroud, Gloucestershire   36
Fleet Air Museum   RNAS Yeovilton, nr Ilchester, Somerset   151
Fleur-De-Lys   Norton St Philip, nr Bath, Somerset   126
Forde Abbey   Chard, Somerset   164
The Fountain Inn Motel   Henstridge, nr Templecombe, Somerset   139
The Fox & Goose   Barrow Gurney, Somerset   114
Franklyns Farm   Chewton Mendip, nr Bath, Somerset   130
The French Horn   Pewsey, Wiltshire   69

G

Garden Café   Lower Lydbrook, Gloucestershire   28
The Gardeners Arms   Cheddar, Somerset   116
Gaulden Manor Gardens & House Exmoor, Somerset   177
The George Inn   Aylburton, nr Lydney, Gloucestershire   26

Glastonbury Abbey	Glastonbury, Somerset	142
The Globe Inn	Somerton, Somerset	156
The Globe	Milverton, nr Taunton, Somerset	175
The Golden Ball	Lower Swell, nr Stow-on-the-Wold, Gloucestershire	51
The Gordons Hotel	Cheddar, Somerset	116

H

Halfway House	Chilthorne Domer, nr Yeovil, Somerset	153
The Happy Return	Chard, Somerset	160
Harry's Bar & Restaurant	Lydney, Gloucestershire	26
Hartwell Farm Cottages	Ready Token, nr Bibury, Gloucestershire	54
Hestercombe Gardens	Cheddon Fitzpaine, nr Taunton, Somerset	172
Hillend Holiday Cottages	Locking, nr Weston-super-Mare, Somerset	123
The Horse & Jockey	Binegar, Somerset	136
The Horseshoe Inn	Bowlish, nr Shepton Mallet, Somerset	136

J

The Jenner Museum	Berkeley, Gloucestershire	46

K

Keith Harding's World of Mechanical Music	Northleach, Gloucestershire	49
King William	Catcott, nr Bridgewater, Somerset	169
The King's Arms Inn & Restaurant	Bishopton, nr Montacute, Somerset	151
The King's Head	Birdwood, nr Huntley, Gloucestershire	25
The Kings Arms Hotel	Shepton Mallet, Somerset	135
The Kings Arms	Monkton Farleigh, nr Bradford-on-Avon, Wiltshire	98
The Kings Head	Lower Coleford, nr Radstock, Somerset	129
The Knowle Inn	Knowle, nr Bridgewater, Somerset	170

L

Laburnum House Lodge Hotel	West Huntspill, nr Highbridge, Somerset	170
Lamb Inn	Clandown, nr Radstock, Somerset	130
Langley House Hotel	Langley Marsh, nr Wiveliscombe, Somerset	176
The Laurels At Inchbrook	Inchbrook, nr Nailsworth, Gloucestershire	38
Lillypool Cheese & Cider	Shipham, nr Winscombe, Somerset	121
Lion Hotel	Dulverton, Somerset	188
Log Cabin At Symonds Yat	Symonds Yat, Gloucestershire	32

M

Manor Farm	Calstone Wellington, nr Calne, Wiltshire	74
Manor FarmDulcote	Dulcote, nr Wells, Somerset	132

The Mariners Arms	Berkeley, Gloucestershire	46
The Masons Arms	Warminster, Wiltshire	89
The Miners Arms	Whitecroft, nr Lydney, Gloucestershire	26
Monkton Inn	West Monkton, nr Taunton, Somerset	168
TV And Radio Museum	Montacute, Somerset	153

N

National Waterways Museum	Gloucester, Gloucestershire	17
The Nelson Arms Inn	Drybrook, Gloucestershire	23
New Inn	Halse, nr Taunton, Somerset	175

O

The Oak Tree Inn	Cromhall, nr Wotton-under-Edge, Gloucestershire	44
The Old Ale House	Salisbury, Wiltshire	77
The Old Bakery	Netton, nr Salisbury, Wiltshire	80
The Old Barn	Wraxall, Somerset	115
The Old Inn	Allington, nr Salisbury, Wiltshire	82
The Old Inn	The Ridge, nr Woodfalls, Wiltshire	83
The Old Neighbourhood Inn	Chalford, nr Stroud, Gloucestershire	36
The Old Rectory	Kilve, Somerset	179
Old Sarum	Salisbury, Wiltshire	79
The Old Ship Inn	Combwich, nr Bridgewater, Somerset	169
Old Station House	Greet, nr Winchcombe, Gloucestershire	8
Old Wardour Castle	Ansty, Wiltshire	86
The Owl	Little Cheverill, nr Devizes, Wiltshire	91

P

The Pelican Inn	Froxfield, nr Marlborough, Wiltshire	65
Pennard Hill Farmast Pennard	Nr Shepton Mallet, Somerset	140
Penscot Hotel & Restaurant	Shipham, nr Cheddar, Somerset	121
The Pheasant Inn	Salisbury, Wiltshire	78
The Pheasant Inn	Worth Wookey, nr Wells, Somerset	145
The Pickwick Inn	Lower Wick, nr Dursley, Gloucestershire	44
The Plaisterers Arms	Winchcombe, Gloucestershire	7
Porlock Vale House	Porlock, Somerset	191
Portquin Guest House	Broadbush, nr Swindon, Wiltshire	60
Poulett Arms	Lopen Head, Somerset	162
Puriton Inn	Puriton, nr Bridgewater, Somerset	170

R

The Railway Inn	Yatton, Somerset	118
The Retreat Inn	Salisbury, Wiltshire	78

Ring o' Roses Inn	Holcombe, nr Bath, Somerset	130
The Rising Sun	Maisemore, Gloucestershire	18
River Barn	Fonthill Bishop, nr Salisbury, Wiltshire	88
Riverside Restaurant	Coxley, nr Wells, Somerset	132
Rock House Inn	Dulverton, Somerset	188
The Rose & Crown	Bower Hinton, nr Martock, Somerset	154
The Rose & Portcullis	Butleigh, Somerset	141
Rose-Ash, Willow and Little Thatch Cottages	Tivington, nr Minehead, Somerset	180
Royal Gloucestershire, Berkshire & Wiltshire Regimental Museum	Salisbury, Wiltshire	77
The Royal Oak Inn	Luxborough, Somerset	186
The Royal Oak Inn	Winsford, nr Exmoor National Park, Somerset	188
The Royal Oak Inn	Withypool, nr Exmoor, Somerset	189
Ruskin Mill	Nailsworth, Gloucestershire	37

S

Seven Stars	Timsbury, nr Bath, Somerset	130
The Seymour Arms	East Knoyle, Wiltshire	87
The Slab House Inn	West Horrington, nr Wells, Somerset	146
Speech House Hotel	Nr Coleford, nr Forest of Dean, Gloucestershire	30
Stable Cottage	Cutwell, nr Tetbury, Gloucestershire	40
STEAM - Museum of the Great Western Railway	Swindon, Wiltshire	61
Stonehenge Inn	Dorrington, nr Amesbury, Wiltshire	81
Stourhead House and Gardens	Stourton, Wiltshire	87
The Strode Arms	West Cranmore, nr Shepton Mallet, Somerset	136
The Sun Inn	Wells, Somerset	132
The Swan Inn	Stroud, Gloucestershire	34

T

The Three Old Castles Inn	Keinton Mandeville, nr Somerton, Somerset	138
Tordown Bed & Breakfast	Glastonbury, Somerset	143

V

The Valiant Soldier	Roadwater, nr Watchet, Somerset	186

W

Wadswick Barns	Wadswick, nr Corsham, Wiltshire	99
Wassells House	Cheddar, Somerset	116
West Park Farm	Market Lavington, nr Devizes, Wiltshire	92

Wharfside Restaurant & Pins And Needles	Devizes, Wiltshire	70
The Wheatsheaf Inn	Stone Allerton, nr Axbridge, Somerset	120
The White Hart Inn	Stow-on-the-Wold, Gloucestershire	50
The White Hart	Lyneham, Wiltshire	62
The Wig and Quill	Salisbury, Wiltshire	76
The Wiltshire Yeoman	Chirton, nr Devizes, Wiltshire	71
Wood Advent Farm	Roadwater, Somerset	186
Woodcutters Arms	Whiteshill, nr Stroud, Gloucestershire	36
The Woolpack	Beckington, nr Bath, Somerset	126

Hidden Places Order Form

To order any of our publications just fill in the payment details below and complete the order form *overleaf*. For orders of less than 4 copies please add £1 per book for postage and packing. Orders over 4 copies are P & P free.

Please Complete Either:

I enclose a cheque for £ [   ] made payable to Travel Publishing Ltd

Or:

Card No: [   ]

Expiry Date: [   ]

Signature: [   ]

NAME: [   ]

ADDRESS: [   ]

POSTCODE: [   ]

TEL NO: [   ]

Please either send, telephone or e-mail your order to:

Travel Publishing Ltd, 7a Apollo House, Calleva Park, Aldermaston, Berkshire RG7 8TN

Tel : 0118 981 7777   Fax: 0118 982 0077

e-mail: karen@travelpublishing.co.uk

	Price	Quantity	Value

Hidden Places Regional Titles

	Price	Quantity	Value
Cambs & Lincolnshire	£7.99	....	....
Chilterns	£8.99	....	....
Cornwall	£8.99	....	....
Derbyshire	£7.99	....	....
Devon	£8.99	....	....
Dorset, Hants & Isle of Wight	£8.99	....	....
East Anglia	£8.99	....	....
Gloucs, Wiltshire & Somerset	£8.99	....	....
Heart of England	£7.99	....	....
Hereford, Worcs & Shropshire	£7.99	....	....
Highlands & Islands	£7.99	....	....
Kent	£8.99	....	....
Lake District & Cumbria	£8.99	....	....
Lancashire & Cheshire	£8.99	....	....
Lincolnshire & Nottinghamshire	£8.99	....	....
Northumberland & Durham	£8.99	....	....
Sussex	£7.99	....	....
Thames Valley	£7.99	....	....
Yorkshire	£8.99	....	....

Hidden Places National Titles

	Price	Quantity	Value
England	£9.99	....	....
Ireland	£9.99	....	....
Scotland	£9.99	....	....
Wales	£9.99	....	....

Hidden Inns Titles

	Price	Quantity	Value
Heart of England	£5.99	....	....
Lancashire & Cheshire	£5.99	....	....
South	£5.99	....	....
South East	£5.99	....	....
South and Central Scotland	£5.99	....	....
North of England	£5.99	....	....
Wales	£5.99	....	....
Welsh Borders	£5.99	....	....
West Country	£5.99	....	....
Yorkshire	£5.99	....	....

For orders of less than 4 copies please add £1 per book for postage & packing. Orders over 4 copies P & P free.

Hidden Places Order Form

To order any of our publications just fill in the payment details below and complete the order form *overleaf*. For orders of less than 4 copies please add £1 per book for postage and packing. Orders over 4 copies are P & P free.

Please Complete Either:

I enclose a cheque for £ [   ] made payable to Travel Publishing Ltd

Or:

Card No: [   ]

Expiry Date: [   ]

Signature: [   ]

NAME: [   ]

ADDRESS: [   ]

POSTCODE: [   ]

TEL NO: [   ]

Please either send, telephone or e-mail your order to:

Travel Publishing Ltd, 7a Apollo House, Calleva Park, Aldermaston, Berkshire RG7 8TN

Tel : 0118 981 7777   Fax: 0118 982 0077

e-mail: karen@travelpublishing.co.uk

	PRICE	QUANTITY	VALUE

HIDDEN PLACES REGIONAL TITLES

Cambs & Lincolnshire	£7.99	....	....
Chilterns	£8.99	....	....
Cornwall	£8.99	....	....
Derbyshire	£7.99	....	....
Devon	£8.99	....	....
Dorset, Hants & Isle of Wight	£8.99	....	....
East Anglia	£8.99	....	....
Gloucs, Wiltshire & Somerset	£8.99	....	....
Heart of England	£7.99	....	....
Hereford, Worcs & Shropshire	£7.99	....	....
Highlands & Islands	£7.99	....	....
Kent	£8.99	....	....
Lake District & Cumbria	£8.99	....	....
Lancashire & Cheshire	£8.99	....	....
Lincolnshire & Nottinghamshire	£8.99	....	....
Northumberland & Durham	£8.99	....	....
Sussex	£7.99	....	....
Thames Valley	£7.99	....	....
Yorkshire	£8.99	....	....

HIDDEN PLACES NATIONAL TITLES

England	£9.99	....	....
Ireland	£9.99	....	....
Scotland	£9.99	....	....
Wales	£9.99	....	....

HIDDEN INNS TITLES

Heart of England	£5.99	....	....
Lancashire & Cheshire	£5.99	....	....
South	£5.99	....	....
South East	£5.99	....	....
South and Central Scotland	£5.99	....	....
North of England	£5.99	....	....
Wales	£5.99	....	....
Welsh Borders	£5.99	....	....
West Country	£5.99	....	....
Yorkshire	£5.99	....	....

For orders of less than 4 copies please add £1 per book for postage & packing. Orders over 4 copies P & P free.

Hidden Places Reader Reaction

The *Hidden Places* research team would like to receive reader's comments on any visitor attractions or places reviewed in the book and also recommendations for suitable entries to be included in the next edition. This will help ensure that the *Hidden Places* series continues to provide its readers with useful information on the more interesting, unusual or unique features of each attraction or place ensuring that their stay in the local area is an enjoyable and stimulating experience. To provide your comments or recommendations would you please complete the forms below and overleaf as indicated and send to:

The Research Department, Travel Publishing Ltd,
7a Apollo House, Calleva Park, Aldermaston, Reading, RG7 8TN.

Your Name:

Your Address:

Your Telephone Number:

Please tick as appropriate: Comments ☐   Recommendation ☐

Name of *"Hidden Place"*:

Address:

Telephone Number:

Name of Contact:

Hidden Places Reader Reaction

Comment or Reason for Recommendation:

....

....

....

....

....

....

....

....

....

....

....

....

Hidden Places Reader Reaction

The *Hidden Places* research team would like to receive reader's comments on any visitor attractions or places reviewed in the book and also recommendations for suitable entries to be included in the next edition. This will help ensure that the *Hidden Places* series continues to provide its readers with useful information on the more interesting, unusual or unique features of each attraction or place ensuring that their stay in the local area is an enjoyable and stimulating experience. To provide your comments or recommendations would you please complete the forms below and overleaf as indicated and send to:

The Research Department, Travel Publishing Ltd,
7a Apollo House, Calleva Park, Aldermaston, Reading, RG7 8TN.

Your Name:

Your Address:

Your Telephone Number:

Please tick as appropriate: Comments ☐ Recommendation ☐

Name of *"Hidden Place"*:

Address:

Telephone Number:

Name of Contact:

Hidden Places Reader Reaction

Comment or Reason for Recommendation: